ROUTLEDGE LIBRARY EDITIONS:
INDUSTRIAL ECONOMICS

Volume 28

REGULATION AND ORGANIZATIONS

REGULATION AND ORGANIZATIONS

International perspectives

Edited by
GLENN MORGAN AND LARS ENGWALL

Routledge
Taylor & Francis Group
LONDON AND NEW YORK

First published in 1999 by Routledge

This edition first published in 2018
by Routledge
2 Park Square, Milton Park, Abingdon, Oxon OX14 4RN

and by Routledge
711 Third Avenue, New York, NY 10017

Routledge is an imprint of the Taylor & Francis Group, an informa business

British Library Cataloguing in Publication Data
A catalogue record for this book is available from the British Library

ISBN: 978-1-138-30830-5 (Set)
ISBN: 978-1-351-21102-4 (Set) (ebk)
ISBN: 978-1-138-56904-1 (Volume 28) (hbk)
ISBN: 978-1-138-56907-2 (Volume 28) (pbk)
ISBN: 978-0-203-70442-4 (Volume 28) (ebk)

Publisher's Note
The publisher has gone to great lengths to ensure the quality of this reprint but points out that some imperfections in the original copies may be apparent.

Disclaimer
The publisher has made every effort to trace copyright holders and would welcome correspondence from those they have been unable to trace.

Regulation and Organizations

International perspectives

Edited by Glenn Morgan and Lars Engwall

London and New York

First published 1999
by Routledge
11 New Fetter Lane, London EC4P 4EE

Simultaneously published in the USA and Canada
by Routledge
29 West 35th Street, New York, NY 10001

Routledge is an imprint of the Taylor and Francis Group

Typeset in Baskerville by Helen Skelton, London
Printed and bound in Great Britain by Biddles Ltd,
Guildford and King's Lynn

British Library Cataloguing in Publication Data
A catalogue record for this book is available from the British Library

Library of Congress Cataloging in Publication Data
Regulation and organizations: international perspectives / [edited by] Glenn Morgan and Lars Engwall
p. cm. – (Routledge Advances in Management and business studies; 5)
"This edited collection of papers arises from a workshop held at Manchester Business School, the University of Manchester in 1996" – Preface.
Includes bibliographical references and index.
1. Industrial laws and legislation – Economic aspects. 2. Industrial laws and legislation – Social aspects. 3. Trade regulation – Economic aspects. 4. Trade regulation – Social aspects. 5. Financial services industry – Europe – State supervision.
I. Morgan, Glenn. II. Engwall, Lars. III. Series.
K3840.R436 1999
338.9–dc21 98-54691
CIP

ISBN 0–415–18391–X

The European Science Foundation is an association of fifty-six member research councils, academics and institutions devoted to basic scientific research in twenty countries. The ESF assists its member organizations in two main ways: by bringing scientists together in its scientific programmes, networks and European research conferences to work on topics of common concern; and through the joint study of issues of strategic importance in European science policy.

The scientific work sponsored by ESF includes basic research in the natural and technical sciences, the medical and biosciences, the humanities and social sciences.

The ESF maintains close relations with other scientific institutions within and outside Europe. By its activities, ESF adds value by cooperation and coordination across national frontiers and endeavours to offer expert scientific advice on strategic issues.

This volume arises from the work of the ESF Scientific Programme on European Management and Organizations in Transition (EMOT). Further information on ESF activities can be obtained from:

European Science Foundation
1 quai Lezay-Marnésia
F-67080 Strasbourg Cedex
France
Tel. (+33) 03 88 76 71 00
Fax (+33) 03 88 37 05 32

Contents

PART III
The evolution of regulatory processes: formal and informal mechanisms of change

PART IV
Regulation, power and inequality

Illustrations

Tables

Figures

Preface

This edited collection of papers arises from a workshop held at Manchester Business School, the University of Manchester, in 1996. The workshop was sponsored by the European Science Foundation's EMOT Programme (European Management and Organizations in Transition) co-directed by Richard Whitley and Anna Grandori and was organized jointly by Glenn Morgan (based then at Manchester Business School) and Lars Engwall. As well as the contributors to the book, valuable contributions to the discussions were made by other participants, including Robert Boyer, Jeff Henderson, Mick Moran, Saskia Sassen, Nigel Thrift, Richard Whitley and Karel Williams.

The editors would like to thank all the contributors to the book for their patience and cooperation in the process of editing and revision. Special thanks are also due to Lesley Gilchrist and Sue Grey at Manchester Business School. Lesley provided valuable help in organizing the original workshop and Sue took on the task of ensuring the final manuscript was completed in an acceptable form.

Glenn Morgan and Lars Engwall
September 1998

1 Regulation and organizations

An introduction

Glenn Morgan and Lars Engwall

One of the most important issues for business over the next decade will be that of regulation. In the 1980s and 1990s there was a great deal of discussion about the need for 'deregulation'. Free-market liberals and their supporters argued that in many industries regulation had become a form of protection for organizations and their existing business practices. Regulation tended to create entry barriers and encourage managers and regulators to develop cooperative relations which benefited themselves rather than customers. In order to release the dynamic forces of market competition into these areas, it was argued that there needed to be deregulation. New entrants would then be able to compete more easily and new business practices would be encouraged. In this way, customers could be expected to benefit from new products, cheaper prices and better service. Deregulation was part of a wider movement to extend the range of the market and its 'high powered incentive structure' (in Williamson's terms: e.g. Williamson 1994: 90) into areas which had previously been managed through hierarchy and authoritative modes of coordination.

In some countries and industries, this led to a significant restructuring of the ways in which business was conducted. Deregulation, privatization and the creation of quasi-markets in healthcare and education were part of a major restructuring of economic and social relations in Britain throughout the 1980s and 1990s. In other European countries and industries, however, deregulation developed more slowly and in a piecemeal fashion. This was reflected in the different ways in which policy makers and academics in particular countries responded to the rhetoric of deregulation and its impact on traditional ways of understanding and managing economies, organizations and social systems. In some societies, deregulation became a rallying cry for politicians and academics seeking to sweep away old established rules of the game based on corporatist and cooperative modes of industrial organization and planning. The rhetorical association of 'deregulation' with high-profile values such as efficiency, competition and markets as propounded in the Anglo-Saxon business environment has been successfully exported to many other societies. However, the balance of institutional forces in these other societies has meant that the discourse of regulation has had to pass through the lens of national experience resulting in a distinctive patterning of policy and practice in each society.

This fragmented experience has been reflected in the range of academic approaches which have been used to understand the process. For example, the major contributions of economists have been concerned with analysing formal regulation and deregulation of the market with a view to identifying the costs and benefits of deviations from the free-market model arising from different types of regulation (Armstrong *et al.* 1994; Bishop *et al.* 1995). There is little concern with the historical construction of systems and styles of regulation, nor with the social interaction of consumers, governments and firms in the regulatory process. In the field of legal studies, the move away from a purely juridical approach to regulation is led mainly by authors influenced by Williamson's theory of market failure; thus the goal is to link types of market failure with types of regulatory process, using a transaction cost framework that illuminates the relative efficiency of the different types of formal and informal regulation (Ogus 1995). This approach also is driven by a heavy economic determinism and does not take account of the ways in which actors' interpretative frameworks and understandings of how markets and organizations operate affects the nature and shape of regulatory processes. In the field of political science, the focus is on the policy process, and how and why different modes of formal regulation emerge in particular industries and societies. These studies are related mainly to the nature of the political system, the state and the relationship between democratic styles, administrative structures and traditions of policy management. The dynamics of markets and the ways in which organizations and managers understand and construct forms of regulation form the background to these processes rather than an integral part of the analysis (e.g. Francis 1993).

Beyond these approaches, however, lie those theories which link the notion of 'regulation' to patterns of order and control in both the macro and the micro contexts and practices of social life. For example, in the French 'regulation school' it is the manner in which the social, political and economic ordering of societies and systems is achieved that defines what is meant by regulation (Boyer 1990). In this approach, regulation is an informal process of social ordering shaped by the overall nature of markets and societies at particular periods of capitalist development. It is generally less concerned with regulation as a formal process of control exercised through regulatory bodies. At the micro level, the idea of regulation can be linked to discussions of how order is constructed within workplaces; as well as the formal notion of management control, regulation can be linked to the construction of employee identities and subjectivities (see e.g. Jacques 1996; also the discussion in Reed, this volume) and the ordering of economic life through 'manufacturing the employee'. In turn, the Foucauldian concept of 'governmentality' also encompasses the relationship between forms of knowledge, subjective identities and the regulation of economic and social life (see e.g Donzelot 1980; Burchall *et al.* 1991; Miller and Rose 1990).

The range of different experiences, different meanings and different explanatory frameworks which have been embedded in discussions of regulation and deregulation has created a particular difficulty for the study of business, organizations and management. As a perusal of the main journals in the field (such as *Organization Studies, Organization, Journal of Management Studies, Administrative Science Quarterly*) in both the USA and the UK reveals, there are few articles on regulation. This is reflected in the fact that there are no notable monographs in the field and few textbooks that deal with the issue other than in very general terms as part of the organizational context (though see Morgan and Knights 1997 for an attempt in this direction within one industry sector – financial services). Instead, anybody within the field who is interested in the topic inevitably gravitates to an existing disciplinary-based literature in which management and organizational issues either disappear completely or are subsumed within the particular theoretical perspective. There is clearly a failure to develop a common research agenda or conceptual framework which enables the theme of regulation to be made directly meaningful to the field of organizations and management. This book has been designed to address this gap and present a range of ways of studying regulation and its relationship to issues of business and management. No attempt has been made to impose a single theoretical approach on the authors but rather to reveal the variety of potential approaches to the topic. In this introductory chapter, however, we offer our own view of how regulation can be constructed as a relevant field of study for business and management before showing how the various sections and chapters fit together.

Regulation, risk and corporate action: towards a theoretical framework

As has already been indicated, the concept of regulation is understood in many different ways. Our approach begins from the perspective that the broad concept of regulation can be understood as referring to all the formal and informal norms and expectations which social actors generate about how to act in particular contexts. It also refers to the mechanisms which are generated to monitor conformance with expectations and the rewards and disciplinary systems developed to ensure conformity. Regulation, together with monitoring and disciplining, can be embedded in formal structures and organizations as well as arising informally. In this sense, regulation is different from law, which must ultimately be codified in some form and backed up by the state, with, in Weber's terms, its 'monopoly over the legitimate use of physical force' (Weber 1948: 78). Regulation may or may not be embedded in law, codified or enforceable through the actions of the state. A system of regulation, however, must possess principles of ordering and stability; a successful system of regulation is defined by its ability to reproduce those principles. This approach combines the sociological conception of 'regulation' (i.e. the concern with social institutions and norms, their origins, monitoring and disciplining as well as the process of change that occurs over time) with the more common-sense understanding of regulation as a formal system of control exercised over a particular social group or set of organizations or activities. Thus societies (and international relations between states) consist of multiple modes of regulating social and economic life.

There is clearly a danger that such an approach becomes so all-encompassing that it lacks any analytical precision. We therefore suggest narrowing down the concept in a number of ways.

First, we wish to locate the issue of regulation historically as an aspect of modernity. As we have already suggested, regulation refers to the process of monitoring and disciplining social actors. In this sense, regulation is a reflexive activity. Giddens identifies this link between modernity and reflexivity in the following passage:

> Modernity is essentially a post-traditional order. The transformation of time and space, coupled with the disembedding mechanisms, propel social life away from the hold of pre-established precepts or practices ... Modernity's reflexivity refers to the susceptibility of most aspects of social activity, and material relations with nature, to chronic revision in the light of new information or knowledge. Such information or knowledge is not incidental to modern institutions, but constitutive of them.
>
> (Giddens 1991: 20)

Second, the regularity/regulation of social life under modernity is not preordained; in Giddens' terms, it is constituted by the everyday reproduction of order and stability which occurs when social actors 'abide by the rules' and are in effect rewarded for their conformity by achieving their expected outcome. The rewards for conformity, however, do not necessarily outweigh the rewards for what may be described negatively as deviance, rebellion and revolution or positively as innovation, improvement and change. On the contrary, in a social order imbued with reflexivity, the automatic reproduction of norms and institutions is increasingly unlikely. In other words, the risk arises that the conditions of reproduction may be changed either intentionally or unintentionally. Innovations in ways of doing things or deviance and rebellion against existing institutions are continually generated in complex societies. Risk is therefore the obverse of 'regulation'; the more societies, individuals and groups become reflexive on the conditions and rules of action, the less likely it becomes that these conditions will be accepted on the basis of 'habit' and 'tradition'. As a result, formal structures of regulation have to be constructed to replace or supplement informal values and norms. However, these formal structures can never be imbued with the certainty characteristic of social order in premodern societies. They are always subject to reflexivity and change. As a broad generalization, we can therefore state that it is in order to reduce socially produced risk (however that is defined or constructed in particular times and settings) that regulatory processes develop. However, they can never achieve this goal due to the process of reflexivity; the result is a continual negotiation and renegotiation of social order through formal and informal structures of regulation.

Third, market relations are particularly central to the production of regulation and risk. Once economic relations are primarily coordinated through the market, a range of risks arise, e.g. that contracts may not be observed, that economic production will generate externalities that adversely affect the social, political and natural environment, that fraud and crime will escape unpunished, that markets may not clear, that consumers may not have the information to act rationally in market contexts, that information asymmetry between producers and consumers will generate market failure, etc., etc. The more a society is dominated by market processes (as opposed to administered systems of rule or traditional norms and values), the more risky social and economic relations become. Formal regulatory processes under conditions of modernity are generally attempts, either in explicit systems of rules or in implicit norms of conduct and action, to reduce risks, particularly those arising from the market. The 'risk society' (Beck 1992) is therefore also simultaneously the 'regulatory society'.

Fourth, there is a spatial element to the 'regulatory society', in the sense that markets and risks are not confined within national boundaries. Although societies may develop specific and distinctive ways of regulating themselves, in an international system, there must, of necessity, be a level of regulation and ordering *between* nations. The more complex the level of interaction between nations (i.e. the more economic, social and political transactions which occur), the more areas of regulation, either formal or informal, that are needed. Areas and types of regulation are also affected by the degree to which relations between nations are multilateral; where nations are organized in blocs (either voluntary blocs such as the EU or coerced blocs such as empires), regulatory processes may be simplified. On the other hand, where negotiations are multilateral or at least multiple (with a small number of dominant nations or blocs having the greatest influence), the complexity of the process increases. Most authors would agree that since the 1960s, the range of activities that require the coordination and regulation of relations between nations has increased dramatically. Whether there is any value to be had in labelling these varied processes under one simplifying concept such as 'globalization' as opposed to investigating in detail the interaction between the national and the international levels is not yet clear. Nevertheless, from the point of view of regulation, risk and disorder stemming from the incongruence of expectations and actions which arises from the confrontation of different national systems must clearly be a central part of our framework.

Fifth, the idea that reflexivity, risk and regulation go together implies that, at the organizational level, managers are involved in the construction of regulatory systems. How managers perceive risks, how they respond to attempts at regulation, how regulation impacts on company performance and how different international and national regulatory frameworks shape business and management practices is therefore an essential part of understanding the dynamic of the regulatory process. Similarly, other groups, most obviously those involved in formal regulatory systems but also others such as consumer and environmental pressure groups, also contribute to the complexity of this dynamic. From this point of view, it is important to see regulation as a process with an *output*. This output is the impact which regulation has on social, economic and political relationships, conceived both in general terms as to whether risk is controlled and handled by the system and also more specifically in terms of the impact on competition, distribution, efficiency and social welfare within sectors, nations or regions.

From this perspective, therefore, our particular view of regulation is as a *process* involving various actors in attempting to create orderly *relationships* between firms, markets and organizations. Order implies a knowledge of outcomes and a reduction of risk in the sense of unanticipated outcomes. This requires the development of certain rules of action which constitute the means through which order is achieved. These rules may be explicitly monitored and controlled through specialist bodies which in turn have their own rules of action and resource bases. Alternatively, the system of regulation may be more loosely coordinated through informal and institutional constraints on action. In practice, the regulatory process will probably be a mixture of both of these. For example, the existence of a regulatory body with powers of monitoring and control cannot guarantee the acceptance or implementation of certain rules of action; frequently, the central issue in the regulatory process is indeed how far the formal rules have become embodied in the informal and institutional practices of organizations and firms as it is often impossible for the regulators to exercise detailed control over individual firms. Achievement of order is, however, continually threatened by a number of factors, including the intensive reflexivity of modern societies which leads to a continual questioning of the process of regulation, and the complexity and dynamism of market relations which lead to discontinuous and continuous processes of innovation and change at the national and the international levels. At the centre of all these processes are social actors attempting to come to terms with and shape this order. Managers are one of the key groups in that shaping process.

The organization and content of the book

The book is organized into four main sections. The first section, 'Concepts of regulation, rules and control', examines the various ways in which regulation can be linked to the ordering of social and economic life. The second section, 'Regulatory regimes and governance', considers at the macro level how particular ways of regulating the relationship between major social institutions contribute to stability, order and change in particular national contexts. The third section, 'The evolution of regulatory processes: formal and informal mechanisms of change', examines the interaction of regulators and regulated in the construction of changing modes of regulation. The final section, 'Regulation, power and inequality', examines how the operation of particular regulatory systems impacts on the relationship between the powerful and the powerless.

The first section presents two chapters which examine the conceptual issues from very different and distinctive points of view. Whilst Reed's chapter is based within sociological accounts of the nature of society and work systems, Grandori and her colleagues draw on organizational economics. The resulting contrast illustrates the breadth of theoretical approaches to the study of regulation.

Reed's analysis is located in debates within organizational sociology concerning the nature of the transition in modern societies (variously characterized as from Fordism to post-Fordism, from modernity to post-modernity, etc.) and its impact on systems of management control. He examines the thesis that control of work-based activities is evolving from an externalized system of rules and regulations overseen and enforced by supervisors and managers towards a system where the workforce internalize the necessity for efficiency and high levels of effort. He describes this as the shift from the 'cage' to the 'gaze', i.e. the shift from the external imposition of rules to internal incorporation of management goals located within a system of surveillance that rewards conformity and punishes deviance. Examining a range of work-based initiatives, he remains sceptical of the more extreme versions of the thesis.

Grandori and colleagues consider the issue of rules and regulations from a more micro and economic perspective. They are interested in the various ways in which economic actors coordinate together. Their argument is that the process of coordination requires a range of short cuts; actors cannot calculate on each occasion how a particular transaction is to be conducted. Therefore, certain rules and informal regulations emerge which give actors confidence about transactions. This argument is familiar from institutionalist economists such as North (1990). However, they go further by distinguishing between types of rules and regulations from at the most general level, what they term 'constitutions', through 'procedures and heuristics' down to 'programming and routines'. They argue that the degree to which the rules and regulations on these various levels are formalized will vary depending on industry context. Through discussing two sectors, they reveal the complex interaction between the various levels and between the formal and informal aspects of regulation. This chapter reveals the complexity of the notion of rules and regulation and the need to clarify in both organizational- and industry-level studies the type of regulatory process which is occurring. It opens up a potentially fruitful area of research for those interested in the interaction between different types of regulation and specific industry contexts.

The second section of the book is particularly concerned with 'national' spaces of regulation and how they are changing. The chapters are all implicitly based on a broad macro-sociological view that societies consist of a range of core institutions that have evolved historically in complex, interdependent ways. Although the notion of 'business system' (see the discussions in Whitley and Kristensen 1996, 1997) is only explicitly taken up by Engwall and Morgan, it is worth briefly elaborating on this perspective and its relationship to regulation. In the business-system perspective, particular national contexts are taken as the framework of analysis. Within these national contexts, it is argued that core institutions (of political order, capital financing, education and training, and culture) shape the way in which business is conducted (at the level of the work system, the authority structure of the firm, relations between firms and forms of ownership of firms). This interaction creates a path-dependent form of development for the society as it responds to changes in technology and the global economic order. In other words, there are certain principles which govern the way in which institutions within a particular national context interact. These aspects of governance may be either formalized or informal; they become part of the rules of action within particular spheres of economic and social life, where they can be described as creating a 'regulatory regime'.

One of the most important patterns of governance in modern societies is that which relates the financial sector to both the state and the economy more generally. There is a long tradition of studies which have examined the national contexts of this relationship (see e.g. Zysman 1983 and more recently Morgan and Knights 1997). These studies show the necessity of considering the inter-relationship between formal structures of supervision and control within the financial sector and the more informal way in which these structures impact on industry, the state and structures of inequality more generally. In this section, all three chapters are concerned with the financial sector (though Engwall and Morgan also consider the university sector). Central to these analyses is the problem of how these national systems of governance are responding to the growing interdependence of financial systems and the rise of global financial markets.

Salomon's chapter examines the French case in detail. She describes how the French banking system was deeply embedded in certain expectations about how the state and the banking sector should contribute to the modernization of France post-1945. However, during the 1980s, there was an increase in support for neo-liberal approaches to managing the economy. She shows how the dominance of these arguments led to a rush for change by dismantling existing controls and regulations. However, she argues that merely changing the rules does not change the capabilities of firms and managers. Her argument is that there was a form of 'organizational' path dependence. Those large universal banks which were expected to be at the forefront of these changes proved inept and incompetent. They used the removal of restrictions on lending to provide liberal amounts of credit throughout the economy but they had not developed adequate systems of risk assessment. As the economy entered a recession, they could not recover their loans. In response to these losses, they instituted a credit freeze which actually worsened the situation. Salomon's work is a corrective to those analyses of deregulation which assume a simple linear relationship between deregulation and economic efficiency. As the experience in Eastern Europe shows, free markets and deregulation can lead to chaos and failure if adequate social and managerial competences do not exist.

D'Alessio and Oberbeck examine the case of German banking. Once again, they are concerned with debates about whether the international context and its knock-on effects in a particular system are capable of inducing change. The German system has long been seen as based on a particularly effective mode of governance and regulation linking the financial sector to manufacturing (see e.g. its role in Will Hutton's work as an exemplar of how to manage the relationship: Hutton 1995; also Zysman 1983). More recently, a number of authors have challenged this view, arguing either that the German system of governance was never quite as well organized as its supporters thought or that, in the last decade, it has started to change fundamentally (see e.g. Edwards and Fischer 1994). D'Alessio and Oberbeck argue that the German system of governance should not be written off too quickly. Although there are aspects of it which are under pressure and have changed, there are so many complex ways in which a certain type of regulation of relations between finance and manufacturing capital is constructed in Germany, that these will not disappear quickly. Like Salomon, therefore, they reinforce the idea of path-dependent development in which societies move along certain trajectories and cannot be shifted off them without major upheaval. On the other hand, it is not surprising that first France and now Germany have turned away from proponents of deregulation and have elected social democratic governments. The conflicts between free-market liberals and their opponents is reaching new levels in these societies as unemployment shows no signs of falling and social inequalities become larger. It may yet be therefore that such a shift will occur, possibly engineered through the emergence of a powerful European Central Bank managing the single European currency.

Engwall and Morgan also consider the financial sector in their discussion of regulatory regimes. They are also concerned with the way in which societies construct distinctive modes of governing aspects of economic and social life and embed them in formal and informal processes of regulation. They focus particularly on the different ways in which the state can regulate entry and behaviour in certain activities. They argue that within specific societies we can see a commonality of approach across such diverse sectors as university education and financial services. They show how a society like the USA has tended to leave regulation to the market. For example, anybody can set up a university in the USA; the key question is will anybody buy its services, not is it competent to perform the role of a university? In European countries, on the other hand, recognition of university status is given by the state. However, they show that there is a complex interaction between entry controls and what they term performance controls. Performance controls shift the emphasis from a one-off recognition process to an ongoing interaction between regulators and the regulated body. Thus achieving the status of a university no longer confers the freedom which it once did. These distinctions between state-based and market-based systems of control and the shift between the two evolve over time within particular sectors and national contexts. Thus Engwall and Morgan emphasize like Grandori and her colleagues the need to be clear about the nature and level of rules and their evolution.

The third section focuses more explicitly on the evolution of regulatory processes. This involves both the interaction between the formal and informal aspects of the regulatory system *and* the emergence of unexpected outcomes in the regulatory process. Once again, the notion that regulation is a rationally planned process that can lead to economic efficiency is unpacked in a series of studies of the political, social and economic contexts of regulation.

Holland's chapter is particularly concerned with the interface between public and private systems of regulation and control. Most advanced Western economies (though not yet all) have sought to outlaw what is termed 'insider trading' from their stock exchanges. Insider trading refers to the ability of someone to use knowledge not yet publicly available to 'beat the market' either by selling or buying stocks in advance of the rest of the trading community. Insider trading was, until the last two decades, an endemic feature of stock exchanges and continues to be so on many, though as capital markets become more interlinked, international regulatory bodies and the most powerful national regulators are combining to outlaw it from as many exchanges as possible. In the British case, with which Holland is concerned, regulators have sought to outlaw this activity by describing what is termed as 'price-sensitive information'. Price-sensitive information cannot be selectively leaked nor can somebody who comes across this information by insider knowledge use it to trade stocks and shares. However, the definition of what is price-sensitive information is not clear. Moreover, interpreting this over-strictly can undermine what is becoming a central feature of the relationship between large institutional investors and firms, i.e. regular discussions of future activities and present performance. It is increasingly the case that large firms have investor relations departments where they seek to establish long-term links to the institutional investors. An over-strict interpretation of the regulations would undermine these contacts. In fact, of course, this is part of the German model of governance which D'Alessio and Oberbeck examine. However, the closer the investors come to the managers of the firm in terms of understanding its strategy and performance, the more danger there is that they are receiving price-sensitive information which will affect their decision to sell or buy the company's stock. Holland shows how a system has evolved which tries to overcome these dangers. Thus the formal system has to be supplemented by an informal system if it is going to have any chance of working at all.

Wallerstedt's chapter examines the evolution of the Swedish auditing profession. She shows how regulation in this sector is a response to a series of critical events. The regulatory structure emerges out of competition between actors as they seek to establish their rights to practise (preferably as a monopoly) certain activities which are central to the coordination of economic activity in a market economy. The state's role in this is crucial as it acts to mediate between the various groups. The issue of professional power and the different modes of regulation which surround these groups is clearly of central importance in modern societies and worthy of continued investigation.

Morgan and Soin's chapter is again concerned with financial services. They suggest that it may be possible to identify a specifically 'organizational' approach to the study of regulation. They define this in terms of a regulatory space examined from two perspectives. First, they argue that a regulatory space is generally occupied by a range of regulatory bodies with some overlapping responsibilities. One of the factors which drives the regulatory process is frequently the way in which relations between these bodies as organizations evolve. Second, they argue that the regulatory process involves the shaping of companies and, as organizations, these are more complex than may at first sight appear. With regard to the first point, they trace the evolution of the regulatory space for retail financial services in the UK. They argue that relations between the higher-level regulator, the Securities and Investment Board (SIB), and the so-called lower-tier regulators, the self-regulatory organizations (SROs) was complex and competitive. They show that the purpose of the regulatory system was not clear at first and different views emerged which were reflected in the different regulators. Although the Labour government has created a single overarching regulator (the Financial Services Authority), it is not clear that these conflicts have been resolved. They reinforce this by reference to a series of firm-level studies of responses to regulation which reveal differences and conflicts within the financial services companies themselves about the role and effectiveness of the regulators. Their general point is that there is a need for more organizational studies of regulation at the level of the regulators themselves and the companies which they regulate.

Hultén and Helgesson's study draws on evolutionary economics to discuss the notion of path dependency within sectors arising from the interaction of technology and regulatory structure. Their chapter makes the interesting point that the way in which the regulatory system develops creates a certain incentive structure for actors within that system. Thus factors like technology, which are often treated as exogenous causes of a certain type of regulation, can be better understood as endogenous to the system, their evolution determined by the incentive structure embedded in the regulatory process. Their argument is illustrated by case studies of two network industries in Sweden at different stages of evolution. They show how the early stages of creating a telephone network in Sweden in the period from 1900 to 1925 were affected not just by technology but the way in which the state was regulating the industry. The discussion of their second case, the changing regulatory structure for Swedish railways in the 1980s and 1990s, reinforces the argument that technology is not determinant but rather part of a regulatory space in which various actors and tendencies towards path dependency are in a dynamic relationship.

The final section of the book, 'Regulation, power and inequality', looks at the issue of outcomes from a variety of perspectives. It is characteristic of market systems that their outcomes are unequally distributed. Formal structures of regulation are often (though not always) legitimated on the basis that they will counteract these inequalities. However, the actual processes of regulation often do not seem to work that way. It is important to subject regulatory processes and their outcomes to some sort of evaluation along the lines of 'who benefits?'. This, after all, was the initial impetus behind the free-market liberals' call for 'deregulation'. Their claim was the fairly simple one that regulation usually brings with it some sort of collusion between regulators and regulated companies to achieve benefit at the expense of outsiders, usually customers.

Clarke's chapter on retail financial services regulation in the UK relates to this argument. Although he does not claim 'industry capture' of the regulatory process, he is scathing about its effectiveness in achieving its overt goals of investor protection. Instead, he shows how in case after case, the industry has acted in its own interests. He demonstrates in particular that the industry has continued to obfuscate the nature of its own activity, vacillating between an ideology of professionalism and an ideology of market-conscious consumers. Professionalism is used as a way of lulling customers into believing that they are receiving 'disinterested advice' when in fact that is not the case. The vision of the market-conscious consumer is held up as an alternative, but one that is as yet far from existence. The result is that large companies have been able to continue to sell inappropriate products and exploit their power over individual consumers. Although there are overlaps between Clarke's argument and that presented by Morgan and Soin, he emphasizes more the power inequality that continues to exist between companies and consumers and the inability of the regulators to counteract this.

Waddams Price's study of price setting in UK utilities looks at a very specific set of arrangements which were put in place under the legislation creating the privatized companies and their regulators. She demonstrates that there are some underlying incompatibilities between the rules drawn up to enhance competition and people's expectations about pricing. In particular, the regulators have been conscious that the introduction of competition could only be effective if the large privatized companies (beginning from a position of monopoly strength) could be stopped from using their financial power to cross-subsidize between their monopoly businesses and their competitive ones, the assumption being that such subsidies would allow the former monopoly to undercut its competitors' prices. However, rules against cross-subsidy can have other less expected effects, particularly raising the question as to whether the notion of equal prices between, for example, rural and urban areas is not in effect a potentially illegal cross-subsidy. Also, the process of targeting customers according to their means of payment has left those without bank accounts (i.e. the poorest) paying more than the rest of the population for their utilities. This example reveals the complexity of creating a market through regulation because the concept of a market is fundamentally social; as economic sociologists such as Granovetter have argued, markets are socially embedded (Granovetter 1985). Formal regulation therefore works in a broader context of inequality between groups and individuals.

Sikka and Willmott's final chapter in the book raises these issues in stark form. Through their detailed analysis of a court case involving money laundering, they paint a damning picture of how those who are supposed to be regulating a profession are unwilling to take action where powerful interests are involved. Their chapter reveals an unwillingness in both professional and political circles to take on responsibility for what is a massively important area in modern societies – the cross-border transfer of funds, some of which have been illegally procured, others of which are on the move to avoid legitimate tax demands from national governments. This final chapter raises by implication the question of international cooperation over regulation. As national borders become more permeable, how can new forms of regulation be constructed that can re-establish control?

In conclusion, the chapters in this book provide a wide overview of regulation from a business and management perspective. Although they reflect different disciplinary perspectives and substantive concerns, together they provide a host of interesting examples and possible tracks for future research. Regulation of business and management will become increasingly important to modern economies and the international trading system. It is therefore crucial that academics contribute to understanding these phenomena. We hope that this book will make a contribution in that direction.

References

Armstrong, M., Cowan, S. and Vickers, J. (1994) *Regulatory Reform: Economic Analysis and British Experience*, London: The MIT Press.

Beck, U. (1992) *The Risk Society*, London: Sage.

Bishop, M., Kay, J. and Mayer, C. (1995) *The Regulatory Challenge*, Oxford: Oxford University Press.

Boyer, R. (1990) *The Regulation School*, New York: Columbia University Press.

Burchall, G., Gordon, G. and Miller, P. (1991) *The Foucault Effect: Studies in Governmentality*, London: Harvester.

Donzelot, J. (1980) *The Policing of Families*, London: Hutchinson.

Edwards, J. and Fischer, K. (1994) *Banks, Finance and Investment in Germany*, Cambridge: Cambridge University Press.

Francis, J. (1993) *The Politics of Regulation*, Oxford: Blackwell.

Giddens, A. (1991) *Modernity and Self-Identity*, Cambridge: Polity Press.

Granovetter, M. (1985) 'Economic action and social structure: the problem of embeddedness', *American Journal of Sociology* 91: 481–510.

Hutton, W. (1995) *The State We're In*, London: Jonathan Cape.

Jacques, R. (1996) *Manufacturing the Employee*, London: Sage.

Miller, P. and Rose, N. (1990) 'Governing economic life', *Economy and Society* 19(1): 1–31.

Morgan, G. and Knights, D. (eds) (1997) *Regulation and Deregulation in European Financial Services*, London: Macmillan.

North, D. C. (1990) *Institutions, Institutional Change and Economic Performance*, Cambridge: Cambridge University Press.

Ogus, A. (1995) *Regulation*, Oxford: Clarendon Press.

Weber, M. (1948) *From Max Weber: Essays in Sociology* (trans. and ed. H. H. Gerth and C. W. Mills), London: Routledge and Kegan Paul.

Whitley, R. and Kristensen, P. H. (eds) (1996) *The Changing European Firm: Limits to Convergence*, London: Routledge.

—— (eds) (1997) *Governance at Work: The Social Regulation of Economic Relations*, Oxford: Oxford University Press.

Williamson, O. (1994) 'Transaction cost economics and organization theory', in N. Smelser and R. Swedberg (eds) *The Handbook of Economic Sociology*, Princeton, NJ: Princeton University Press.

Zysman, J. (1983) *Governments, Markets and Growth*, Ithaca, NY: Cornell University Press.

Part I

Concepts of regulation, rules and control

2 From the 'cage' to the 'gaze'?

The dynamics of organizational control in late modernity

Michael Reed

Introduction

This chapter focuses on changing forms of internal regulation in contemporary work organizations. It overviews the 'control debate' in organizational research and analysis, as well as assessing its implications for our understanding of the governance structures and practices through which intraorganizational coordination and order are sustained. This 'control debate' has crystallized around three inter-related issues: first, the trajectory followed by changing control logics; second, the overall effect of these putative changes on the dominant institutional locations and forms of regulation discovered in work organizations; third, the cumulative impact of this general process of restructuring on control regimes as a whole. In each of these domains, fundamental questions are being raised about potential transformations in compliance structures, knowledge systems and surveillance technologies within work organizations as existing models of organizational governance and regulation come under attack from various directions.

Underlying contemporary research and analysis on each of these themes is the growing perception that a potential 'paradigm shift' in organizational control regimes is underway, if by no means completed, which signals the decay of Weberian-style bureaucratic regulation ('the cage') and its eventual replacement with Foucauldian-style 'panopticon discipline' ('the gaze'). Four inter-related sets of changes are identified as bringing this paradigm shift about. First, a new phase of 'globalized' capitalist production and consumption which requires much more flexible and mobile control regimes equipped to transcend temporal and spatial barriers to intensified capital accumulation. Second, the structural implosion of bureaucratic control under the pressure exerted by technological change. Third, the erosion of the ideological foundations of bureaucratic control consequent upon the collapse of 'collectivist' belief systems and the rise of 'individualist' cultures in which market values (re)emerge as the dominant institutional norms. Fourth, the operational decomposition of bureaucratic control due to the relative efficiency and effectiveness of decentralized and dispersed – that is, 'localized' – modes of political management and governance in which the organizational subjectivities and identities of actors emerge as the major focus for managerial control strategies. Taken together, these changes are deemed to initiate a logic of organizational restructuring in which structurally based forms of intraorganizational regulation are in the process of being superseded by internalized modes of discipline and control in which the reshaping and manipulation of actors' subjectivities and identities is the primary concern. While the diffusion of the latter is highly uneven, partial and contested, there is a growing perception of an immutable paradigm shift in control regimes within contemporary work organizations which moves them away from continuing dependence on traditional mechanisms of bureaucratic control and towards socially constructed networks of self-regulation and discipline.

Initially, the chapter will provide an exposition of the arguments and evidence which have been advanced in support of 'from the cage to the gaze' thesis in relation to the package of technological, cultural and political changes deemed to be corroding the very institutional foundations and identity of the Weberian control model. This will be followed by a consideration of the ways in which Foucault's conception of panopticon surveillance and control has been mobilized to provide explanatory leverage on the new locations and forms of intraorganizational regulation which have taken shape out of the structural debris left in the wake of 'bureaucratic meltdown'. Finally, the chapter will develop a somewhat sceptical evaluation of the thesis that a radically new model of intraorganizational governance is forming in late modern or advanced capitalist political economies. It will suggest that exponents of the 'postbureaucratic' control thesis have intellectually traded on a model of bureaucratic regulation and discipline which seriously underestimates its inherent adaptability and flexibility as a control mechanism – a fact which did not escape the attention of an older generation of researchers more keenly attuned to its cognitive, cultural, political and structural versatility (March and Simon 1958; Perrow 1986).

The cage

Weber's (1947, 1978a, 1978b) model of bureaucratic domination and control has provided the analytical benchmark against which subsequent developments in organizational governance have been interpreted and assessed (Clegg 1990; Dandeker 1990; Turner 1992, 1996; Dean 1994; Ray and Reed 1994). As an integrated configuration of structures and practices, bureaucratic control imposes a regulative system on individuals which subjects their physical, psychological and social condition 'to the maximum degree of clarity, calculability, systematicity and consistency' (Dean 1994: 67). While Weber is quite aware that social life can be rationalized from very different points of view and very different directions, bureaucratic rationalization instigates an apparatus of control based on generalized structures of domination and administration that trap the individual within an 'iron cage' of subjugation and containment (Weber 1978b: 987–8).

For Weber, it is the modern capitalist enterprise which epitomizes the inexorable force of bureaucratic rationalization and domination. Rational economic conduct and management become institutionalized within an organizational form which imposes the structural mechanisms and operational techniques through which capital accumulation can be routinely maximized (Weber 1927). These intraorganizational governance mechanisms take on a 'life of their own insofar as they establish a logic of economic, and hence social, action that is fateful, even demonic' (Turner 1996: 11–14). Within the capitalist enterprise, logics of socioeconomic action are institutionalized in such a way that they work themselves out irrespective of the subjective preferences of owners, managers and workers. There will be resistance and conflict within and between various social groups over capitalist control regimes and the distributional outcomes they reproduce. In turn, these control struggles will modify the substantive functioning of specific capitalist enterprises in particular situations. Nevertheless, Weber insists that historical and situational contingencies cannot prevent the inherent logic of social structures, such as rational bureaucratic control within capitalist enterprises, imposing themselves on social actors. In this sense, there is a significant and inviolable degree of sociological determinism inherent in Weber's analysis of bureaucratic rationalization and domination which cannot be eradicated or 'glossed over' by 'culturalist' reinterpretations of his work (Collins 1986; Turner 1996). At their worst, the latter ignore the coercive power that Weber ascribes to social structures and administrative systems once they have become fully institutionalized, 'and compel individuals and groups to behave in certain ways whatever they may wish to do – not indeed by destroying their freedom of choice but by shaping their choosing mentalities and by narrowing the range of possibilities from which to choose' (Schumpeter 1974: 130).

The detailed components of Weber's model of bureaucratic control are itemized in Figure 2.1. This model combines, in one conceptual archetype, the interlocking configuration of ideological, structural and operational elements through which organizational control can be routinely exercised on the basis of specialized and centralized knowledge. It highlights the intimate relationship between instrumental rationality, hierarchical authority structures, functional specialization and routinized task activities that defines the organizational basis on which bureaucratic control is secured. The structural backbone of this control model is located in the core mechanisms through which everything is reduced, as far as possible, to a standardized routine through which all action is framed by a rational

1 Extended hierarchy
2 Specialized division of labour
3 Direct supervision
4 Formal rules
5 Vocational occupational culture
6 Standardized knowledge/centralized authority
7 Technically based selection, promotion and removal
8 Impersonal/disinterested value system
9 Time scheduling and programming
10 Fixed administrative jurisdictions

Figure 2.1 Bureaucratic control.

calculation of the technically most efficient and effective means of realizing predetermined ends. In particular, the triptych of hierarchical coordination, functional specialization and formalized rules provides the overall structural framework within which temporally based coordination and control is routinely secured.

However, two crucial contextual features of the Weberian control model should not be forgotten. First, that it is an integral component of Weber's analysis of the process of rationalization and the institutional and ideological constraints which it inevitably imposes on actors. Second, that there is an inherent tendency for rational bureaucratic control systems, in all areas of economic, social and political life, to exceed their purely technical or functional role (Weber 1947: 339). From a Weberian perspective, technocratic governance ideologies, authority structures and rationalized work systems are not simply, or even primarily, neutral control mechanisms uncorrupted by vested interests. They are strategic resources and instruments in the ongoing struggle for power between collective actors located within institutionalized power structures which provide them with unevenly distributed opportunities and capacities 'to make a difference' (Layder 1994).

In both of these respects, Weber is suggesting that the room for manoeuvre or negotiation available to actors progressively declines as bureaucratic regulation structures 'ultimately become immovable objects of control' (Barker 1993: 410). We literally entrap ourselves within an 'iron cage' of control with its own immutable developmental logic working its way through modern institutions and organizations such as the capitalist state and business enterprise. A less deterministic and fatalistic interpretation of Weber's diagnosis of and prognosis for the 'iron cage' of bureaucratic control can be formulated (Ray and Reed 1994). But the underlying logic and dynamic of the latter seem to push inexorably in the direction of an increasingly stabilized system of control from which there is no escape (Dandeker 1990: 16–22). As a control system, bureaucratic organization indelibly shapes – through the matrix of behavioural norms and rules which it generates and legitimates – the whole panoply of cognitive presuppositions and regulative injunctions through which its institutional power is established and consolidated (Blau and Schoenherr 1971; Perrow 1986).

Yet, more recent organizational research and analysis has indicated that the logic of bureaucratic control may be collapsing under the weight of its own internal contradictions within the intense cumulative pressure exerted by technological, cultural and political change in contemporary capitalism. Are we living through another phase of radical, fundamental and intense Schumpeterian 'creative destruction' in long-term capitalistic development, such that the conventional model of Weberian-style bureaucratic control is in terminal decline? Is a major structural transformation in organizational control occurring, such that the core components of the Weberian model can no longer be sustained and are in the process of being replaced by alternative control mechanisms? If this is occurring, do we not require very different theories of organizational regulation and control that 'speak to' these new, unimagined realities which Weberian analysis can no longer recognize, much less explain?

Bureaucratic meltdown

A number of factors have been identified as bringing about the dissolution of bureaucratic control as specified by the Weberian model. First, a qualitative shift in the logic of capital accumulation such that highly centralized, formalized and static bureaucratic regulatory regimes become an impediment to, rather than a precondition for, effective corporate competition within a globalized market. Second, a transformation in the material technologies, work systems and corporate forms through which this much more reflexive, flexible and mobile process of advanced capital accumulation is realized and maintained. Third, a dismantling of the regulative infrastructure of 'corporatist' political and juridical relations through which capital accumulation had been administratively coordinated and ordered in Keynesian welfare states. Finally, a revolution in cultural values and beliefs in which the strength and relevance of communal norms have been irreparably damaged by a process of social fragmentation which prioritizes sectional and individual interests over collectivist ideologies.

Taken together, the cumulative impact of these developments, it is contended, generates a process of 'conjunctural change' in which bureaucratic modes of organizational control simply implode in on themselves under the accumulated burden of several forms and layers of change acting in deadly combination. Rather than evolutionary or incremental change – in which partial modifications to existing regulative structures and technologies of control are gradually absorbed within the established regime as it adapts to altered conditions – 'bureaucratic implosion or meltdown' presupposes a complex and escalating chain of interacting changes that destroys and transforms the core elements of the Weberian control regime as a whole. This emphasis on 'transformational change' (Ferlie *et al.* 1996) in control regimes reflects Harvey's (1996: 240) argument that 'Capitalism is a revolutionary mode of production, always restlessly searching out new organisational forms, new technologies, new lifestyles, new modalities of production and exploitation, and, therefore, new objective definitions of time and space. Periodical re-organisations of space relations and of spatial representations have had an extraordinarily powerful effect.' It is exactly this generalized perception of an intense process of globalized spatial/temporal restructuring and its fundamental destabilizing impact on organizational control regimes that underpins the 'cage to gaze' thesis reviewed in this chapter.

The argument that a radically different logic of capital accumulation has taken hold in advanced capitalist political economies over the last two decades which spells the 'death knell' of centralized bureaucratic control regimes typical of Fordist production and corporatist regulation has been developed by a number of researchers in recent years (Lash and Urry 1987, 1994; Castells 1989, 1996; Harvey 1989, 1996; Zukin 1991; Jessop 1994). While these accounts differ considerably in their theoretical predilections and substantive prognoses, they collectively agree that a new round of intensive 'time–space compression and extension' has occurred in all the advanced capitalist societies which makes conventional modes of bureaucratic regulation and control largely redundant. In place of the cumbersome administrative mechanisms typical of welfare-state bureaucracy and the sclerotic managerial routines characteristic of Fordist production and consumption, the era of flexible specialization/accumulation is seen to usher in new control regimes in which temporal and spatial barriers to globalized capital accumulation can be transcended by technological and organizational forms which literally shrink and stretch time/space boundaries at will. Thus, Castells (1989: 32, italics added) argues that 'there is a shift away from the centrality of the organisational unit to the network of information and decision. In other words, *flows rather than organisations become the units of work, decision and output accounting.*'

In the domain of consumption, which becomes of strategic importance for contemporary capitalist enterprises, flexible specialization/accumulation and its accompanying control regimes are focused on 'quick changing fashions and the mobilisation of all the artifices of need inducement and cultural transformation that this implies' (Harvey 1989: 156). Again, highly centralized and formalized corporate planning systems and standardized marketing techniques are seen to give way to decentralized and dispersed control systems in which rapidity of response to fast-moving consumer needs and continuous product innovation become the over-riding imperatives (Best 1990; Nonaka and Takeuchi 1995). Overarching these transformations in capitalist production and consumption is the complete reorganization of the global financial system in which legal deregulation, accelerated geographical mobility and instantaneous telecommunications have created 'a single world market for money and credit supply' (Harvey 1989: 161). As a result, flexible specialization/accumulation looks much more to finance capital – in itself an increasingly unstable and unpredictable configuration of circuits and interests – as its strategic coordinating power, rather than to the giant industrial, commercial and governmental bureaucracies which were once the critical integrating organizational nodes in Fordist production/consumption and corporatist regulation.

In many respects, Lash and Urry (1987, 1994) offer the most far-reaching and all-encompassing analysis of advanced capitalist 'economies of signs and spaces' in which structures of corporate organization and work control undergo a dramatic metamorphosis into social forms which make them virtually unrecognizable in Weberian terms. Their analysis indicates that the organized capitalist core of the old Fordist era and corporatist order has largely disintegrated to be replaced by a new institutional core 'clustered around information, communications and advanced producer services, as well as other services such as telecommunications, airlines and important parts of tourism and leisure' (Lash and Urry 1994: 17). They further suggest that the strategic informational, material and cultural 'flows' going through this new core are coordinated and regulated through social and economic networks which effectively lead to the displacement and eventual dismantling of the old, organized Fordist/corporatist system (Williamson 1989). The bureaucratic command and control structures which previously dominated the latter have been 'hollowed out' and disaggregated (Scarbrough and Burrell 1996) in various ways, such that their functional roles have either been completely rationalized out of existence or relocated in more flexible and mobile organizational forms – such as professional service organizations, consultancies, joint ventures and 'virtual organizations'.

As other versions of the 'globalization thesis' (Albrow 1996; Hirst and Thompson 1996; Scott 1997) have indicated, what is being emphasized here is the 'organisation of diversity' rather than a 'replication of uniformity' (Scott 1997: 7). The control systems appropriate to the former, it is argued, participate in a logic of organizing which is fundamentally different from Fordist/corporatist regimes to the extent that they reject the bureaucratic homogenization and standardization characteristic of the latter. Instead, the 'organization of diversity' engages in a logic of organizing in which heterogeneity, localism, fragmentation, diversity and dispersion are the dominant structural trends and cultural motifs.

These arguments about globalized capital accumulation and their long-term implications for organizational control regimes have been significantly reinforced by recent research on new information technologies and their corrosive effect on the 'iron cage' of bureaucratic rationality and domination (Zuboff 1988; Burris 1993; Lyon 1994; Nohria and Berkley 1994; Casey 1995; Poster 1995; Webster 1995; Castells 1996). This research suggests that the new information and communication technologies now available to organizations generates an

> implosion of our older structures of co-ordination and control: a simultaneous miniaturization, concentration and dispersion of these mechanisms that render them both less visible and more flexible ... As this occurs, much of the Weberian model is implicitly or explicitly overturned: we witness the vilification of hierarchy, the physical abolition of the 'office', the disappearance of office rules, the re-integration of the levels of planning and execution, and other such inversions of Weber's ideal type.
>
> (Nohria and Berkley 1994: 116)

If 'bureaucratic administration means fundamentally the exercise of control on the basis of knowledge' (Weber 1947: 339), then information technology is seen to bring a qualitatively different form of knowledge-based control to bear within work organizations. It achieves this to the extent that it dispenses with the highly mechanistic, rigid and static structures on which bureaucratic domination and control relied. In their place, information technology offers supple networks and manoeuvrable processes through which transparency, surveillance and discipline can be realized in ways that overcome the limitations of time and space endemic to bureaucratic control regimes. Thus, information technology 'withdraws the structures of co-ordination and control from the plane of everyday life' (Nohria and Berkley 1994: 121) and relocates them within nodes of strategic monitoring and control geographically and socially remote from operational activity. Information and communication control systems are designed and implemented in such a way that total and complete transparency of organizational behaviour becomes a realizable, if not realized, managerial aspiration. While poor design, system overload and operational breakdown are routine aspects of organizational life, Zuboff's (1988) focus on the 'drive to automate', underpinning managerial rationality in the domain of technological change, is well taken to the extent that it highlights the control imperatives at the ideological and political core of the latter. The managerial desire to 'transmit the presence of the omniscient observer and so induce compliance without the messy conflict-prone exertions of reciprocal relations' (Zuboff 1988: 323) may be corrupted and deformed by all sorts of cognitive, political and cultural contingencies. But information and communication technologies seem to possess the inherent capacity for delivering an organizational control regime in which self-regulation and discipline through the manipulation of biological, cognitive, emotional and moral identities – rather than structurally imposed behavioural constraints and demands – is a realizable project for management.

The third arena in which bureaucratic control is seen to be under severe pressure is in relation to a series of ideological and cultural changes which undermine its legitimatory and ethical base (Ray 1985; Deetz 1992, 1994; Casey 1995; DuGay 1996; Jacques 1996; Albrow 1997). Broadly speaking, cultural research and analysis indicates that the economically and technologically driven collapse of the structural scaffolding on which bureaucratic control relies has its roots in the seismic movements which have occurred in the latter's normative foundations. Insofar as bureaucratic control rests on norms of objectivity, universality, rationality, service and progress, then the relativizing and individualizing thrust of contemporary ideological and cultural transformation is seen to corrupt and eventually destroy these core values. For Weber, bureaucratic control is the institutional culmination and organizational embodiment of a long-term process of sociohistorical rationalization in which instrumental or technical rationality comes to dominate all aspects of cultural and symbolic life (Habermas 1981; Albrow 1997). But, if the core values and principles on which this rationality are based are seriously eroded by competing symbolic forms and representations which do not recognize, much less share, its cultural and ethical 'domain assumptions', then the very legitimacy and validity of the control regime which it supports are also fundamentally called into question. If we accept Albrow's (1997) argument, that there is now no accepted cultural template for administrative structure and process, such that organizational governance and regulation have to be completely reinvented without the ideological legitimation and ethical certainty provided by instrumental rationality, then the consequences for bureaucratic control are very severe indeed.

In a similar vein, Albrow (1997: 88) identifies the trend towards

> postmodern organising where individuals negotiate their respective relations on the basis of their cultural capital and acquired portfolio of skills. Organisational structure as imperative co-ordination becomes ephemeral, an instrumentality for all involved in it and not invested with an aura of superior rationality. Negotiating authority becomes the medium for the new organising work.

This conception of the culturally fragmented and deratiocinated mode of 'postmodern organizing' is entirely consistent with contemporary analyses of individualized, even 'atomized', enterprise cultures and market-driven relations that finally eviscerate the vocational, occupational and professional ideologies associated with bureaucratic organization. The discursive formations through which 'postmodern organizing' is represented and communicated reconstruct the 'bureaucratic personality' as a 'corporatized or colluded self' which is 'dependent, over-agreeable, compulsive in dedication and diligence, passionate about the product and the company. The colluded self is comforted by primary narcissistic gratifications of identifications with a workplace free of the older attractions of occupation and class-based solidarities' (Casey 1995: 191). This may be an inherently fragmented, contradictory and unstable organizational identity based on simulated myths of community, consensus, family and solidarity bereft of any meaningful grounding in everyday material and social practices. However, the discourses of enterprise and excellence open up new vistas of sociopsychological manipulation and regulation for management in which innovative, work-based subjectivities and identities can be reconstructed around the notion of the 'sovereign consumer/customer' in the marketplace, workplace and 'polityplace'. Tired and jaded norms related to values of service, continuity, equity and rationality are swept away by cultural re-engineering programmes in which corporate bureaucracy is 'progressively reshaped, watered down or reversed' (Kanter 1991: 83). The discourse of 'repressive tolerance' and 'impersonal functionality' characteristic of bureaucratic coordination and control (DuGay 1994) is replaced by a discourse of 'symbolic seduction' and 'personalized consumption' definitive of the excellent business enterprise. Within the latter, 'the function of surveillance in consumer culture is now placed in the hands of the market, social surveillance gives way to auto-surveillance' (Du Gay 1996: 79).

Thus, the general move towards more indirect, culturally based organizational control regimes – in which the pervasive communication and internalization of the 'correct' way to perceive and relate to changed realities is the dominant concern of organizational elites – followed by large corporations in the 1980s and 1990s (Alvesson 1993; Willmott 1993) is entirely consistent with the new temporal and spatial configurations that information technology imposes. A recognition of the fact that 'the *identity* of the players and *the culture of the corporation*, acquired under a certain regime of spatio-temporality prevents doing what obviously ought to be done in order to survive under another' (Harvey 1996: 244, italics in original) underpins a great deal of the cultural re-engineering that large corporations have undertaken in recent years. Again, the move towards individualized corporate cultures and fragmented organizational identities, consequent upon the shift towards market-based ideologies and computer-based surveillance, is seen by many as the normative correlate of an ongoing process of economic restructuring in which vertical disintegration, labour-market segmentation (at all levels of the skill/expertise hierarchy) and flexible decentralization are the dominant trends (Storper and Walker 1989; Sabel 1991; Mandel 1996).

For many commentators (Barry *et al.* 1996; Dumm 1996; Mandel 1996; Offe 1996) the final 'nail in the coffin' of bureaucratic control relates to the political changes and reorganizations connected with the economic, technological and cultural transformations previously discussed in this section. The escalating disenchantment with overcentralized and bureaucratized modes of corporatist regulation experienced in the 1980s and

1990s has encouraged major institutional actors within both the public and private sectors to experiment with more 'localized', targeted and modest forms of political intervention in which delegated control and regulated autonomy are the prime characteristics (Miller and Rose 1993; Reed 1995; Ferlie *et al.* 1996; Hoggett 1996; Power 1997). In turn, this has encouraged the development of novel and innovative organizational control regimes directed to the contained expansion of economic freedom and the enhancement of personal autonomy, enterprise and choice. Miller and Rose (1993: 98) describe this shift towards 'regulated autonomy' in the following terms:

> No longer is citizenship construed in terms of solidarity, contentment, welfare and a sense of security established through the bonds of organizational and social life. Citizenship is to be active and individualistic rather than passive and dependent. The political subject is henceforth to be an individual whose citizenship is manifested through the free exercise of personal choice amongst a variety of options. Programmes of government are to be evaluated in terms of the extent to which they enhance that choice. And the language of individual freedom, personal choice and self-fulfilment has come to underpin programmes of government articulated from across the political spectrum from politicians and professionals, pressure groups and civil libertarians alike.

Thus, both in public and private sector organizations a new 'apparatus of rule' has crystallized around these local regulative interventions and 'molecular'-level control initiatives which drastically reduces the dependence of dominant political and economic groups on state-centred and corporate-centred mechanisms of governance. In turn, new forms of technical, managerial and professional expertise take shape within these localized modes of governance to the extent that they provide the organizational technologies and practices which make indirect, decentralized and pluralistic control a realizable project. The liberated, empowered and proactive political subject, alongside its counterpart, the enterprising, entrepreneurial and calculating economic subject, are both relocated within a web or network of control practices in which regulatory sensitivity – 'a sensitivity which involves decisions about how to leave individuals alone to get on with their work as much as about how to monitor them' (Power 1997: 145) – replaces imperative coordination as the underlying principle of organizational life.

Under sustained assault from interconnected economic, technological, cultural and political changes occurring at multiple levels of social organization which eat away at its very moral foundations and corrode its administrative infrastructure, bureaucratic control is seen to be literally collapsing in on itself and disintegrating as a viable regulatory regime. Unable to free itself from its ideological moorings in outmoded and otiose conceptions of externally imposed structural regulation, bureaucratic control gives way to a new control regime ideally suited to the dynamic, shifting and uncertain world in which contemporary organizations must operate – 'panopticon control'.

The gaze

Bureaucratic control is based upon an interconnected set of regulative mechanisms coordinating temporal, spatial and social relations in such a way that they become contained and fixed within a relatively stable and enduring regime of administrative structures (Giddens 1984). Previous discussion has indicated that temporal, spatial and social fixity have become debilitating weaknesses in conditions where 'smart control' – based upon much more highly mobile, miniaturized and dispersed control technologies and practices – emerges as a prerequisite for organizational survival in a globalized economic, political and cultural marketplace. In these latter conditions, a continuum of control technologies and practices are required which conquer and organize time/space relations through much more flexible and discriminating means than those made available by a pre-existing regulative regime in which bureaucratic structures play the strategic coordinating and ordering role.

Foucault's (1979, 1981, 1991) analysis of 'panopticon control' has provided the major theoretical inspiration for contemporary researchers attempting to understand the dynamics of a shift towards a new model of organizational regulation and governance which seems to break with the core structural logic and elements of the Weberian control model. Many commentators (O'Neil 1986; Gordon 1987; Burrell 1988; Turner 1992; Dean 1994) have drawn attention to the similarities between Weber's formal analysis of the anatomy of bureaucratic domination and Foucault's processual interpretation of the physiology of disciplinary power and control. Nevertheless, more recent interpretations and applications of Foucault's work in the domain of changing organizational control dynamics and forms have stressed the clear differences with Weber in relation to theoretical presuppositions and substantive analyses (Turner 1996).

Foucault (1981: 135–45) analyses the development and design of panopticon control as an integral sociohistorical feature of a form of 'bio-power' in which increasing areas of individual and collective life are subjected to a continuum of political technologies and administrative mechanisms directed to the subjugation of bodies and population management. In this sense, panopticon control, as originally conceived and applied by Foucault, refers to the widespread diffusion of specialized techniques of surveillance and control – at every level of the 'social body' and utilized by a very diverse set of organizations (the army, police, schools, asylums, hospitals, clinics, prisons, etc.) – geared to the construction and maintenance of a new moral order. The latter signifies

> nothing less than the entry of life into history, that is, the entry of phenomena peculiar to the life of the human species into the order of knowledge and power, into the sphere of political techniques ... a relative control over life averted some of the imminent risks of death. In *the space for movement thus conquered, and broadening and organizing that space*, methods of power and knowledge assumed responsibility for the life processes and undertook to control and modify them.
>
> (Foucault 1981: 141–2, italics added)

Thus, Foucault contrasts panopticon control with older, traditional and legalistic forms of 'sovereign power' which deal with public life in society and economy, rather than the much more 'inaccessible substrate' of private sociobiological existence discovered in carceral institutions such as prisons, clinics and hospitals. Biological existence becomes organizationally mirrored in political existence. A new discourse of organizational practice and control emerges in the nineteenth century which reconstructs and redefines bio-political life as the strategic terrain of modern life on which continuous regulatory interventions and corrective mechanisms would be enacted to ensure the 'normalization' of the 'social body'.

In contradistinction to Weber, Foucault's model and analysis of panopticon control are advanced within a conception of instrumental or functional rationality as an overlapping series of discourse and practices, rather than as an overarching world view or cultural Zeitgeist facilitating the institutional structuring of social action in definitive and often coercive ways (Fischler 1995: 42). Instead, panopticon control is described and analysed as a loosely coordinated set of organizational 'micro-practices' through which 'discipline organises an analytical space' (Cousins and Hussain 1984: 185). At the theoretical core of Foucault's model lies a processual analysis of organizational control based on a network of spatial, temporal, observational and normative practices dedicated to the realization of internalized self-surveillance and discipline that largely dispenses with the need for the externally imposed structural controls so strongly emphasized in Weber's model.

Panopticon control is based on four interconnected sets of surveillance and control practices through which carceral organizations strive to realize their mission of transforming recalcitrant, disordered and potentially threatening individuals into docile and obedient subjects: spatial separation, segregation and enclosure; continuous and remote supervisory observation and monitoring; hierarchical ranking and distribution; and pedagogical internalization and normalization (Foucault 1979: 135–228; Cousins and Hussain 1984: 168–98; Merquior 1991: 91–107; Townley 1994: 25–33). The art and technique of spatial distribution is critical to panopticon control, Foucault argues, because it operationalizes the ideal of a 'disciplinary space' in which spatial ordering and surveillance can become much more closely linked – as in military academies based on monastic cellular models, factories split up into specialized but functionally interconnected and decentrally supervised units or boarding schools and clinics in which pedagogical and medical practice are integrated with the spatial allocation of pupils/patients. Once spatial enclosure and distribution had been achieved, then effective control of everyday organizational activity could be achieved through the detailed temporal scheduling and observational monitoring of individual behaviour down to the very movements and motions of the body. Thus, discipline based on surveillance needed to delegate supervision through a form of decentralized control as realized through temporal and ocular monitoring technologies such as timetables, scanning towers and observational galleries. Hierarchical ranking and pedagogical normalization completed the model of panopticon control to the extent that they facilitated an internalized form of self-surveillance and discipline in which the individual prison inmate, school examinee or factory worker would automatically subject themselves to the 'normalizing judgements' of warders, teachers and foremen. As Foucault (1979: 178) sees it, panopticon control employed a series of micro-level techniques geared to a thorough and intensive scanning of individual and collective conduct where 'each subject finds himself caught in a punishable, punishing universality'.

For Foucault, panopticon control can refer both to a particular regulative regime in a relatively compact and integrated form, such as the modern prison (Garland 1990), or to a much more diffused and generalized 'system', such as the loosely coupled network of localized carceral organizations that gradually replaces the violent spectacle of centralized 'sovereign power' from the second half of the eighteenth century onwards. But in both cases he envisages the gradual dissemination of 'the subtle segmentations of discipline on to the confused space of internment' (Foucault 1979: 60) and more 'therapeutic' control apparatuses which come to displace the physically coercive and hierarchically legimated systems of public punishment typical of the prebourgeois era (Garland 1990). In this sense, panopticon control becomes, particularly during the course of the nineteenth century, a generalized regime of 'privatized' disciplinary power which, in most respects, is far more durable and formidable than its premodern precursor because it gives organizational and cultural expression to one of the great social inventions of bourgeois society. As Merquior (1991: 113) summarizes this view: 'Unlike random sovereign power, which was chiefly exercised over the earth and its products, disciplinary power concentrated on human bodies and their operations. So, instead of discontinuous levies, modern man got constant surveillance. Carceral society was born.'

The major analytical elements of Foucault's model of panopticon

1 Spatial distribution
2 Delegated supervision
3 Remote surveillance
4 Continuous observation
5 Ocular monitoring
6 Normalising judgement
7 Temporal scheduling
8 Operational transparency

Figure 2.2 Panopticon control.

control are summarized in Figure 2.2. This model of a form of continuous, unobtrusive and pervasive surveillance combined with internalized, cultural self-management and discipline has provided the theoretical benchmark against which the emergence of a new organizational control regime that radically breaks with its bureaucratic predecessor has been analysed in recent years. It seems to resonate with the much more intensive, discrete and detailed organizational control technologies and practices that have taken shape over the last two decades as they come to displace, and then subsequently replace, bureaucratic control regimes ill-suited to 'new times'. In particular, panopticon control is seen to signal the arrival of a totally integrated circuit of surveillance and control with minimum levels of externally imposed intervention and direct supervision as conventionally enshrined in the structural mechanisms that are situated at the core of the Weberian control model. The latter, it is contended, simply cannot deal with – at an explanatory or managerial level – the spatial practices, temporal instruments and cultural discourses through which new regimes of organizational control are crystallizing in late modern societies. While bureaucratic control is obtuse, static and rigid, panopticon control is sharply focused, mobile and flexible; only the latter is appropriately equipped to provide the simultaneous 'tight-loose' control processes and practices required by the new regime of globalized capitalist accumulation.

Panopticism in action

Three, relatively recent, innovations in intraorganizational control regimes, which are viewed by many commentators as further reinforcing the underlying shift from Weberian bureaucratic control to Foucauldian panopticon control, will be reviewed in this section. First, corporate re-engineering, as most explicitly reflected in 'lean production', 'total quality management' (TQM) and 'business process re-engineering' (BPR) initiatives undertaken by a number of major private and public sector organizations during the 1980s and 1990s. Second, corporate re-enchanting as symbolized in the new cultural control processes and practices associated with 'corporate culture', 'human resource management' and 'emotional labour'. Third, corporate reimagining as expressed in the emergence of organizational forms – such as the 'network' or 'virtual' organization – which seem to dispense with the physical, technological and social realities that previously defined the ontological foundations of corporate bureaucracy such as factories, offices, filing cabinets, clerks and secretaries. Each of these three clusters of innovatory control programmes and technologies will be reviewed and assessed against the thesis of the putative collapse of bureaucratic control – as a relatively coherent, stable and resilient regulative regime – and its replacement with panopticon control as discussed in previous sections of this chapter. A more broadly based evaluation of the 'cage to gaze' thesis will be provided in the penultimate section of this chapter.

Re-engineering

The major focus for corporate re-engineering initiatives undertaken in both the private and public sectors over the last decade or so has been the rationalization of organizational operations in order to cut overhead costs – such as labour – to the bone and to establish effective managerial control over the production process. Thus, Womack *et al.* (1990: 99) maintain that 'lean production' has two key organizational features: 'It transfers the maximum number of tasks and responsibilities to those workers actually adding value ... and it has in place a system for detecting defects that quickly traces every problem, once discovered, to its ultimate cause.' There is also sufficient evidence to suggest that the adoption of lean production methods, and other production practices identified with 'Japanese-style' manufacturing organization (Elger and Smith 1994), entails the continuous rationalization and intensification of work, as well as the delegation of work-process control to 'dynamic teams' in which traditional notions of individual craftsmanship and collective worker organization are finally eradicated. As Tomaney's recent review of empirical research on lean production reorganization methods reveals, the reintegration of production operations and delegated managerial control over production flow

> is leading to a growing importance, for management, of creating active vigilance, responsibility and initiative among workers on its behalf ... To the extent that new production systems attempt to harness the subjective aspects of workers' abilities, this is seen as overcoming certain inherent limitations in hierarchical forms of work organization in ways which reflect a continuing logic of rationalization.
>
> (Tomaney 1994: 191)

This technologically mediated delegation and internalization of organizational control is reflected in recent case study research on lean production restructuring by Sewell and Wilkinson (1992), Garrahan and Stewart

(1992), Delbridge and Turnbull (1992) and Barker (1993). Barker (1993: 412–33) provides an illuminating summation of these kinds of developments when he refers to the emergence of a form of 'concertive control' in self-managing teams and the adoption, by management and workers alike, of a new substantive rationality that

> created an omnipresent tutelary eye of the norm with the team members as themselves the eye, that continually observes their actions, ready either to reward, or more importantly punish. The tutelary eye of the norm demanded its observants to become super-involved or risk its wrath ... The team members had become their own masters and their own slaves.

This form of concertive or normative control, Barker suggests, is entirely consistent with Foucault's prognosis that organizational control regimes will become less apparent and even more powerful as they inscribe themselves into the sociopsychological textuality of everyday organizational existence as 'natural', 'uneventful' and 'inevitable'.

Similar developments can be identified in relation to the new sociotechnical practices linked to total quality management and business process re-engineering. TQM-type initiatives have been interpreted as another managerial strategy for internalizing surveillance and control to the extent that they subject workers and lower-/middle-level managers to a form of organizational discipline in which the dictates of market rationality become unchallengeable (Munro 1995; Reed 1995; Tuckman 1995a, 1995b; Walsh 1995). As Zeitz and Mittal's (1993) research on the institutionalization of TQM ideology and practice in the USA demonstrates, powerful corporate interests have supported the widespread diffusion of values and techniques directed to the internalization of control regimes in which work intensification, casualization and disciplining are accepted as inevitable concomitants of the 'new competition'. By internally restructuring the organization in such a way that customer-driven performance standards and market (externalized or internalized) relations pervade all aspects of its operations, managers effectively debureaucratize their control systems and delegate the burden of responsibility for 'quality' to their employees. They achieve this by instilling behavioural norms and implementing more indirect self-surveillance technologies through which customer feedback can be routinely monitored and used as a basis for disciplining workers (Fuller and Smith 1991; Hill 1991; DuGay and Salaman 1992; Wilkinson *et al.* 1992). Formal authority hierarchies, centralized rule systems and standardized work performance measurement schemes are dispensed within in a new regime of control that transforms the organization into a microcosm of the market and the individual employee or manager into its willing and eager agent.

BPR can also be analysed as the latest organizational expression of a series of re-engineering initiatives in which work processes and authority structures – particularly in service sector organizations (Head 1996) – are radically transformed from narrow, task-based routines and bureaucratic hierarchies into broad, activity-based patterns and dynamic networks (Hammer and Champy 1993; Conti and Warner 1994; Grint 1994; Willmott 1995). At the centre of BPR-type restructuring initiatives lie three, interconnected changes in the organization and control of work: first, a move from functional departments to multiskilled process teams; second, a rapid transition from simple, routinized tasks to multidimensional work; and third, a flattening of authority hierarchies and streamlining of administrative procedures (Grint 1994: 182–91). These changes, it is contended, strip out all the excess activities, transferences and regulations that massively increase organizational overheads and delays in organizational responses to customer demands. They also entail an over-riding emphasis on 'centralized decentralization' whereby operational control is internalized by self-disciplining work groups and teams, while strategic control over corporate policy making and implementation is concentrated at the apex of a delayered management structure. As Conti and Warner (1994: 100–1) argue, BPR seriously disrupts established frameworks of bureaucratic control and decision making in order that more ubiquitous and unobtrusive forms of work monitoring and control can be routinely implemented with the minimum of opposition. Viewed as a form of 'mediated Taylorism' – that is, the extensive use of new production technologies and work routines to rationalize organizational operations more thoroughly and consistently – BPR creates the scaffolding for a new regime of control in which team-based self-surveillance and disciplining are combined with rationalized production and administration to form a very powerful tool in the hands of management.

Underlying the various forms of re-engineering discussed above there emerges a consistent focus on the substantially enhanced control potential of new information and communication technologies which seem to make panopticon control a realizable organizational objective rather than a mere theoretical possibility. These technologies can be seen as setting in motion a deeper and more general process of intensive monitoring and extended supervision which directly contributes to the further individualization and isolation of employees (Webster and Robins 1993; Webster 1995). While this interpretation has been challenged (Lyon 1994; Thompson and Ackroyd 1995), research on corporate re-engineering has sensitized us to the possibilities for 'the invisibility of inspection, its automatic character, the involvement of subjects in their own surveillance and … decentralized self-policing' (Lyon 1994: 67–8) made available by new technology and the organizational restructuring it has facilitated.

Re-enchanting

Re-enchantment refers to a symbolic or discursive, rather than material or structural, reworking of the ways in which organizations discipline and control their members. It shifts the focus of attention away from material technologies and organizational structures to the cultural and linguistic forms through which members represent and communicate their organizational identities. As DuGay (1996: 75–6) has argued, re-enchantment highlights the increasing significance of new discursive constructions of subjectivity and identity through which 'people are made up' and 'make themselves up'. By crafting and promulgating new conceptions of the 'organizational subject' – as, say, dynamic self-entrepreneur and/or discerning and autonomous consumer rather than staid bureaucratic servant and/or constrained and regulated producer – innovative forms of cultural discourse and practice are made available for colonizing and controlling the 'internal life' of the organization. In this way, the Weberian vision of a disenchanted and deracinated organizational world, totally bereft of value and emotion, is reversed by a process of cultural revitalization in which the emotional, symbolic and mystical essence of organizational life is rediscovered and put to work. Kanter's (1989, 1991) 'giants learn to dance' by hearing and playing new cultural melodies that reverse the decline of individual autonomy and the increase in communal anomie under the driving force of bureaucratic rationalization. Our individual and collective fate, the 'culture gurus' strive to convince us (Thrift 1997), will not be the same as that suffered by the fellahin of ancient Egypt – slaves to the dictates of a despotic and implacable bureaucratic regime – but as imaginers and masters of our own destinies in culturally pluralistic organizations which offer untold possibilities for personal growth and group solidarity (Haferkampf 1987).

A range of symbolic discourses and representational practices has been linked with the process of organizational re-enchantment such as corporate culture, human resource management and emotional labour. Several researchers (Ray 1985; Kunda 1992; Willmott 1993; Anthony 1995; Casey 1995; Thompson and McHugh 1995) have highlighted the strategic role played by the reconstruction and manipulation of cultural discourse and practices by corporate elites as they search for conceptions of organizational identity which will be internalized by employees as self-disciplining symbolic orders. Casey (1995: 13) summarizes much of the underlying thrust of this research when she suggests that cultural re-enchantment – particularly in high technology and advanced service sector companies – is directed to the securing of general

> employee internalization of and identification with a caring corporate employer. Employees identify with their own team and family (and consequently the corporation) rather than their occupation. They

> believe, or want to believe, that they are needed and valued in a familial, caring relation to each other, that they are 'all in this together'. They are 'smart' believers developing 'smart' technologies.

She sees this as a sustained effort on the part of corporate elites to reverse the Weberian bureaucratic culture of 'specialists without passion, hatred or spirit' by restoring and manipulating preindustrial notions of family, community and solidarity in which organizational membership – at least for those who are fortunate enough to survive successive waves of downsizing, delayering and deregulation – takes precedence over all other social ties and involvements.

This attempt to realize Barnard's dream of the 'immolation of the self' within a revitalized organic solidarity of communal values and practices – symbolically relocated from its original social siting in the village, craft guild and township to the business organization through various cultural transpositions, such as those entailed in corporate paternalism (Anthony 1986) and participative self-management (Besser 1995) – is resurrected as the solution to economic survival and organizational reintegration within an unforgiving and merciless global order. In turn, the rediscovery and revitalization of the organic community within the networked business organization is complemented by the growing emphasis on 'emotional labour' (Hochschild 1983, 1990; Fineman 1993; Grey 1994; Newton 1995) as the key to high levels of customer satisfaction and hence retained, if not enhanced, market share. Thus, companies with strong, that is unitary, corporate cultures lay greater and greater stress on skilful impression management on the part of all their employees as the primary indicator of organizational commitment and the rewards, both material and symbolic, which it is guaranteed to deliver.

Human resource management (HRM) rhetorics and techniques establish a patina of humanized managerial control under which cultural re-enchantment and emotional reconstruction can be attempted (Townley 1994; Legge 1995; Jacques 1996). By disciplining the interior of the organization through spatial, temporal and sociopsychological practices which facilitate the systematic calculation of and detailed control over the work performances required of employees, HRM codifies and normalizes the values and rules through which people can be distributed, monitored and ranked. It also provides a rhetoric of empowerment and a language of involvement through which the intensification and commodification of labour can be culturally overlaid and glossed with a 'discourse of transition' to a new moral order in which the soul of the corporation and the employee become as one (Keenoy and Anthony 1992). Prosaic techniques such as job evaluation, performance appraisal and work redesign are now infused with the moral significance of cultural transformation towards a new vision of the organization as a revitalized community in which the age-old conflicts between individual freedom and collective duty become obsolescent. Under this regime, the individual employee can serve their employing organization no better than when they assert their individuality, enterprise and expertise – as long as these are performed within the normative parameters and behavioural expectations that re-enchanted corporate cultures prescribe.

Reimagining

Reimagining initiatives have been focused on the inherent power of advanced information and communication technologies to reconfigure visual, spatial and cognitive representations of 'organization' in such a way that the latter literally ceases to exist as a physically materialized and instantiated entity. If re-engineering is concerned with structural redesign and re-enchantment with cultural rerepresentation, then reimagining signifies the arrival of an interconnected series of technologies which radically transform our understanding of organizational ontology by suspending, if not destroying, the accepted temporal and spatial norms on which the existence and relevance of Weberian bureaucracy are premised. Conventional conceptions of rationalized and commodified spatial/temporal relations that once provided the ontological foundations for bureaucratized systems of coordination and control (Adam 1995: 84–106) seem to be destroyed by representational technologies that allow, indeed force, organizational existence to break free from its anchoring in a pre-existing material and social reality. Continuous self-organization and reorganization through technologies 'that shatter the traditional physical instantiation of information and knowledge' (Nohria and Berkley 1994: 119) become more widespread. They also anticipate the demise of 'organization' as a stabilized, structural entity constrained by temporal, spatial and social conditions that drastically circumscribe its inherent capacity for reshaping its identity and development.

The theme of reimagining the organization is most clearly expressed in connection with debates about the virtual organization, complexity, networks and the globalization of all manner of deregulated markets for capital, labour, information, knowledge and anything else which can be translated into the binary code of digital technology (Kallinikos 1994; Nohria and Berkley 1994; Ligget and Perry 1995). The concept of the virtual organization is based on the power of new information and communication technologies – such as electronic databases (Poster 1995), computer writing and conferencing, and virtually generated realities – to dematerialize and deconstruct organizing processes in such a way that all externalized manifestations of structure are eliminated. The latter are transformed into constantly moving and unfolding transactions that converge and dissolve as their participants demand. As Kallinikos (1994: 127) tries to encapsulate these developments, digital technology

> brings about a totalizing attitude that seeks to embrace and codify the entire range of tasks that is supposed to make up the texture of work, and suppress any other mode of involvement ... and almost totally erases action and experience as a testing context and source of representations.

Dematerialized as a physical entity and social reality, virtual organization – and its accompanying information and communication networks – entails a transformational change in the way in which social interaction is ordered and controlled. Hierarchies, functional divisions of labour and formalized rules systems collapse in on themselves and are replaced by computer-generated and -mediated encounters that constitute their subjects as textual cyphers and symbolic images to be manipulated in a similar fashion to any other 'virtual resource'. This is consistent with the logic of the global market which treats individuals, organizations, states and nations as mobile nomads whose innate capacity for agency is denuded by their incorporation within a globalized information highway that is unable to recognize, much less respect, their capacity to resist.

Both the discourse and practice of reimaginization hold out the promise of panopticon control to the extent that they ontologically reconfigure the organizational subject as an inherently dispersed, fragmented and unstable identity rather than the universal rational actor underpinning Weber's model of bureaucratic domination and control (Poster 1995: 78–94). Once this reconstitution of the 'ontologically decentered' organizational subject is complete, then, it is argued, it becomes feasible to develop continuous and indirect processes of surveillance and control which are internalized by those who are subjected to them. Indeed, reimagining technologies can be seen as instigating a form of 'super-panoptic control' in which the

> unwanted surveillance of one's personal choice becomes a discursive reality through the willing participation of the surveilled individual ... Individuals are plugged into the circuits of their own panopticon control, making a mockery of theories of social action, such as Weber's, which privilege consciousness as the basis of self-interpretation ... The individual is interpellated by the super-panopticon through technologies of power, through the discourses of databases that have little if anything to do with 'modern' conceptions of rational autonomy. For the super-panopticon, this perfect writing machine constitutes subjects as decentered for their ideologically determined unity.
>
> (Poster 1995: 86–7)

The model of the rational actor which provided the ontological and analytical foundations for Weber's model of bureaucratic control can no longer be sustained within a sociotechnical world in which the biological, physical, cognitive and cultural unities on which they were premised have been destroyed by the dividing and fragmenting power of digital technology.

Each of the three forms of organizational change which have been discussed in this section can be interpreted as signalling a decisive and irreversible shift in the organizational means and mechanisms through which corporate control is realized. Deetz (1992: 37–8) attempts to articulate the wider transformational significance of these changes when he traces the emergence and diffusion of a form of disciplinary power that 'is omnipresent as it is manifest and produced in each moment ... The focus on order with accompanying surveillance and education shifts control away from the explicit exercise of power through force and coercion and places it in the routine practices of everyday life.' Thus, panopticon control suppresses, deflects and marginalizes alternative sources of meaning and resistance within a newly configured contested terrain of values and interests in which the sovereign power of the ruling class, power elite or technocratic cadre are conspicuous by their absence. A new, micro-level disciplinary power and politics seems to be in the ascendancy in late modernity within corporate sites in which new modalities of surveillance and control fill the ideological and cultural vacuum left by the collapse of class-based politics and the systems of bureaucratic regulation through which it was previously managed (Deetz 1994).

Beyond the iron cage?

The 'cage to gaze' thesis reviewed in this chapter raises some fundamental questions about the dynamics of changing organizational control regimes and their implications for wider debates about the emergence of new forms of institutional regulation and governance. In its strongest form, the 'cage to gaze' thesis suggests that a fundamental shift in intraorganizational compliance bases and structures is well underway, which presages a more fundamental transformation in the relationship between power and knowledge. The latter is seen to drive towards forms of organizational surveillance and control more accurately captured in Foucault's model of panopticon control than Weber's model of bureaucratic control. This shift from the Weberian 'iron cage' of bureaucratic control to the Foucauldian 'tutelary gaze' of panopticon control is summarized in Figure 2.3.

What this figure conveys is the idea of a deep-seated restructuring of intraorganizational control regimes in relation to three inter-related domains: first, the trajectory of change, second its underlying logic, and third, the implications of this trajectory and logic of change for the dominant location and form of organizational control in late modernity. In relation to the trajectory of change, the 'cage to gaze' thesis suggests a fundamental redirection of organizational control regimes away from institutionalized structures based on rational planning and external regulation

Cage	**Gaze**
Temporal ordering	Spatial ordering
Hierarchical structure	Network process
Centralized authority	Dispersed power
Direct supervision	Ocular surveillance
Social differentiation	Cultural normalization
External regulation	Internalized discipline
Vertical coordination	Decentralized control
Partial transparency	Total transparency

Figure 2.3 From the cage to the gaze.

towards localized networks of political management and internalized discipline. This redirection is interpreted as constituting a fundamental break with the underlying logic of bureaucratic rationalization and control originally identified by Weber. Not only are once critical but now superfluous elements of bureaucratic control – such as centralized authority structures – incrementally discarded and replaced with more effective means of panopticon control – such as dispersed supervision and indirect monitoring – but the core elements of the former are seen to be totally collapsing in on themselves with such destructive force that they can no longer sustain the underlying momentum of structurally based forms of organizational rationalization. Finally, the break with bureaucratic rationalization and domination through imperatively coordinated collective action leads to a relocation and redefinition of organizational control within the interstices of increasingly remote, unstructured, dispersed and dematerialized processes of surveillance and discipline. Structures of bureaucratic regulation dissolve away into a myriad of micro-level circuits of surveillance and control where no central locus or 'sovereign power' can be identified and captured by a dominant class, elite, movement or party (Dyrberg 1997). The power/knowledge nexus is transformed from a structural reality into a discursive construction and relocated in a highly fragmented series of spatio-temporal sites unconstrained by the conventional limitations of physical existence.

What are we to make of the 'cage to gaze' thesis? In most respects it is too early to pronounce with any certainty on this issue. Most of those sympathetic to a 'Foucauldian reading' of longer-term changes to organizational control regimes are focusing on a concatenation of developments that are, as yet, incomplete but which, they insist, contain the generative potential for a radical break with the Weberian prognosis of irreversible bureaucratic rationalization and regulation. Thus, Sewell (1996) has recently argued that panopticon control radically reformulates the problem of procuring and manipulating knowledge in highly rationalized production systems. Bureaucratic organization and Taylorized work systems provide mechanisms for identifying, sanctioning and correcting deviations from 'the norm'. But they are much less adept 'at identifying positive divergences from existing managerially-imposed norms and incorporating them within new ones' (Sewell 1996: 793). Panopticon control, in direct contrast, provides an extremely flexible set of disciplinary practices focused on manipulating the pressures acting on the subjectivity of individuals in such a way that 'deviance' – in whatever form it occurs, such as avoidance, over-conformity or overt resistance – can be readily absorbed and turned to the advantage of the prevailing regime by deftly incorporating it in appropriately modified norms. While reinforcing the 'project of instrumental rationalism', panopticon control attempts to realize it in fundamentally different ways and means from those relied upon by bureaucratic corporations. In so doing, it also fundamentally questions the cogency and accuracy of Weber's analysis of bureaucratic control and its supposed institutional longevity.

However, the overall interpretation which Foucauldians have offered of contemporary organizational restructuring and its wider implications for control regimes has been the object of considerable criticism. Commenting on the 'flexibilization of labour' component of the Foucauldian case, Peck (1996: 126–7) has insisted that

> surface manifestations of flexibility and fragmentation – such as vertical disintegration or the breaking-up of collective labour market structures – are often associated with powerful tendencies towards the further concentration of social capital and the extension of oligopolistic control. Disintegration and fragmentation on the surface often reflect underlying processes of integration and centralisation. This is certainly true of labour markets, where many of the 'new' flexibility strategies ... are in fact long-established means of deepening control over the labour process and commodifying labour market relations.

In a related context, Aronowitz and DiFazio (1994) have argued that the 'dedifferentiation' thesis – that is, a drastic reduction in the intra- and interorganizational divisions and boundaries characteristic of Fordist production and Weberian administration – which lies at the theoretical and empirical core of Foucauldian analysis, can readily be reinterpreted as entailing an extension of managerial domination over technical, professional and skilled workers through conventional means of rationalized coordination and control.

There has also been a considerable amount of debate about 'hybridization' of control forms (Starkey *et al.* 1991; Harrison 1994; Ferlie *et al.* 1996; Hoggett 1996) – particularly in relation to developments in public sector organizations – which suggests that delegated autonomy and remote control are in the process of being recombined in novel organizational designs which more effectively manage the inevitable tensions and contradictions between economic competitiveness and sociopolitical regulation. Thus, Hoggett (1996) identifies the emergence, in the British public sector, of a new form of organizational governance based on the principle of 'regulated autonomy' – that is, innovative organizational technologies and practices which facilitate the balanced integration of 'hands-on' intensive control and 'hands-off' remote control. Nevertheless, this analysis of hybridized control regimes is still based on the premise that 'organizations' – in both the public and private sectors – are disappearing as distinctive and bounded social units which are regulated on the basis of core structural mechanisms resembling Weber's model of imperatively coordinated association.

Criticisms of the substantive claims made for panopticon control have also encouraged a deeper evaluation of its epistemological and theoretical foundations (Aronowitz and DiFazio 1994; Thompson and Ackroyd 1995; Reed 1998). In particular, the tendency towards 'discursive reductionism' inherent in Foucauldian analysis and its implications for an 'ascending theory of power' (Foucault 1980), implacably opposed to any conception of power as an institutionalized, structural reality (Merquior 1991; McNay 1994), have been identified as a debilitating explanatory weakness for theories of panopticon control. Foucauldian analysis brilliantly excavates the micro-level mechanisms and practices – particularly the discursive and representational practices through which conceptions of the 'organizational subject' are constructed – by means of which panopticon control emerges as an embryonic regime of organizational surveillance and discipline. But, insofar as it carries out this micro-level excavating work in isolation from the wider, institutionalized structures of power and domination within which panopticon control takes shape, then it is in danger of providing an extremely limited and one-sided view of this development. This is so to the extent that it drastically overestimates the extent to which micro-level developments in control practices can, in and by themselves, seriously undermine the overarching structures of power and domination within which they are institutionally embedded.

It also risks overgeneralizing the extent to which structurally based control is giving way to processually based control within contemporary organizations. There is clearly sufficient evidence to support an increasing selective emphasis on panopticon-type control mechanisms and practices by dominant class groupings and organizational elites as they struggle to come to terms with the new pressures and uncertainties that another intensive phase of globalized capitalist restructuring imposes. This is often occurring at the expense of the more peripheral aspects of bureaucratic control, such as secure career structures, elaborate rule systems and strong occupational ideologies. However, it is highly questionable, certainly at this point in time and for the foreseeable future, as to whether this is inevitably driving towards an overall collapse or implosion of the core structural components of bureaucratic coordination and order as the major mechanisms through which regulative power and control has been maintained in modern organizations and societies. As a number of researchers (Pollitt 1993; Nohria and Berkley 1994; DuGay 1994; Ritzer 1996) have recently suggested, the political and economic dominance of neo-liberal ideology throughout the 1980s and 1990s – particularly in the Anglo-American economies – has usually led to an extension and strengthening of the core components of bureaucratic control within work organizations in parallel with the simultaneous weakening of macro-level and meso-level regulative structures. Centralized decentralization or regulated autonomy necessarily depend upon the reinforcement, rather than the simple retention, of micro-level organizational control mechanisms and practices anchored in the Weberian model of bureaucratic control – such as hierarchical authority, specialized divisions of labour and close supervision. These may be overlaid with an infrastructure of discursive, technological, cultural and political control innovations making the core structural components of bureaucratic regimes more implicit, indirect and invisible – but they are still 'there' as the foundational elements on which more complex control forms may be developed.

Conclusion

This chapter has provided an exposition and assessment of the thesis that bureaucratic control is giving way to a qualitatively different regime of control based on a contrasting trajectory and logic of regulative ordering in which intensive, but remote and dispersed, scanning of organizational behaviour and its 'normalizing' effects are the key features. This 'cage to gaze' thesis, it has been argued, is based on four interconnected sets of developments – respectively, economic, technological, cultural and political – which seem to generate an underlying process of conjunctural or transformational change in which the core structural elements of bureaucratic control become locked into a vicious circle of decline from which they are unable to escape. In turn, the latter is seen to be clearly manifest in contemporary processes of structurally, culturally and technologically driven organizational change which further reinforce the downward spiral of institutional degeneration in which bureaucratic control has been ensnared.

While significant elements of panoptican control can be discerned in contemporary organizational restructuring, this chapter has suggested that these are most appropriately viewed as complementary to a further enhancement of the inherent versatility of bureaucratic control (Adler and Borys 1996) – a key factor which is often ignored in current debates about the rise of 'postbureaucratic organization'. As Weber, and his more subtle interlocutors, have always recognized, bureaucratic organization provides a highly flexible and adaptable form of coordination and control which researchers, employees and citizens ignore at their cost. Even something as mundane as organizationally dependent bureaucratic career structures may be more resilient in the face of economic and technological change than some commentators have suggested (Halford and Savage 1995). Consequently, the core structural features of bureaucratic control are also likely to be more difficult to remove than is often supposed.

Indeed, too much of the debate on new trajectories and forms of organizational control has been based on a caricature of bureaucratic organization which seriously underestimates its capacity to provide regulative mechanisms and practices well suited to the changing pressures and demands exerted by an accelerated phase of capitalist restructuring on a global scale. The latter is evolving a globalized system of interorganizational networks of various kinds, but this 'in no sense constitutes a reversal – let alone a negation – of the 200-year-old tendency towards concentrated control within industrial capitalism, even if the actual production activity is increasingly being decentralised and dispersed' (Harrison 1994: 171). Neither is it likely to entail the imminent dissolution of intraorganizational control regimes that divide, contain and regulate individual and collective behaviour through established bureaucratic mechanisms such as hierarchical structuring and work rationalization. If the core of bureaucratic control is, as Weber suggested, the exercise of control on the basis of knowledge, then the strategic organizational and political issue of the next century will continue to be the question of who has the power to acquire, store, develop and manipulate the forms of knowledge through which capital accumulation will be sustained and regulated in even more intensive regimes of capitalist competition on a global scale (Jacques 1996).

References

Adam, B. (1995) *Timewatch: The Social Analysis of Time*, London: Allen and Unwin.

Adler, P. S. and Borys, B. (1996) 'Two types of bureaucracy: enabling and coercive', *Administrative Science Quarterly* 41: 61–89.

Albrow, M. (1996) *The Global Age*, Cambridge: Polity Press.

—— (1997) *Do Organisations Have Feelings?* London: Routledge.

Alvesson, M. (1993) 'Cultural–ideological modes of management montrol', in S Deetz (ed.) *Communication Yearbook Volume 16*, Newbury Park, CA: Sage.

Anthony, P. D. (1986) *The Foundation of Management*, London: Tavistock.

—— (1995) *Managing Culture*, Buckingham: Open University Press.

Aronowitz, A. and DiFazio, W. (1994) *The Jobless Future*, Minneapolis, MN: University of Minnesota Press.

Barker, J. R. (1993) 'Tightening the iron cage: coercive control in self-managing teams', *Administrative Science Quarterly* 38: 408–37.

Barry, A., Osborne, T. and Rose, N. (1996) *Foucault and Political Reason*, London: UCL Press.

Besser, T. L. (1995) 'Rewards and organisational goal achievement: a case study of Toyota manufacturing in Kentucky', *Journal of Management Studies* 32: 383–99.

Best, M. (1990) *The New Competition*, Cambridge: Polity Press.

Blau, P. and Schoenherr, P. (1971) *The Structure of Organizations*, New York: Basic Books.

Burrell, G. (1988) 'Modernism, postmodernism and organizational analysis 2: the contribution of Michel Foucault', *Organization Studies* 9: 221–35.

Burris, B. H. (1993) *Technology at Work*, Albany, NY: State University of New York Press.

Casey, C. (1995) *Work, Self and Society: After Industrialism*, London: Routledge.

Castells, M. (1989) *The Informational City*, Oxford: Blackwell.

—— (1996) *The Rise of the Network Society*, Oxford: Blackwell.

Clegg, S. (1990) *Modern Organisations: Organisation Studies in the Postmodern World*, London: Sage.

Collins, R. (1986) *Weberian Sociological Theory*, Cambridge: Cambridge University Press.

Conti, R. F. and Warner, M. (1994) 'Taylorism, teams and technology in re-engineering work organisation', *New Technology, Work and Employment* 9: 93–102.

Cousins, M. and Hussain, A. (1984) *Michel Foucault*, London: Macmillan.

Dandeker, C. (1990) *Surveillance, Power and Modernity*, Cambridge: Polity Press.

Dean, M. (1994) *Critical and Effective Histories*, London: Routledge.

Deetz, S. (1992) 'Disciplinary power in the modern corporation', in M. Alvesson and H. Willmott (eds) *Critical Management Studies*, London: Sage.

—— (1994) 'The new politics of the workplace: ideology and unobtrusive controls', in H. W. Simons and M. Billing (eds) *After Postmodernism: Reconstructing Ideology Critique*, London: Sage.

Delbridge, R. and Turnbull, P. (1992) 'Human resource maximization: the management of labour in just-in-time manufacturing systems', in P. Blyton and P. Turnbull (eds) *Re-assessing Human Resource Management*, London: Sage.

DuGay, P. (1994) 'Colossal immodesties and hopeful monsters', *Organization* 1: 125–48.

—— (1996) *Consumption and Identity at Work*, London: Sage.

DuGay, P. and Salaman, G. (1992) 'The cult[ure] of the customer', *Journal of Management Studies* 29: 615–34.

Dumm, T. L. (1996) *Michel Foucault and the Politics of Freedom*, Newbury Park, CA: Sage.

Dyrberg, T. B. (1997) *The Circular Structure of Power: Politics, Identity, Community*, London: Verso.

Elger, T. and Smith, C. (1994) *Global Japanization*, London: Routledge.

Ferlie, E., Ashburner, L., Fitzgerald, L. and Pettigrew, A. (1996) *The New Public Management*, Oxford: Oxford University Press.

Fineman, S. (1993) *Emotion in Organisation*, London: Sage.

Fischler, R. (1995) 'Strategy and history in professional practice: planning as world making', in H. Liggett and D. C. Berry (eds) *Spatial Practices*, Newbury Park, CA: Sage.

Foucault, M. (1979) *Discipline and Punish: The Birth of the Prison*, Harmondsworth: Penguin.

—— (1980) *Power/Knowledge*, London: Harvester Wheatsheaf.

—— (1981) *The History of Sexuality, Volume 1: An Introduction*, Harmondsworth: Penguin.

—— (1991) 'Governmentality', in G. Burchell, C. Gordon and P. Miller (eds) *The Foucault Effect: Studies in Governmentality*, London: Harvester Wheatsheaf.

Fuller, L. and Smith, V. (1991) 'Consumers' report: management by customers in a changing economy', *Work, Employment and Society* 5: 1–16.

Garland, D. (1990) *Punishment and Society: A Study in Social Theory*, Oxford: Clarendon Press.

Garrahan, P. and Stewart, P. (1992) *The Nissan Enigma: Flexibility at Work in a Local Economy*, London: Mansett.

Giddens, A. (1984) *The Nation State and Violence*, Cambridge: Polity Press.

Gordon, C. (1987) 'The soul of the citizen: Max Weber and Michel Foucault on rationality and government', in S. Lash and S. Whimster (eds) *Max Weber, Rationality and Modernity*, London: Allen and Unwin.

Grey, C. (1994) 'Career as a project of the self and labour process discipline', *Sociology* 30: 479–98.

Grint, K. (1994) 'Re-engineering history: social resonances and business process re-engineering', *Organization* 1: 179–201.

Habermas, J. (1981) *Knowledge and Human Interests*, London: Heinemann.

Haferkampf, H. (1987) 'Beyond the iron cage of modernity? Achievement, negotiation and changes in the power structure', *Theory, Culture and Society* 4: 31–54.

Halford, S. and Savage, M. (1995) 'The bureaucratic career: demise or adaptation?', in T. Butler and M. Savage (eds) *Social Change and the Middle Classes*, London: UCL Press.

Hammer, M. and Champy, J. (1993) *Re-engineering the Corporation: A Manifesto for a Business Revolution*, New York: Harper Business.

Harrison, B. (1994) *Lean and Mean: The Changing Landscape of Corporate Power in the Age of Flexibility*, New York: Basic Books.

Harvey, D. (1989) *The Condition of Postmodernity*, Oxford: Blackwell.

—— (1996) *Justice, Nature and the Geography of Difference*, Oxford: Blackwell.

Head, S. (1996) 'The new, ruthless economy', *The New York Review of Books*, February: 47–52.

Hill, S. (1991) 'How do you manage a flexible firm?: the total quality model', *Work, Employment and Society* 5: 397–415.

Hirst, P. and Thompson, G. (1996) *Globalization in Question: The International Economy and the Possibilities of Governance*, Cambridge: Polity Press.

Hochschild, A. R. (1983) *The Managed Heart*, Berkeley, CA: University of California Press.

—— (1990) 'Ideology and emotion management: a perspective and a path for future research', in T. D. Kempner (ed.) *Research Agendas in the Sociology of Organizations*, Albany, NY: State University of New York Press.

Hoggett, P. (1996) 'New modes of control in the public service', *Public Administration* 74: 9–32.

Jacques, R. (1996) *Manufacturing the Employee: Management Knowledges from the 19th to 21st Centuries*, London: Sage.

Jessop, R. (1994) 'Post-Fordism and the state', in A. Amin (ed.) *Post-Fordism: A Reader*, Oxford: Blackwell.

Kallinikos, J. (1994) 'The architecture of the invisible: technology is representation', *Organization* 2: 117–40.

Kanter, R. (1989) *When Giants Learn to Dance: Mastering the Challenges of Strategy, Management and Careers in the 1990s*, New York: Simon and Schuster.

—— (1991) 'The future of bureaucracy and hierarchy in organizational theory: a report from the field', in P. Bourdieu and J. S. Coleman (eds) *Social Theory for a Changing Society*, Boulder, CO: Westview Press.

Keenoy, T. and Anthony, P. (1992) 'HRM: metaphor, meaning and morality', in P. P. Blyton and P. Turnbull (eds) *Re-assessing Human Resource Management*, London: Sage.

Kunda, G. (1992) *Engineering Culture: Control and Commitment in a High Technology Corporation*, Philadelphia: Temple University Press.

Lash, S. and Urry, J. (1987) *The End of Organised Capitalism*, Cambridge: Polity Press.

—— (1994) *Economies of Signs and Space*, London: Sage.

Layder, D. (1994) *Understanding Social Theory*, London: Sage.

Legge, K. (1995) *Human Resource Management: Rhetorics and Realities*, London: Macmillan.

Ligget, H. and Perry, D. C. (1995) *Spatial Practices*, Newbury Park, CA: Sage.

Lyon, D. (1994) *The Electronic Eye: The Rise of Surveillance Society*, Cambridge: Polity Press.

McNay, L. (1994) *Foucault: A Critical Introduction*, Cambridge: Polity Press.

Mandel, M. (1996) *The High Risk Society: Peril and Promise in the New Economy*, New York: Random House.

March, J. and Simon, H. (1958) *Organizations*, New York: Wiley.

Merquior, J. G. (1991) *Foucault*, 2nd edn, London: Fontana Press.

Miller, P. and Rose, N. (1993) 'Governing economic life', in M. Gane and T. Johnson (eds) *Foucault's New Domains*, London: Routledge.

Munro, R. (1995) 'Governing the new province of quality: autonomy, accounting and the dissemination of accountability', in H. Willmott and A. Wilkinson (eds) *Making Quality Critical: New Perspectives on Organisational Change*, London: Routledge.

Newton, T. (1995) *Managing Stress: Emotion and Power at Work*, London: Sage.

Nohria, N. and Berkley, J. D. (1994) 'The virtual organization: bureaucracy, technology and the imposition of control', in C. Heckscher and A. Donnollon (eds) *The Post-Bureaucratic Organization: New Perspectives on Organizational Change*, Newbury Park, CA: Sage.

Nonaka, I. and Takeuchi, H. (1995) *The Knowledge-Creating Company: How Japanese Companies Create the Dynamics of Innovation*, Oxford: Oxford University Press.

Offe, C. (1996) *Modernity and the State*, Cambridge: Polity Press.

O'Neil, J. (1986) 'The disciplinary society', *British Journal of Sociology* 3: 42–60.

Peck, J. (1996) *Work-Place: The Social Regulation of Labour Markets*, New York: Guilford Press.

Perrow, C. (1986) *Complex Organizations: A Critical Essay*, 3rd edn, New York: Random House.

Pollitt, C. (1993) *Managerialism and the Public Services: The Anglo-American Experience*, 2nd edn, Oxford: Blackwell.

Poster, M. (1995) *The Second Media Age*, Cambridge: Polity Press.

Power, M. (1997) *The Audit Society: Rituals of Verification*, Oxford: Oxford University Press.

Ray, C. (1985) 'Corporate culture: the last frontier of control?', *Journal of Management Studies* 21: 287–97.

Ray, L. J. and Reed, M. I. (1994) *Organising Modernity: New Weberian Perspectives on Work, Organisation and Society*, London: Routledge.

Reed, M. (1995) 'Managing quality and organisational politics: TQM as a governmental technology', in I. Kirkpatrick and M. Martinez (eds) *The Politics of Quality in the Public Sector*, London: Routledge.

—— (1998) 'Organisational analysis as discourse analysis: a critique', in D. Grant, T. Keenoy and C. Oswick (eds) *Discourse and Organisation*, London: Sage.

Ritzer, G. (1996) *The McDonaldization of Society*, revised edn, London: Sage.

Sabel, C. (1991) 'Mobeius-strip organizations and open labour markets: some consequences of the re-integration of conception and execution in a volatile economy', in P. Bourdieu and J. S. Coleman (eds) *Social Theory for a Changing Society*, Boulder, CO: Westview Press.

Scarbrough, H. and Burrell, G. (1996) 'The axeman cometh: the changing roles and knowledges of middle managers', in S. R. Clegg and G. Palmer (eds) *The Politics of Management Knowledge*, London: Sage.

Schumpeter, J. A. (1974) *Capitalism, Socialism and Democracy*, London: Allen and Unwin.

Scott, A. (1997) 'Globalization: social process or political rhetoric?', in A. Scott (ed.) *The Limits of Globalization*, London: Routledge.

Sewell, G. (1996) 'Be seeing you: a rejoinder to Webster and Robins and to Jenkins', *Sociology* 4: 785–97.

Sewell, G. and Wilkinson, B. (1992) 'Someone to watch over me: surveillance, discipline and just-in-time labour process', *Sociology* 26: 271–89.

Starkey, K., Wright, M. and Thompson, S. (1991) 'Flexibility, hierarchy, markets', *British Journal of Management* 2: 165–76.

Storper, M. and Walker, R. (1989) *The Capitalist Imperative: Territory, Technology and Industrial Growth*, Oxford: Blackwell.

Thompson, P. and Ackroyd, S. (1995) 'All quiet on the workplace front? A critique of recent trends in British industrial sociology', *Sociology* 29: 615–34.

Thompson, P. and McHugh, D. (1995) *Work Organisations: A Critical Introduction*, 2nd edn, London: Macmillan.

Thrift, N. (1997) 'The rise of soft capitalism', unpublished manuscript.

Tomaney, J. (1994) 'A new paradigm of work organisation and technology?', in A. Amin (ed.) *Post-Fordism: A Reader*, Oxford: Blackwell.

Townley, B. (1994) *Reframing Human Resource Management: Power, Ethics and the Subject at Work*, London: Sage.

Tuckman, A. (1995a) 'Ideology, quality and TQM', in H. Willmott and A. Wilkinson (eds) *Making Quality Critical: New Perspectives on Organisational Change*, London: Routledge.

—— (1995b) 'The yellow brick road: TQM and the restructuring of organisational cultures', *Organization Studies* 16(4): 27–42.

Turner, B. S. (1992) *Max Weber: From History to Modernity*, London: Routledge.

—— (1996) *For Max Weber: Essays on the Sociology of Fate*, London: Sage.

Walsh, K. (1995) 'Quality through management: the new public service management', in H. Willmott and A. Wilkinson (eds) *Making Quality Critical: New Perspectives on Organisational Change*, London: Routledge.

Weber, M. (1927) *General Economic History*, London: Allen and Unwin.

—— (1947) *Theory of Social and Economic Organization*, New York: Free Press.

—— (1978a) *Max Weber: Selections in Translation*, ed. W. G. Runciman, Cambridge: Cambridge University Press.

—— (1978b) *Economy and Society*, Volumes 1 and 2, ed. G. Roth and C. Wittich, Berkeley, CA: University of California Press.

Webster, F. (1995) *Theories of the Information Society*, London: Routledge.

Webster, F. and Robins, K. (1993) 'I'll be watching you: comment on Sewell and Wilkinson', *Sociology* 27: 243–52.

Wilkinson, A., Marchington, M. and Goodman, J. (1992) 'TQM and employee involvement', *Human Resource Management Journal*, 2: 24–31.

Williamson, P. J. (1989) *Corporatism in Perspective: An Introductory Guide to Corporatist Theory*, London: Sage.

Willmott, H. (1993) 'Strength is ignorance; slavery is freedom: managing culture in modern organization', *Journal of Management Studies* 30: 515–52.

—— (1995) 'The odd couple: re-engineering business processes, managing human resources', *New Technology, Work and Employment* 10: 89–98.

Womack, J. P., Jones, D. and Roos, D. (1990) *The Machine That Changed the World*, New York: Simon and Schuster.

Zeitz, G. and Mittal, V. (1993) 'Total quality management: the Deming method as new management ideology; institutionalization patterns in the USA', unpublished manuscript.

Zuboff, S. (1988) *In the Age of the Smart Machine: The Future of Work and Power*, London: Heinemann.

Zukin, S. (1991) *Landscapes of Power: From Detroit to Disneyworld*, Berkeley, CA: University of California Press.

3 Rules as a mode of economic governance

Anna Grandori, Giuseppe Soda and Alessandro Usai

Introduction[1]

Institutions have been often and increasingly considered – in new institutional economics as well as in neo-institutionalist sociology – as background or 'embedding' human constructs, setting constraints to feasible economic actions and behaviours, on the basis of various sources of legitimacy. North (1990) defines institutions as 'the rules of the game in a society or, more formally, the humanly devised constraints that shape human interaction', thereby differentiating them from the choices that are made within the rules by teams, organizations and individuals in order to win economic games played under these rules. In the field of organizational sociology, it has been argued that economic actions are often shaped by the models of behaviour and organization that have become historically established and accepted as legitimate within particular sectors or societies leading to 'institutional isomorphism' (Powell and DiMaggio 1991).

These ideas derive partly from the notion that it is practically impossible for groups or individuals to take all decisions on a case-by-case basis. Substituting a rule for current decision making can economize on cognitive effort and conflict resolution (Simon 1960, 1990; Nelson and Winter 1982; North 1990; Brennan and Buchanan 1985). Institutionalization is one aspect of bounded rationality in the sense that once a model of behaviour becomes 'institutionalized' – i.e. becomes established, relatively stable, and followed without further scrutiny on the basis of customs, habits or laws – then it plays the role of a constraint, a decision premise and an embedding framework for discretionary behaviours. It acts as a mode of coordination of economic behaviour. However, identifying the impact of institutionalization on subsequent behaviour is distinct from explaining why it was that some behaviours became institutionalized in the first place (as opposed to being coordinated through alternative mechanisms) and why they have taken on a particular form (since, there are, as will be argued, different types of rules). In fact, rule-guided and institutionalized behaviour is but one mode of generating suitable actions among many alternative modes. As March stated:

> Calculated rationality ... is only one of several forms of intelligence, each with claim of legitimacy. Learned behaviour, with its claim to summarize an irretrievable but relevant personal history, or conventional behaviour and rules, with their claims to capture the intelligence of survival over long histories of experience more relevant than that susceptible to immediate calculation, are clear alternative contenders ... The superiority of learned or conventional behaviour depends, in general, on the amount of experience it summarizes and the similarity between the world in which the experience was accumulated and the current world.
>
> (March 1978: 604)

In a similar spirit, in this chapter, rules and conventions will be conceived as a distinctive mode of selecting economic actions and achieving effective and efficient coordination among different economic activities and actors, based on a particular class of decision-making models, which are distinct from those based on the attempted prediction of outcomes and the selection of either acceptable or optimal actions through calculative rationality. Models based on institutionalization assume that actions are generated through the application of long-standing rules, either learned or conventional, which prescribe 'appropriate' behaviours in particular situations (Grandori 1997, forthcoming).

In addition, this chapter addresses in detail the nature of rules and what types of rules may be effective in governing what types of behaviour. It explores the significance of rules as a mode of regulation of economic behaviour by examining in detail their nature and properties before turning to two empirical cases of institutionalized rules in operation. The analysis reveals that as rules vary along the following dimensions, their governance properties change:

- the level of generality versus action-specificity of rules, i.e. the extent to which rules guide behaviours through a few key principles or through many applied and specific precepts
- the level of formalization of rules, i.e. the extent to which they are embodied in and enacted as formal laws or alternatively remain informal norms of behaviour
- the level of externality of rules, i.e. the relative incidence of external laws guaranteed by public authorities and courts or of internal rules guaranteed by private system-specific authorities and 'courts'.

Once these differences are identified, it becomes possible to identify the factors which explain the effectiveness of different rule systems in specific contexts.

Rules as a governance alternative

In this section, we examine rules from two points of view; first, the way in which they solve certain information-processing problems, and second, how they relate to processes of conflict resolution.

The advantages of rules in information-processing respects have been widely analysed, as have the conditions under which those advantages can be realized. These advantages and functions include:

- the reduction of uncertainty through the provision of the 'rules of the game' within which players can calculate and play their strategies and moves (North 1990)
- the reduction of ambiguity through the provision of cognitive frames defining languages and meanings within which decision making and problem solving can take place (Weick 1979)
- the reduction of information processing costs in repeated actions, especially when many actors are involved, through the codification of learned feasible or effective actions into programmes and routines (Simon 1960; Nelson and Winter 1982) or into procedures, as in the case of traffic rules (Brennan and Buchanan 1985).

It is worth noting, however, that these reasons for rules mix together two subtly different properties. On the one hand, the suspension of critical judgement and the acceptance of conventions, principles and rules 'out of discussion' has a cognitive foundation in the lack of critical knowledge about our background concepts, the potentially huge variety of behavioural options and the ultimately arbitrary nature of all starting assumptions (Kuhn 1962; Lakatos 1970). In this case, learned or rule-guided behaviour is linked to situations of high uncertainty about what the relevant information is in the first place, i.e. to situations of ambiguity (March 1976). Rules therefore emerge as ways of mitigating high uncertainty, providing participants with ready-made solutions to potentially intractable problems. On the other hand, the adoption of a rule is, by contrast, linked to conditions of low uncertainty brought about by past learning of effective actions in a given domain. In this scenario, case-by-case critical problem solving is not cognitively unfeasible but would be costly and time consuming, particularly when there is a 'proven' solution at hand. In this case, the rules become embedded in programmes, routines and procedures for the very reason that there is low uncertainty. The distinction between rules incorporating background knowledge and rules incorporating learned action programmes indicates a way out of the paradox that, if considered all together, rules may reflect either high or low information uncertainty.

The use of rules also has important properties in terms of conflict resolution. In the first place, it can help in making the theoretical possibility that the freely stated preferences of different actors lead to situations of 'impossible' integration (Arrow 1951) unlikely in practice. The fact that preferences are not 'exogenous' or random but are formed through learning within networks of social relationships and shared information domains, imposes limits to their variation thereby reducing conflict among interests at its very origin (March and Shapira 1982; Etzioni 1985). In the second place, it is known that while the problem of choosing specific actions and positions for a set of actors in a game can be highly conflictual, the choice of the rules for the game behind 'a veil of ignorance' about one's own specific position is by this very condition much more cooperative (Rawls 1979; Brennan and Buchanan 1985). Therefore a shift from a mode of governance based on case-by-case decision making, which may often involve the use of negotiation, power and authority, to a mode of governance in which procedural rules for the settlement of disagreements have been agreed in advance of any particular dispute can lead to the solution of otherwise disruptive conflicts (Fisher and Ury 1981). In the third place, when interdependent actors are numerous and preferences are unclear or highly divergent, actions that proved to be feasible in the past (albeit for unclear or unanalysed reasons) can often provide the basis for decision rules that generate new solutions in a quasi-automatic way (Davis *et al.* 1974; Lindblom 1977). In the fourth place, conflict resolution through case-by-case negotiation is the most expensive mode of governance in terms of transaction and process costs, and therefore, even when feasible, it is often efficient to replace it by the automatic application of accepted rules (Nelson and Winter 1982). Institutionalized rules of action can therefore emerge as ways of reducing conflicts between individuals and groups.

How do these rules emerge? A number of alternative explanations exist. Traditional economic accounts privilege the process of rational choice, but two other arguments need emphasizing. First is the idea of adaptive learning as developed by evolutionary economists and bounded-rationality theorists, in which rules become established through a sequence of experimental steps, each one of which shapes the conditions under which the next step is undertaken. Thus, the existence and content of rules is 'path dependent'. Second, the processes of rule formation could be based on a natural or social 'selection' of subjects 'programmed' according to different rules in a given domain (Campbell 1960; Hannan and Freeman 1977). In spite of these differences in the motives and processes leading to their formation, rules can be evaluated in terms of the governance functions they perform. Critical to this purpose is their structuration in hierarchically ordered logical layers.

The pyramidal structure of rule systems

What do we mean by rules in this context? Drawing on the organizational culture literature (e.g. Duncan and Weiss 1978; Trice and Beyer 1984;

Schein 1985), one can identify the level of cognitive frames and paradigms. This type of knowledge is incorporated in social norms – often widely held at the level of entire societies – such as the norm of reciprocity (Gouldner 1960; Ouchi 1980), or the shared values about 'fair dealing' in a sector. With reference to the regulation of industrial districts, Sabel (1993) has recently and aptly defined these principles and norms as 'constitutions', thereby stressing the analogous role of embedding principles played by formal constitutional laws and informal unwritten constitutions. The organizational literature on formal regulation within firms has given less consideration to this 'constitutional' level of ruling. However, the recent emphasis on governing through statutes, basic charts of rights and mission statements, can be read as a response to the growing needs for 'flexible formalization' in dynamic industries and service sectors, and as a sign that the distinction between different levels of rules is important.

The other end of the spectrum of rule types in terms of level of generality has been well analysed both in its formal and informal manifestations. Programmes, procedures, routines, habits and business practices have been widely described empirically and well analysed in their heuristic cognitive nature. However, as Sidney Winter (in Cohen *et al.* 1996) has recently noticed, two cognitive levels are often meshed in these concepts. The level of 'routines' in a strict sense – no matter whether informal or formalized into programmes of action – is made up of rules prescribing what action to take in a specific area in response to what stimulus. Examples can be the sequence of actions automatically taken by a clerk in processing a cheque or by an artisan for producing a hand-made traditional good. A higher-level type of rules is represented, according to Winter, by 'heuristics' or empirical laws and 'rules of thumb' that are believed to generate correct actions in specific fields. In other terms, these type of rules incorporate procedural rather than substantive knowledge and leave more discretion to the actor for some implementative decision making. Examples can be linear decision rules in budget allocations or procedures on how to evaluate performances and calculate rewards.

The distinction between these three main levels of rules (summarized in Figure 3.1) is conducive to an evaluation of the effective level and intensity of ruling. A maximum degree of flexibility can be achieved by containing rules and norms at the constitutional and paradigmatic level. These rules will be performing mainly a function of resolving ambiguity and their effective application will be compatible with high degrees of uncertainty and variability in specific action conditions. The more intense the use of lower-level rules, procedures or heuristics and programmes or routines, the more economic action will be prescriptively and rigidly constrained. These types of rules perform mainly an information cost-reduction function and their effective application will be contingent upon stable and repetitive action conditions.

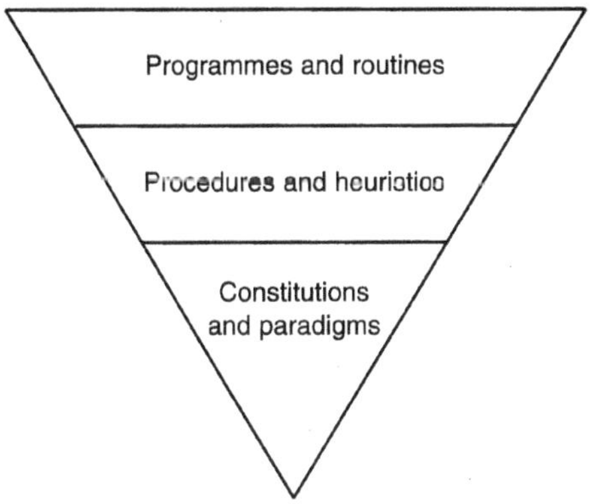

Figure 3.1 The inverted pyramid of rule systems (Grandori, forthcoming).

Effective levels of formalization

Defining different levels of rules is a separate issue from the degree to which such rules are formalized. Constitutional principles, for example, may be written down and formalized or they may be more informal. The level of the rule does not prescribe its degree of formalization. It is not formalization *per se* that drives rigidity, but it is the level of detail or prescriptiveness of a norm – no matter whether social or formal. For achieving flexible rather than rigid regulation, corporate and public legislators can and do act upon the level of generality of norms, i.e. use constitutions and basic statements of values and objectives rather than more substantive and detailed prescriptions.

What causes the formalization of rules (as opposed to situations where they remain unspoken and not written down)? Some of the antecedents of effective formalization are generally agreed.

In spite of the harsh criticisms that have been directed at the pioneering studies of the Aston group (Pugh *et al.* 1969), few would argue against the proposition that the size of a system of economic action is positively related to the degree of formalization of the rules by which it is governed, if it is to be effective (reach some performance objective) and efficient (at a reasonable cost). Another claim that seems to be subject to little doubt is that the need for accountability and justifiability towards interested third parties – such as, for example, in bank and insurance activities towards the clients – raises the level of effective formalization of procedures. Less often recalled but still well documented in organizational decision-making research (Witte and Zimmermann 1986) and in some structural contingency work is the need for formalization of decision-making processes stemming from computational complexity. When the number of elements and the variety of information to be taken into account is high, information storage and retrieval needs to be supported by formalizing the information into documents or other IT-based support systems. This relationship explains why the processes of conducting 'large' and complex activities or transactions – such as product development in high technology sectors or the sale of complex equipment – are highly formalized, in spite of their uncertainty.

A more debated question is whether the need to protect against opportunism in conditions of incomplete contracts leads actors to seek internal explicit formal safeguards and procedures for solving conflicts. Two additional conditions help to explain why uncertainty and contract incompleteness *per se* do not always lead to integrative formal regulation. When conflict amongst different interest groups (to a contract) is high (Grandori, forthcoming) and the amount of possible losses is also high (Nooteboom *et al.* 1995), then the formalization of the rules and of the other mechanisms governing a relationship is often found. For example, an interfirm collaboration in the area of research and patent development, in which both parties can learn and none exposes critically important proprietary know-how, should not be expected to be highly formalized into contracts and hierarchically supervised internal rules – even in the presence of uncertainty and specificity. But the reverse would be true if risks of loss were high and the parties had clearly divergent interests. This can help explain why highly conflictual and risk-loaded transactions – such as labour transactions – are regulated in a highly formalized way, irrespective of their degree of specificity.

The example of employment relations also illustrates the importance of another antecedent of the formalization of rules – the requirement of procedural justice – that remained for too long analysed only in the specialized literature on organizational justice (Greenberg 1987). The idea that the formalization of explicit rules could be the best defence against arbitrariness, personalistic power and domination was not at all unknown in organization studies, being one of Max Weber's main arguments in favour of bureaucracy. But it seems to have been lost in later treatments of formalization. Organizational justice studies have consistently shown how the transparency of controllable procedures is of paramount importance for the efficient and effective regulation of work relations – even more important than the substantive terms of the exchange.

Other instructive examples of the improvements in the justice of governance systems that could be achieved through the formalization of governance rules abound in interfirm relationships characterized by asymmetric bargaining power. For example, it has been widely observed that the relationships between 'hub' firms and their satellites (especially where the hub is for many reasons much less replaceable for the satellites than the satellites are for the hub firm) are very informal and are not regulated by written contract or explicit private rules. Although this reality may be partly explained by long-standing acquaintance and 'trust' among firms, deeper inspection and the reported opinion of the 'satellites' often reveals that the preferences of the latter would be for a more guaranteed and formalized relationship, because without such formality their exposure to risk is totally unregulated (and unpredictable). In the absence of formal regulation they are often made to bear unilaterally the costs of adapting to the changing requests of the dominant firm (Grandori 1991). So informality may hide a 'corrupted' authority relation in which risk is allocated inefficiently and transaction costs and quasi-rents are allocated unfairly.

A final unconventional note regards the consequences of the formalization of rules for organizational change. A traditional tenet in organization studies has been that systems of action that are highly formalized – in the sense of being governed by extensive application of explicit and written rules, procedures and programmes – show high inertia and low capacity for change. However, according to the argument developed here, the equation between the intensity of regulation and the intensity of formalization is not necessary and possibly due to the neglect of the important regulatory function of informal norms in traditional organization studies (in which 'informal organization' has often been seen as counterdependent and deviant with respect to rational-legal organization and as performing psychological defence rather than economic governance functions). If we accept the hypothesis that it is the prescriptiveness of rules and norms that drives rigidity, we could even argue, as North (1990) recently did, that the explicitness and formalization of rules can improve organizational change capacities. In fact, informal social norms, exactly because they are often interiorized as 'natural' rather than artificial human constructs, and because they may not even be clearly recognized by the actors following them, are likely to be more difficult to change.

The fungibility between external and internal regulation

Recent contributions in law and economics have argued that the systems of rules supervised by hierarchy that largely govern the internal activities of firms are a 'continuation' and integration of the incomplete regulation that can be achieved through external laws and contracts supervised by judicial authority (Williamson 1993). This perspective can be useful for evaluating when external or internal regulation is going to be more effective, and for predicting more reliably the consequences of specific changes in 'external' regulation on economic behaviour.

However, for this purpose, the usual explanatory framework employed in transaction cost economics needs to be enriched substantially. That framework sets out two main predictors of a required shift from external to internal regulation: uncertainty about the possible states of the world in which exchange will take place, leading to contract incompleteness; and 'small numbers' contracting seen as deriving from bilateral monopolies based on asset specificity (Williamson 1975). Some of the required extensions may be outlined starting from this formulation of Williamson's organizational failures framework. First, monopolies are not always bilateral and the consequences of unilateral monopolies for effective regulation may be different. Second, not all monopolies are due to asset specificity, and again, the regulatory implications of monopolies with different sources are different (Williamson 1987). Third, transaction costs analyses of regulation consider the costs for the transacting firms; but a correct evaluation of when external regulation should prevail on internal regulation should include also the costs borne by external third parties, such as consumers or neighbourhoods. Fourth, when both external and internal regulation and arbitration are feasible, corporate actors will assess the comparative advantages of relying on external law and courts or on private settlement, taking into account the cost and time entailed by the two systems as well as the probability of winning under the two systems. Therefore, the relative use of internal and external regulation will depend also on cognitive variables such as attitudes towards risk and probability assessments.

With regard to the first point, Klein *et al.* (1978) and Monteverde and Teece (1982) have analysed the case of asymmetric specific investments and unilateral monopoly in a transaction and have observed that the party which foresees fewer and less attractive alternative partners, because of the specific investment it has made, is exposed to the expropriation of the quasi-rent generated by the specific transaction up to the value that it can realize in its best alternative transaction. Given that this arrangement would be inefficient and unfair, they prescribe integration or at least quasi-integration among the two parties as a possible solution. However, that solution will be reached only if the weaker party does not enter the asymmetric relation and demands safeguard *ex ante.* Once asymmetric specific investments are made, given that the expropriating party has no incentive for changing the arrangement and the expropriated party has no bargaining power for obtaining a change, it seems that an efficient and fair solution is not likely to be implemented. Rather, it seems that the case of asymmetric specific investments, as more generally the case of unilateral monopolies, once formed, is a situation that calls for external regulation, if efficient and fair contracts are to be reached.

A different situation arises in the second case when there are small numbers and high transaction costs but they are not due to asset specificity. For example, Williamson (1975) discusses the problem of 'conspiring oligopolists' incurring high transaction costs for devising and maintaining aligned behaviours, e.g. price levels, in the face of uncertain events and free-riding potential. He concludes that even though an integrated firm would be superior because of small numbers, uncertainty and high transaction costs, the creation of an integrated dominant firm (even if transaction-cost efficient) should be opposed firmly and fiercely by anti-trust law. This illustrates how the implications of transaction-cost economics for anti-trust regulation need to be considered as one input among others and do not lead directly to designing efficient regulatory solutions. And it leads to our third and related point about the need for considering externalities.

This issue is strictly connected to the former because the reasons justifying anti-trust blockage of integration, in spite of high transaction costs for the involved firms, lie mainly in the costs that increased concentration and private ruling are likely to generate for other external actors. Finally, the reasons for accepting external regulation (i.e. an imposed public rule system for resolving conflict) as opposed to internal regulation (a private rule system negotiated and agreed by the parties to the conflict) are affected by other factors, such as the cost of administering the two systems, and expectations about the relative probability of gaining/winning in the two systems. If a particular issue is poorly regulated in the public law system, then there may be more informal and private attempts to regulate. Inefficient and ineffective systems of public law and regulation tend to lead to the use of internal regulation and private agreements. Even a process of deregulation on the part of public authorities is likely to be responded to by private interest groups installing their own systems of private regulation rather than by 'competing'. An interesting example of the last contention is provided by a study on the effect of deregulation in the airline industry in the US (Lang and Lockhart 1990) in which an increase in board interlocking was found both between airline companies (in the form of indirect interlocks through participation in a third firm's board, given the legal limits to direct interlocks between competitors) and between airlines and financial institutions, representing sources of critical resources. Among the possible signs that the first hypothesis is also reasonable, the consistent rise of a profession of business arbitrators (Bazerman and Lewicki 1983) assisting and supervising private systems of rules, can be mentioned. In addition, the diffusion of obligational arbitrated contracts could be interpreted as an interesting 'hybrid' regulatory solution capable on one hand of replacing cumbersome public regulatory and judicial systems, and on the other hand to help the directly involved parties to find agreements that they would not be able to see by themselves.

Case studies

The following two studies illustrate some of the ideas previously developed. The structure of regulation in the television sector is analysed to show how the prevalence of 'constitutional' and 'paradigmatic' rules and of codes of conduct, with respect to applied routines and procedures, allow 'flexible regulation' to take place. The evolution of regulation in the construction industry illustrates the interaction and interlockedness between external and internal regulation, and between formal and informal regulation.

Flexible regulation in the television industry: a flat and reversed rule pyramid

The European television sector reveals the complexity of forms of institutionalized rules and regulation. It is often said that the television industry is one of the most regulated and institutionalized but, in reality, the case of broadcasting companies demonstrates that it is not possible to speak about the nature of governance without considering the level of detail of the regulations, be they formal or informal. In other words, the extent to which an organizational decision maker is restricted in his/her choices by external rules is not always directly proportional to the degree of regulation of the business sector.

Television companies, particularly public television companies, live in a highly complex context (Soda *et al.* 1998). On the one hand, they operate in an industry that is one of the most highly regulated by the state; on the other, they are called upon to construct a creative and innovative product that is capable of competing in the highly competitive market of audience ratings. This means that the highly social nature of television (Bourdieu 1996) gives rise to a great deal of background regulation, but the artistic nature of the product and the 'postmodern' instability of competitive success simultaneously encourage greater flexibility in terms of the detailed regulatory context.

Programming decision making, which is the main manifestation of broadcasting activities, is therefore part of a multilayered context of institutionalization. Formal and social norms are widespread at the level of underlying values and general regulations. Decision makers are above all bound by the national legislation governing broadcasting: for example, the amount of advertising allowed or the proportion of programmes that must be produced nationally or in Europe. At this first level of regulation, the television sector appears to be restricted and constrained. However, the laws of the state are not the only types of rules that can be found in television companies, some of which have formalized detailed codes of conduct and decision making ('producers' guidelines'), that have to be followed by programming managers. These latter norms regulate programming content by providing what may be called 'ethical' directives. In some countries, these take the form of physical manuals (as in the case of the BBC); in others, they are simply tacit elements of the cultural patrimony of programming managers (as in the case of RAI, the Italian state television company). The norms include general guidelines concerning such questions as good taste and decency, the representation of violence within the programming structure, the protection of privacy, programming impartiality and the transmission of scenes of sex and violence. These norms represent an intermediate level of ruling – what has been earlier termed the level of 'procedures and heuristics'. These rules still leave the programme makers and the programme planners with the issue of what is actually to be produced. In this respect, they retain discretion. Nor can this discretion be removed by the application of routines – the most detailed level of rules and regulations – for the simple reason that there is no sure way of predicting success in the industry. Uncertainty at this level is high and therefore programme planners and makers ultimately base all of their decisions on highly personal decision-making heuristics that are influenced by their own direct experience. There are extremely few programming decisions that can be routinized and these generally relate to some highly particular types of transmission, such as weather forecasts.

In conclusion, the pyramid of rules existing inside television companies seems to be highly unbalanced towards 'constitutional' or core norms, becoming less rich as it moves in the direction of rules of thumb, and virtually disappearing in the case of programmes and routines. This particular configuration of the pyramid of rules shows that even apparently highly regulated sectors – simply because they are rich in the more visible macro forms of regulation – may seem to be relatively 'anarchic' if the entire range of rules is analysed. Second, the differentiation of the roles of the different types of rules seems to be confirmed: in the case of television companies, 'constitutional' rules serve to guarantee and safeguard the public interest in the offered services, though the rule system also seems to provide decision makers with freedom in making operational programming decisions. This lightness of the system of detailed norms is consistent with the complex and creative nature of the product. In brief, television programming decision makers enjoy a relatively high degree of discretion despite the fact that they are strongly influenced by constitutional indications, as they are not tightly constrained by low-level rules and routines.

In order better to describe the different structures of ruling systems we can use the metaphor of the pyramid, introduced before. There are structures of rules that have very light bases of constitutional norms but highly constraining systems of procedures and routines. The production decision in a manufacturing plant within a firm competing in a mature industry can be the example of this configuration of a rule system. The structure of ruling in the case of television programming seems to be opposite. In this case the pyramidal structure of rules is characterized by a heavy base of constitutional norms and lighter layers of more constraining rules such as procedures and routines.

State regulation and industry self-regulation in the Italian construction industry

This second example considers the relationship between formal and informal rules of behaviour and the role of public-versus-private regulation of the rules, through an examination of the Italian construction industry. In this context, the formal rules refer to the legislation governing the certification of the competence of the companies to undertake particular types of building activity and the way in which competition for public-works contracts was managed. By 'industry self-regulation' we refer to how the large firms within the industry established their own informal norms to govern competitive and cooperative behaviour.

A historical reconstruction of the legislative interventions aimed at regulating the industry (Soda and Usai 1999) has highlighted the production of formal regulations on the part of the state. The construction industry in Italy still seems to be characterized by the fact that it has a large number of legal provisions governing the way in which it works. It is an industry that enjoyed almost forty years of continuous growth in Italy until it was struck by a profound crisis in the 1990s. Before this crisis, the large Italian construction enterprises had developed a system of cooperative relationships aimed at ensuring that they all received some part of the large public-works building contracts that were issued by the state each year. State legislation favoured the formation of coalitions of companies to manage major public-works contracts. The companies took this formal set of regulations and gradually constructed their own system for self-regulating the competition. This private and informal system was based on rules that were unwritten because they frequently involved illicit behaviours. Industry self-regulation was complementary to rather than substitutive of state regulation. It was a case of the perfect coexistence of formal, public and informal, private regulation. In practice, the state had created conditions in which industry self-regulation was particularly profitable for the companies (for example, by creating a mechanism that allowed groups of companies to qualify for particular contracts by summing the individual certifications of the different partners). In this way, the Italian construction industry reflects the argument that 'the greater the potential benefits to an industry of self-regulation, the greater the likelihood of such regulation' (Gupta and Lad 1983: 421).

By means of the cohesion of the network of alliances among the companies, which created a network of reciprocal obligations or indebtedness, the large construction firms managed the relationship between supply and demand in the market of public works. In practice, a process was generated in which the laws of the state created the perfect conditions for the development of private regulation which, in turn, created the conditions for increasing the volume of the business managed by the industry.

No bankruptcies occurred for many years because the enterprises colluded with each other simply to divide the resources made available by the state by means of its financing of public works. The construction companies exerted pressure on the state in order to formalize the tacit norms already existing as industry rules or to create new norms that would be useful for strengthening the private system of regulation. This illustrates the way in which internal, private rules and external, public rules are embedded in each other, and neither one, or both, play the role of a 'context' for the other.

There are a number of reasons for the profound crisis that has afflicted the industry in the 1990s, but the main reason can be attributed to the institutional crisis involving a large part of the national political system as a result of its many and substantial illicit relationships with the large construction companies. The political crisis both undermined the formal norms governing the functioning of the industry and the informal, social norms that governed the way in which it worked. The social norms which governed the industry have been upset, the clash among institutional powers has led to the lapse of the rules and practices that had governed the industry for over thirty years. The effect on the munificence of the environment has been immediate. In the example of the building industry the institutional earthquake occurred through a strong retrenchment of the resources (both economic and 'legitimation') given by the system. While organizational survival is enhanced by legitimacy, it is also enhanced by economic viability. The institutional crisis has, in fact, caused the crisis of a whole economic system based on formal and informal rules and practices which used to keep the industry functioning. Firms were no longer able to control access to the contracts leading to a rapid decline in profitability for many of the large construction companies in the period 1992–93.

The situation following the breakdown of the old system is characterized by uncertainty and the search for new rules. Companies are no longer able to guarantee access to public-works contracts nor are politicians able to ensure that demand is kept constantly high by expanding public finance. There has been some attempt at consolidation through mergers and acquisitions but many companies have gone bankrupt and the network of cooperation that had long governed the industry has dissolved over the last few years.

Summary and conclusions

Rules have been seen as a distinctive mechanism for governing corporate and economic action that can be used as an alternative to or in combination with other mechanisms. The comparative analysis of rule-guided economic behaviours with respect to other forms of governance based on case-by-case decision making, and the comparative analysis of different types of rules with respect to each other, has provided various insights for rule explanation and design. Institutionalized rules and regulations provide actors with ways of acting that avoid the necessity for case-by-case decision making. The degree of certainty/uncertainty in particular contexts is a major influence on the extent of rule-based behaviour. Uncertainty itself may exist on a variety of levels. There may be uncertainty at the level of basic rules of action; this leads to the sort of 'constitution' building where key principles are articulated either formally or informally, as in the case of broadcasting companies. There may be uncertainty at the technical level of operations which militates against routines and the programming of decisions. In other cases there may be certainty at the level of technical operations which leads to rules embedded in routines and programmes.

The 'constitutional' level may be less relevant in these contexts, such as standardized manufacturing.

The degree of formalization of rules is not, however, directly linked to issues of uncertainty and flexibility, but it can be thought of as a function of size, accountability and computational complexity (as information-processing variables); and of the degree of conflict among interests and the requirements for procedural justice (as conflict-resolution variables).

Furthermore, most contexts are characterized by an interaction between internal and private regulation on one side, and external and public regulation on the other side. Changes in either system generally lead to changes in the other system. In particular, changes in the public regulation system, and in particular events of 'deregulation', do not inevitably lead to arms-length exchange and competition. Private systems of rules and supervisory authorities are a likely substitute for public rules and authorities, given that the nature of these mechanisms and the conditions for their effective application are to a large extent equivalent.

In conclusion, this chapter has examined rules and regulations as a particular mode of governing economic transactions. The specificity of this mode of governance is that it provides a way of dealing with complex issues without having to recalculate or re-evaluate all the elements. However, rules exist on different levels and are enforced through different mechanisms. It is important that in the study of regulation researchers identify the particular properties of the rules and in what ways these constrain action. Do they provide programmes and routines, heuristics and procedures or constitutions and paradigms? Are they formalized or not? How far are they embedded in public systems of regulation or private systems of cooperation? By examining in detail these processes, it is possible to go beyond broad caricatures of regulation and deregulation and seek to explain how economic actions are coordinated within complex systems of rules and enforcement mechanisms.

Note

1 The conceptual framework of this chapter is based on Grandori (forthcoming). Both the conceptualization and case studies have benefited from comments by Giuseppe Delmestri.

References

Arrow, K. J. (1951) *Social Choice and Individual Values*, New York: Wiley.

Bazerman, M. H. and Lewicki, R. J. (eds) (1983) *Negotiating in Organizations*, Beverly Hills, CA: Sage.

Bourdieu, P. (1996) *Sur la Télévision*, Paris: Liber-Raison d'Agir.

Brennan, G. H. and Buchanan, J. M. (1985) *The Reasons of Rules*, Cambridge: Cambridge University Press.

Campbell, D. T. (1960) 'Blind variation and selective retention in creative thought as in other knowledge processes', *Psychological Review* 67: 380–400.

Cohen, M. D., March J. G. and Olsen J. P. (1996) 'Routines and other recurring action patterns of organizations: contemporary research issues', *Industrial and Corporate Change* 5(3): 653–98.

Davis, O. A., Dempster, M. A. H. and Wildavsky, A. (1974) 'Toward a predictive theory of government expenditures: US domestic appropriations', *British Journal of Economics* 9: 587–608.

Duncan, R. and Weiss, A. (1978) 'Organizational learning implications for organizational design', in B. Staw (ed.) *Research in Organizational Behavior, Volume I*, Greenwich, CT: JAI Press.

Etzioni, A. (1985) 'Opening the preferences: a socio-economic research agenda', *Journal of Behavioral Economics* 14: 183–205.

Fisher, R. and Ury, W. (1981) *Getting to Yes*, Boston, MA: Houghton Mifflin.

Gouldner, A. G. (1960) 'The norm of reciprocity: a preliminary statement', *American Sociological Review*, April.

Grandori, A. (1991) 'Negotiating efficient organization forms', *Journal of Economic Behavior and Organization* 16: 319–40.

—— (1997) 'Governance structures, coordination mechanisms and cognitive models', *Journal of Management and Governance* 1(1): 29–47.

—— (forthcoming) 'Rules, norms and conventions', in A. Grandori (ed.) *Organization and Economic Behaviour*, London: Routledge.

Greenberg, J. (1987) 'A taxonomy of organizational justice theories', *Academy of Management Review* 12(1): 9–22.

Gupta, A. K and Lad, L. J (1983) 'Industry self-regulation: an economic, organizational, and political analysis', *Academy of Management Review* 8(3): 416–25.

Hannan, M. H. and Freeman, J. (1977) 'The population ecology of organizations', *American Journal of Sociology* 82: 929–64.

Klein, B., Crawford, R. G. and Alchian, A. A. (1978) 'Vertical integration, appropriable rents and the competitive contracting process', *Journal of Law and Economics* 21: 297–326.

Kuhn, T. S. (1962) *The Structure of Scientific Revolutions*, Chicago, IL: University of Chicago Press.

Lakatos, I. (1970) 'Falsification and the methodology of scientific research programmes', in I. Lakatos and A. Musgrave (eds) *Criticism and the Growth of Knowledge*, Cambridge: Cambridge University Press.

Lang, J. R. and Lockhart, D. E. (1990) 'Increased environmental uncertainty and changes in board linkage patterns', *Academy of Management Journal*, 33(1): 106–28.

Lindblom, C. E. (1977) *Politics and Markets*, New York: Basic Books.

March, J. G. (1976) *Ambiguity and choice in organizations*, Bergen: Universitaetforlaget.

—— (1978) 'Bounded rationality, ambiguity, and the engineering of choice', *Bell Journal of Economics* 9: 587–608.

March, J. G. and Shapira, Z. (1982) 'Behavioral decision theory and organizational theory', in G. R. Ungson and D. N. Braunstein (eds) *Decision Making*, Boston, MA: Kent Publishing.

Monteverde, K. and D. J.Teece (1982) 'Appropriable rents and quasi-vertical integration', *Journal of Law and Economics* XXV: 323–8.

Nelson, R. R. and Winter, S. G. (1982) *An Evolutionary Theory of Economic Change*, Cambridge, MA: Harvard University Press.

Nooteboom, B., Berger, J. and Noorderhaven, N. G. (1995) 'Sources, measurement and effect of trust in the supply of electrical/electronic components', paper given at the ESF EMOT Conference: Industry structure and interorganizational networks, Geneva.

North, D. C. (1990) *Institutions, Institutional Change, and Economic Performance*, Cambridge: Cambridge University Press.

Ouchi, W. G. (1980) 'Markets, bureaucracies and clans', *Administrative Science Quarterly* 25: 129–41.

Powell, W. W. and DiMaggio, P. J. (1991) (eds) *The New Institutionalism in Organizational Analysis*, Chicago, IL: University of Chicago Press.

Pugh, D. S., Hickson, D. J., Hinigs, C. R. and Turner, C. (1969) 'An empirical taxonomy of structures of work organizations', *Administrative Science Quarterly* 14: 115–26.

Rawls, J. (1979) *A Theory of Justice*, Cambridge, MA: Harvard University Press.

Sabel, C. F. (1993) 'Constitutional ordering in historical context', in F. W. Scharpf (ed.) *Games in Hierarchies and Networks*, Frankfurt: Campus Verlag.

Schein, E. H. (1985) *Organizational Culture and Leadership*, San Francisco, CA: Jossey-Bass.

Simon, H. A. (1960) *The New Science of Management Decision*, New York: Harper and Row.

—— (1990) 'A mechanism for social selection and successful altruism', *Science* 250: 1665–8.

Soda, G. and Usai, A. (1999) 'The dark side of dense network: from embeddedness to indebtedness', in A. Grandori (ed.) *Inter-firm Networks: Organization and Industrial Competetiveness*, London: Routledge.

Soda, G., Usai, A., Pilati, M. and Salvemini, S. (1998) 'Facing complexity of decision making processes: organisational responses in the European broadcasting industry', unpublished paper, Milan: Bocconi.

Trice, H. M. and Beyer, J. M. (1984) 'Studying organizational cultures through rites and ceremonials', *Academy of Management Review* 9(4): 653–69.

Weick, K. (1979) *The Social Psychology of Organizing*, Reading, MA: Addison-Wesley.

Williamson, O. E. (1975) *Markets and Hierarchies: Analysis and Antitrust Implications*, New York: Free Press.

—— (1987) *Antitrust Economics. Mergers, Contracting and Strategic Behavior*, Oxford: Blackwell.

—— (1993) 'Transaction cost economics and organization theory', *Industrial and Corporate Change* 2(2): 107–56.

Witte, E. and Zimmermann, H. J. (1986) *Empirical Research on Organization Decision-making*, Amsterdam: North Holland.

Part II

Regulatory regimes and governance

4 Deregulation and embeddedness

The case of the French banking system

Danielle Salomon

Since the 1980s, banking activity has been restructured in most industrialized countries, generally through a process of deregulation and reregulation (Majone 1994; Morgan and Knights 1997). In France, the deregulation process began in earnest in the mid-1980s and continued through into the 1990s. The general idea was to change the state's role, which in banking had been characterized since the end of the Second World War by deliberate and planned policies of intervention in the allocation of funds (Zysman 1983). This chapter aims to study the implementation of the deregulation process within the specific French context.

The French banking system had been protected by forty years of 'organized competition' within the sector. This had depended on strong and protective relationships between financial institutions and the state which ensured profits to the companies by shielding them, while ensuring profits from an open, competitive game. The reforms beginning in the mid-1980s were meant to substitute the existing regulatory framework with another one. New principles, rules and modes of interaction between actors had to evolve whilst old methods of state control had to be discarded on the basis of new principles; as a consequence, rules, interactions between actors and practices had also to evolve. Lying behind this was the conviction of senior managers in the industry, influential politicians and higher-level civil servants that in the long run competition would have virtuous consequences for France as a whole (Jobert and Théret 1994).

The complexity of this process was increased by the fact that it took place in the context of two other profound changes. First, there was the growing importance of European integration to the French state which implied a shift towards opening up markets, including those for financial services. Thus it was obvious that the old system was incompatible with the European Single Market and the state had to disentangle itself from the financial sector which, in turn, had to be strong enough to meet competition from other European Union countries. Second, there was the severe recession of the late 1980s and early 1990s which hit financial institutions in all European countries, reducing their capital base and making them vulnerable to bad debts (Pastré 1993). Policy makers sought simultaneously to navigate their way through these difficulties whilst still maintaining their sight on the eventual goal of a liberalized and competitive financial services sector. The result was a rather messy compromise in which some of the old ways of managing the sector were retained even in a supposedly deregulated environment.

French banking on the eve of reform

The French banking system on the eve of its reform had several main characteristics, which stretched back to its origins in the nineteenth century. Its key historical characteristic was the way in which it grew into a series of hermetically sealed sectors. Each time a new demand for specific financing had emerged throughout the nineteenth and twentieth centuries, the French government had authorized the incorporation of private companies designed to meet these particular economic or client needs. This policy led to the coexistence of a series of heterogeneous financial institutions of varying legal status, with various types of capital, oriented towards different types of clients or financing (Gueslin and Lescure 1995), all operating under the guidance of various arms of the state.

In the postwar period, this structure became the basis of a more concerted effort on the part of key actors in the French state to use the financial system to modernize industry whilst supporting agriculture, thus improving France's status on the international stage (Fourquet 1980). State agencies, particularly the Direction du Trésor, part of the Ministry of Economy and Finances, took overall charge of finance, banking and nationalized firms in France. Credit ceilings were defined for each type of financial institution, based on the previous year's activity and the priorities decided by the government (Castel and Masse 1983). These were complemented by other measures like compulsory reserves set by the central bank, the fixing of prices to reduce competition for funds, a ban on interest-bearing deposit accounts, and exchange controls. These practices were fulfilling three aims at the same time: a monetary policy, a supervising policy and an economic policy. Fixing the credit ceilings along with exceptions could, for instance, promote exports, this being accompanied by additional measures such as export policy insurances.

The fragmentation of the financial institutions into clients, sectors, types of financing or financial services and the long stability that growth and a centralized and authoritative policy maintained, led to a compartmentalization of the system. Specific financing channels linked certain categories of lenders and borrowers and created a general inertia in their relationships. Only in the retail sector did the state allow any semblance of real competition in the hope that it could persuade the French population to entrust their savings to banks rather than hide them under the bed! This strategy proved relatively successful as the total amount of money in circulation grew from 11.92 billion francs to 670.2 billion in thirty years. By the late 1980s almost 100 per cent of adults in France had a bank account.

Fragmentation, sedimentation, compartmentalization, stability and centralized policies in a context of growth meant profits for the financial institutions. As a counterpart, laws were very protective and favourable to the clients by providing various types of credit and loans for priority areas and generally holding interest rates to a politically rather than economically determined level, a process which was sustained to a significant degree by the ability of financial institutions to do cross-subsidies from one activity to another with little outside knowledge or interference.

The principles underlying the transformation of French banking

The transformation which the French state attempted was based on the implicit assumption of a fluid banking system, in which the market and competition were to regulate the direction and pricing of funds. Formal regulation was to become merely 'technical'; political and economic goals were no longer to have any influence. The 1984 Banking Act provided a single framework to all banking institutions. This framework was to be managed in its various elements by a range of actors including supervisory authorities (in particular, the Ministry of Economy and Finances, often represented by the Direction du Trésor and the Banque de France) and monitoring bodies (Conseil National du Crédit – National Credit Council – a consultative body; Comité des Etablissements de Crédit – Committee of Credit Institutions – which provides permits to organizations wishing to do business as banks; Comité de la Réglementation Bancaire – Banking Regulations Committee – in charge of developing rules; Commission Bancaire – Banking Commission – in charge of controlling institutions, sanctioning them and making sure rules are complied with) (Noyer 1990). These bodies have the authority to define the policy framework, whenever a question is within their sphere of competence, without having to resort to the legislative process.

The Banking Act was followed by measures taken by the various left- and right-wing governments in power from 1985 on (see Zerah 1993 for a full account). In 1985, measures were taken to allow for the development of financial markets and to ensure access to these markets for large and medium-sized companies. In 1986, credit control rules were announced to be officially eliminated as of 1 January 1987. Exchange control, with its diverse and complex procedures for businesses as well as private individuals, was gradually lifted between 1985 and 1989. Prudential rules were gradually implemented from 1986 onwards, as well as laws adapting the French law to Single Market dispositions and liberalizing the Banque de France from government authority.

Following their victory in the 1986 elections, the Right initiated a privatization movement countering the nationalizations of 1982. Between 1986 and 1988, Société Générale, CCF and Crédit Agricole were privatized, along with other large public companies. Shareholding structures were organized so that 'stable' shareholders would make up the 'core capital' and shield these organizations from possible hostile takeovers. The top managers of the banks remained the same public officers coming from the 'grands corps' educated at the 'grandes écoles'. The aim was to limit the impact of privatization by providing stability in both the ownership structure and management system of the banks. Privatizations were stopped in 1988, and then started again with the return of the Right in 1993. In 1995 the Left continued that movement and progressively all the financial institutions were sold to the public or to private groups.

It is important to note here that very few laws are passed for banking purposes, and that when they are it is often as an incorporation of European directives which leaves little autonomy. Instead, changes in the banking sector are managed by the Trésor and the Banque de France which have the key resources for this, i.e. their extensive knowledge of banking, their privileged situation as supervisors, their capacity to negotiate with all types of financial institutions and their privileged access to the Banking Commission. In other words, the banking framework, until very recently, has hardly been subject to public deliberations, and when it has, debates have been strictly controlled.

Keys to the new paradigm: a virtuous competition

Eliminating central planning and introducing prudential rules was aimed at providing a uniform policy framework for all institutions, placing them all under identical constraints. In theory, prudential rules internalize in banks the need for self-limitation, whilst before, the quantitative credit ceiling was held by the public authorities. Prudential rules tie together the various elements of banks' financial structures, so that a given institution cannot jeopardize its own existence, either because of the overwhelming importance of a single customer or because of overly ambitious total risks. As a consequence, these rules internalize the follow-up and control of operations inside institutions. Supervisory bodies only have to 'control the control', i.e. make sure that banks not only play by the rules, but also have the necessary tools for information and internal management and for the ongoing tracking of operations. Therefore there is one big difference between credit control and prudential control: the first directly limits the activity of the institution, whereas the second does so indirectly by forcing the company to limit its lending to the levels which accord to its prudential position.

Operating in real competition and playing by these new rules, the idea was that French bankers would have to bring their products, their operating conditions, their productivity and their profitability in line with that of other world players. Failure to do so would affect their abilities to raise funds on the international financial markets and thereby threaten their position in both home and foreign markets where banks with better credit ratings would be able to outcompete them. By beginning this process in the 1980s, the French authorities hoped to give the financial institutions enough time to change and to get accustomed to these new practices.

This transformation assumed, between the lines, that operators facing strong competition would be 'rationally' ready to reform their internal operations, change their structure and introduce new ways of working in order to meet new monitoring conditions. Once fair competition was in place, all financial actors would play on an equal footing. However, this was not what happened. Instead, the sector was deeply destabilized: companies experienced either losses or only moderate profits compared with their foreign counterparts. The main financial institutions were not in a position to proceed along the learning curve as expected, and the cut-throat competition on prices which emerged weakened all the players.

Difficulties arising from the transformation process

The frailty of the transformation underway comes from a number of facts. First, the rules of the game were modified before the conditions for its success were changed. Second, the recession burst at a time when the competitors were involved in a crazy race to increase market share without having the appropriate resources to cope with it. On the side of the state, the new regulatory framework did not offer the authorities direct leverage on the internal practices of the financial institutions. In fact, the new regulations assumed an environment ready for implementation, which it was not. The successful application of prudential rules and competition in a declining market context relies on high-performance internal systems, which is just what the large banks lacked. Furthermore, successful competition between credit institutions presupposed that no significant constraints hindered the process of competition, which was far from being the case.

A banking system with multiple regulations

The main characteristic of the French banking system, as recalled earlier, is a strong compartmentalization that the reform tried notably to erase. This objective was partially met. However, differentiating factors remained, stemming from prerogatives and counterobligations set by the state, which were not eliminated by deregulation (see de Fournas 1993 for a comprehensive and polemical list). Banks – joined by the large mutual deposit institutions, by far the largest segment of credit institutions – feeling themselves freed by the lifting of credit ceilings, started to wage an open war against all institutions which enjoyed positive prerogatives (such as, for example, a monopoly on tax exempt savings accounts) different from their own. However, the government, supported by the elected representatives and certain administrations and in need of specific instruments for various patrons and clients with interests in the specific economic sectors affected by these privileges, insisted on maintaining them.

For example, the birth and growth of Crédit Agricole had been fostered in order to help the financing of French agriculture; it had thus been allocated the monopoly of subsidized loans designed for farmers. To make up for that, Crédit Agricole was not allowed to open counters in urban areas, and could not service clients outside rural and agricultural areas. In 1988, when it became a private mutual credit bank, it lost its monopoly on subsidized loans to farmers, but was allowed to do business outside farming areas and to open up its ruling bodies to customers from all walks of life. However, it remains the largest provider of subsidized loans, and with the Post Office the only other institution to provide clients with financial services in rural areas. In addition, its mutual structure remains and, although the clients now come from all areas of the population, the members of its board, especially at regional level, remain in majority farmers. Furthermore, Crédit Agricole is not bound by the 1937 decree requesting all commercial banks to close their counters for two days in a row, including a Sunday. Along the same lines, Caisses d'Epargnes (Savings Banks) were entitled to a monopoly on the distribution of a tax-exempt savings account which had been designed to collect money to finance subsidized housing projects, but which provides them now with a financial manna most commercial banks dispute.

For the commercial banks (and especially the three largest, Crédit Lyonnais, Société Générale and Banque Nationale de Paris), the deregulation process was particularly destabilizing. They pursued new markets, all of which were now more competitive because of decompartmentalization (leading every bank into competing for the same business). At the same time, the recession was reducing the number of potential clients available. As the banks sought new markets, they came into competition with more specialized institutions. In some sectors, where specialist knowledge was effective (such as consumer credit, see Salomon 1997a), the large banks were outcompeted. They found themselves with poor performing loans because of their inability to develop systems of control and monitoring capable of weeding out high-risk borrowers. They operated on a simple dichotomous model of the world and their clients. Conditions were either 'certain' or 'uncertain'; the large banks did not have the systems for analysing degrees of uncertainty which specialist institutions had developed over a long time (Landau 1973; Landau and Chisholm 1992).

Whether or not operators learned how to play the new game depended on several factors: their weight, dominant or marginal; their organization and their internal resources in relation to change; their strategic position, the moment they arrived on the market; and finally, the challenge represented either by a specific segment, or more often by their mere survival in a changing environment. In this respect banks, and notably universal banks, were especially weakened by the new conditions in that many other institutions (which had previously focused on their own particular sector) now also sought to tap what was in effect the banks' main source of income.

The inadequacy of the new regulatory tools in cases of difficulty

The difficulties experienced by operators, clients and sectors came from factors endogenous to the banking scene (destabilization, weaker operators, etc.), as well as from exogenous factors, such as the continuing economic recession, high interest rates or inflation, which condition a great number of financial behaviours or decisions. Authorities, even though endowed with an extensive policy framework, had no formal way of dealing with these difficulties. However, the government, the Banque de France and administrations decided to rescue the actors instead of leaving the market to regulate the process. The most symbolic example is Crédit Lyonnais which was rescued by the state instead of left to bankruptcy. Social peace, political matters, consideration of confidence and the reputation of Paris as a financial centre were probably behind the decision and it became a symbolic message to both actors and market.

The difficulties in the early 1990s affected both specific groups of clients (such as private individuals who had become overindebted, or small and medium-sized enterprises which had gone bankrupt) and particular sectors (especially consumer credit and real-estate lending). In turn, these impacted on specific operators who suffered substantial losses. In all cases, the new regulatory system based on prudential rules and *a posteriori* control left the authorities helpless to intervene immediately and directly in the ways they would have done before deregulation. Prudential rules call for ratios which are hardly ever breached because the size and versatility of large banks always makes the proportion taken up by a single client or a single activity seem in itself relatively insignificant. *A posteriori* control requires long months, if not years, of painstaking analyses before coming up with tangible results allowing for the intervention of the monitoring authority. Crédit Lyonnais is a perfect illustration of this. These mechanisms have no leverage on the collective behaviour of banking institutions or their clientele.

This situation was compounded by two phenomena. The novelty of the rules, the deliberate desire to change the nature of relationships between authorities and operators and the power granted to the Banking Commission placed it in a situation where it had to interpret the rules it controlled. This meant that for the rules to be applied, they had to be interpreted, i.e. they could be negotiated before application. In many cases, the Banking Commission was invested with this role, which, as a consequence, partly released operators from their responsibilities. As an example, the controlling body is supposed to be able to intervene on the basis of a qualitative assessment of, for example, the internal control system, whose definition is governed by a rule designed in 1990. For the Crédit Lyonnais, this internal control system had been analysed by the Banking Commission at the end of the 1980s, and the positive conclusions drawn in their analysis were widely used by Haberer (the president of the bank) when the bank's losses were referred to and analysed by various investigation commissions. The second phenomenon, linked to the central position confidence and reputation play in credit activities, considerably limits authorities' room for manoeuvre. In a competitive environment, actions taken by supervisory bodies and authorities are in full view. For example, simultaneously investigating all internal controlling systems in large banks equates to announcing alarmist news openly, which markets and observers can pick up and use adversely. On the other hand, after experiencing a series of losses and a deterioration of their operating conditions, operators with deficient information systems become reluctant to actively push business. Politicians are always ready to blame bankers for their 'lack of daring', 'bashfulness' or for deploying 'umbrellas' in stormy weather. This holds especially true when recession jeopardizes an economic system based on mass production and mass consumption fuelled by the widespread availability of credit.

In the absence of direct levers provided by the banking policy framework, in an environment where interest rates were maintained way above inflation for monetary policy purposes, authorities were unable to do anything to solve emerging difficulties. However, political considerations dealing with the preservation of social peace and with the promotion of France among the leaders of industrialized countries drove politicians and senior administrators to find other means to allow them to, at least, influence what was going on.

Various levers were implemented or used, according to the challenges and opportunities at hand. Among the main measures were a series of efforts made by administrative bodies to persuade operators to change their practices, such as pushing operators towards integrating new management rules (e.g. in due time, creation of the interbank market), setting up working parties on topical items and bringing together the representatives of major credit institutions, or circulating advisory articles and analyses among the banking community. This work was not devoid of impact, especially since the Banking Commission, with its central role, was in charge of interpreting and negotiating rules and forecasts required for specific risks.

Two levers emerged: the first dealt with the control of differential competition conditions still in the hands of public authorities; the second was the opportunistic derivation of any event which could possibly support, influence or directly reach an objective that normal mechanisms were unable to attain.

The Banque de France and the Ministry of Economy and Finances, mainly through the Direction du Trésor, control the number of players by checking entry into the sector as well as exit from it in case of difficulties. Marketplace mechanisms allow the governor of the central bank to call on shareholders to bail out a potentially failing institution. When the institution is public, the state as shareholder can be called to the rescue, and institutions with public ownership can also be called upon even to bail out a private institution; for example, the Caisse des Depôts rescued the Banque des Travaux Publics, whose clientele interested public authorities.

The various prerogatives which continue to be enjoyed by the financial institutions still provide the authorities with some leverage to negotiate or even force decisions. They can use this leverage to force decisions on competitors (e.g. setting new standards of activities derived from the most profitable institutions), or to obtain arrangements from them by reducing or eliminating a privilege allowed to a single establishment (for example, reducing the interest rate on the Livret A – Savings book – of Caisses d'Epargnes, and creating a new tax-exempt savings account for all credit institutions, in exchange for banks agreeing to decrease their base rate).

Finally, and above all, through privatization the state introduced large banks to international market constraints. Once privatized, Société Générale and Banque Nationale de Paris had to compete strongly against their largest competitor, Crédit Lyonnais, particularly when the government decided to bring fresh capital into the latter, causing the others to argue this was an obvious example of unfair competition. However, by setting up 'core capital', the government helped to ease the learning process by protecting banks from hostile takeovers and by ensuring uniform practices and reciprocal consensus among 'core capital' members (in particular, that they would accept a lower return on equities than would be normal in other sectors).

These negotiation mechanisms met short- and medium-term priorities. In the short term, they provided effective leverage for some challenges. In the medium term, the gradual and timely elimination of prerogatives through negotiations eased the way towards the goal of deregulation. Immediately doing away with all privileges would have produced violent reactions and destabilized the market. Even so, as the consumer credit crisis (Salomon 1997b) and the crisis at Crédit Lyonnais showed, banks were keen to test the new competitive market to its limits and, in doing so, a number of them overstepped the mark before the state was able to intervene.

The authorities in charge of control were well aware that the operators' internal systems were deficient, and therefore they deliberately slowed down the opening and transformation processes. This deceleration was made easier by the fact that industrialized countries and the European Union also faced major difficulties. 1 January 1993 was not marked by the massive arrival of new operators coming from other member states, and in this respect banking was more protected than other sectors, such as airlines, even though the latter also have assets allowing them to brush aside some of their competitors, timewise and geographically. This meant that senior managers in these large corporations found themselves better off generating strategies to bypass internal difficulties in the short term rather than confronting them head on. The paralysing power of junior commercial and administrative staff has long been demonstrated. In the longer term, managers aimed at smoothly generating in-depth changes. Authorities, senior managers and staff needed the evidence of 'hefty' losses before an operator like Crédit Lyonnais, for example, was forced to resort to change.

Faced with competition, institutions became defensive, which made it difficult for industry associations to develop a common position. These associations remained based on their former statutes, even though these were no longer relevant in an environment of alliances and confrontations. The Association Française des Banques (the French Banking Association) for example, which remains the strongest and best-organized association, seemed paralysed by the divergent interests of its members. The administration, pushed by politicians and by the ever-increasing uncertainty, was encouraged to take action alone. Intervention was limited in time, solutions were developed with little coordination or consultation, and old reflexes dating back to the administered period came back on both sides. The objective of internalizing inside institutions the constraints of complying with rules was weakened in the process. The definition of long-term policies and of leverage provided by rules was also in jeopardy. Yet opportunities for public debate arose from these very difficulties and these were turned into public challenges, like the staggering losses suffered by Crédit Lyonnais. However, the way the problem was put on the public agenda was done to the detriment of a more global debate, where banking deregulation could be discussed in terms of its general consequences, with a clear statement of its objectives for French society.

More generally, banking, before changes in regulations, was a stable and closed community of public policies (Kingdon 1984). One of the consequences of the changes is that the financial sector is still broken up according to challenges which are hard to reconcile, but it continues to concentrate knowledge and the ability to define problems and possible alternatives into a very small number of hands, which act behind the scenes in the government, the Direction du Trésor, the central bank and the monitoring institutions. These privileged few are legitimized in their secrecy by the urgency of the situation and the political 'sensitivity' of the consequences of change, as well as the technical aspects and the overbearing importance of the reputation and confidence problem.

On the other hand, the fact that banking deregulation had social consequences and that the cost of it is spread over the community prompted a wider debate when problems came into the open. Elected representatives could easily make political capital out of the action taken, selecting certain institutions or practices as symbolic of wider social solidarities. For instance, the privatization of a group of regional banks (CIC) could be stopped by local elected deputies. However, this has also opened up the discussion to new players (consumer associations, magistrates) who have become part and parcel of the political scene, and are able to present their own arguments on the responsibilities and accountability of the financial sector and its regulators.

Conclusion

Banking, for the most part, is embedded in historical, social, economic, political and territorial specificities. Banks have retained customers through inertia in the past, but this is changing as prices and services become more differentiated. Even so, the level of transparency necessary to promote fluidity and competition is still limited and traditional relationships remain powerful. From the point of view of operators, banking seems to require order, so that competition does not lead to destabilizing anarchy and can provide virtuous consequences (the learning process of less affected players is more efficient than that of more destabilized ones). The earlier period in banking was characterized by a regulatory code managed jointly by senior administrators, politicians and bankers. The present period is marked by a dissociation of concerns. Institutions are more autonomous and can use this to compete with each other. But this new autonomy is in fact limited by the strong protective context of banking. For example, the existing laws involving the commitments of banks towards their indebted clients act as a protection against outside competition in a Single Market context. Facing the foreign institutions, all French institutions defend their specificities against any harmonization that would modify the spirit of the context of laws and practices in which banking is strongly embedded.

In conclusion, the French system has undergone a process of change in which the pattern of interaction between the state, the financial institutions and their various customers have been reconstructed. The orderly system which had been developed in the postwar period by adapting the traditional compartmentalized banking structure of France to a dirigiste state policy became increasingly difficult to sustain as financial markets internationalized and politicians sought to establish a single European market. However, simply legislating for a deregulated competitive market was not sufficient. The institutions could not discard the experiences, competences and relationships which had built up over decades. Their attempts to develop in new markets without first building and developing the skills were therefore disastrous, particularly in the context of the economic depression of the late 1980s and early 1990s. The authorities had to adapt their actions to these problems and therefore old attitudes re-emerged in which the state was asked to provide help and support. Thus the regulatory system evolved out of its old mould but moved hesitantly towards a new model. This evolution was a product of the particular embedded social relationships which characterized France and its financial institutions in the era before deregulation.

References

Castel, M. and Masse, J. A. (1983) *The Credit Ceiling* (*L'Encadrement du Crédit*), Que sais-je, Paris: PUF.

de Fournas, F. X. (1993) *Species of Bankers. Essays on Banking Management and Zoology* (*Espèces de Banquiers. Essai de Management et de Zoologie Bancaires*), Paris: Economica.

Fourquet, F. (1980) *The Accounts of Power. A History of the National Accounting and Planning* (*Les Comptes de la Puissance. Histoire de la Comptabilité Nationale et du Plan*), Paris: Encres.

Gueslin, A. and Lescure, M. (1995) 'Les banques publiques, parapubliques et coopératives françaises (vers 1920–vers 1960)', in *Banks in Western Europe from 1929 to Today* (*Les Banques en Europe de l'Ouest de 1929 à Nos Jours*), Acts of the Bercy Symposium, 7–8 October 1993, Comité pour l'histoire économique et financière de la France, Paris.

Jobert, B. and Théret, B. (1994) 'France: la consécration républicaine du néo-libéralisme', in B. Jobert (ed.) *The Neo-liberal Turn in Europe* (*Le Tournant Néo-libéral en Europe*), Logiques Politiques, Paris: L'Harmattan.

Kingdon, J. W. (1984) *Agendas, Alternatives and Public Policies*, London: HarperCollins.

Landau, M. (1973) 'On the concept of self-correcting organization', *Public Administration Review*, March/April: 1–36.

Landau, M. and Chisholm, D. (1992) 'Success oriented vs. failure avoidance. Management in public administration: a reconsideration', *Symposium: Public Management Modernization, Lessons from Experience* (*Colloque: La Modernisation de la Gestion Publique, les Leçons de l'Expérience*), Institut de Management Public, 26–27 March, Paris.

Majone, G. (1994) 'Communauté Economique Européenne: Déréglementation ou re-réglementation? La conduite des politiques publiques depuis l'Acte Unique', in B. Jobert (ed.) *The Neo-liberal Turn in Europe* (*Le Tournant Néo-libéral en Europe*), Logiques Politiques, Paris: L'Harmattan.

Morgan, G. and Knights, D. (eds) (1997) *Regulation and Deregulation in European Financial Services*, London: Macmillan.

Noyer, C. (1990) *Banks: The Rules of the Game* (*Banques: La règle du jeu*), Paris: Dunod.

Pastré, O. (1993) 'The French banking system, assessment and prospects' ('Le système bancaire français, bilan et perspectives'), *Revue d'Economie Financière, L'Industrie Bancaire* 27: 233–72.

Salomon, D. (1997a) 'When the public policy hides another – the Neiertz Act as a political answer and opportunist act from the supervising authorities' ('Quand une politique en cache une autre … La Loi Neiertz comme réponse politique et acte opportuniste des organismes de tutelle'), in M. Gardaz (ed.) *Debt and its Actors* (*La Dette et ses Acteurs*), Paris: Economica.

—— (1997b) 'The problematic transformation of the banking sector in France. The case of consumer credit', in G. Morgan and D. Knights (eds) *Regulation and Deregulation in European Financial Services*, London: Macmillan.

Zerah, D. (1993) *The French Financial System. Ten Years of Mutation* (*Le Système Financier Français. Dix Ans de Mutation*), Paris: Les Etudes de la Documentation Française.

Zysman, J. (1983) *Governments, Markets and Growth, Financial Systems and the Politics of Industrial Change*, Oxford: Martin Robertson.

5 Regulatory regimes

Lars Engwall and Glenn Morgan

Introduction

In most neo-liberal accounts of developments in markets and organizations there exists an implicit and sometimes explicit assumption that firms and organizations will converge towards a single form of structure and coordination because of the forces of global market competition. The detailed processes whereby such convergence might occur are rarely explained and such empirical work as has been done tends to show that claims of convergence and globalization are exaggerated (see e.g. Berger and Dore 1996; Boyer and Drache 1996; Hirst and Thompson 1996). In contrast to this approach, neo-institutionalist theories of national business systems have emphasized the way in which forms of economic activity are shaped by their embeddedness in specific social contexts. From this perspective, the impact of globalizing markets has to be considered in the context of all the other forces within national settings (such as culture, capital markets, systems of labour relations and education, the nature of the state) that act to reproduce existing forms of economic coordination (see Whitley and Kristensen 1996, 1997). In this chapter, we seek to build on the neo-institutionalist approach by examining how regulatory regimes within particular national contexts shape the structures and capacities of collective economic actors. Even when societies and organizations face similar problems, for example in terms of the crisis of welfare spending or the internationalization of financial markets, their responses are different because of the influence of their specific regulatory regimes.

The first section of the paper presents our framework for understanding regulatory regimes, while the second briefly examines the regulation of two significant institutional sectors: universities, providing intellectual capital, and banks, providing financial capital. If types of regulatory regimes are similar across these two sectors within national contexts, this provides strong prima facie evidence for the existence of a single 'national regulatory regime'. We discuss these sectors in relation particularly to the USA, the UK and France, though we also consider in passing a number of other countries. The final section summarizes our findings.

Regulatory regimes

We use the term 'regulatory regimes' to refer to the way in which political actors relate to the operations of the market. Two extreme forms of such interaction can be easily described for heuristic purposes. At one extreme, there is the idea that the market itself operates as a form of regulation since failure to meet consumer expectations leads to exit. So long as consumers are operating in their own best interests, therefore, there is no need for any external body to make decisions about what sort of economic actor is acceptable and what is not. Proponents of 'free banking' (i.e. banking free from all regulations to do with capital adequacy, etc.) have frequently argued that the costs of maintaining a system of regulation that establishes and monitors standards for banks is not only costly but also inhibits the operation of the market by not allowing consumers to take the risks which they want to take. On the other hand, most economists will admit 'market failure' particularly in areas of 'information complexity and asymmetry' where consumer knowledge is low. There is therefore a recognition that the market cannot supply everything. The state becomes the means whereby these weaknesses are overcome. It becomes a provider of certain services and a regulator of others. At the other end of the spectrum, there is the idea (partially embodied in the Soviet system) that only those groups or actors specifically authorized by the state can participate in economic life.

Most modern industrial societies operate somewhere between these two extremes, developing their own characteristic forms of state–market relations. Two mechanisms, in particular, appear to be utilized as means of regulating economic activities. The first is the exercise of control over who can be a competent actor in a particular economic context; the second is the extent of monitoring of what economic actors are actually doing. The former describes the degree to which economic actors are free to associate and enter markets; the latter refers to their freedom once in the market.

Entry control

Freedom of establishment of economic enterprises is a corner-stone of modern economies. However, this freedom is not unconditional; it is bound by the laws and practices of particular states. Limited liability companies can only be established if they conform to legal requirements (which may include regularly registering accounts, audits, etc.). Other activities are permitted but considered so important that they need more detailed screening with respect to entry. The basic reasons for such encroachment on the freedom of establishment appears to be felt needs for quality control in order to protect consumers or the public at large. This tightened form of entry control therefore tends to be especially developed in industries or occupations where the consumer or the general public run particular risks from, for example, lack of knowledge.

Two forms of entry control can be considered. The first type is where the predominant mechanism of entry control is exercised through the state, the other where the control is the result of private agreements. In terms of the first case European banking can serve as an example, since over the last twenty years, all European Union countries have had to establish detailed rules for what constitutes a bank and only those organizations which meet the criteria (including aspects such as adequate capital and responsible management) can undertake banking business. The second type of entry control, however, can also be illustrated by reference to banks. In Britain, until the 1970s, the title and position of 'merchant bank' – which implied a special relationship with the Bank of England, in particular the Bank's willingness to provide extended credit in the event of financial difficulties – was granted not by the state but by informal agreement between the Bank and the existing merchant houses. The basic distinction is therefore between state-regulated entry procedures and self-regulated entry, though the two are often intertwined. For example, professional groups such as lawyers and doctors traditionally strive for self-regulation backed up by statute, rather than direct state regulation. Private agreements amongst firms to regulate entry tend to avoid state involvement or indeed state knowledge, since such activities may be labelled as anti-competitive practices.

Entry control implies two sorts of processes. One process involves control of the numbers passing through the entry barrier. This clearly has implications for the economic power of those allowed through the barrier and therefore makes control of this position a vital mechanism of power. Professional self-regulation generally uses this control to maintain economic privilege partly by maximizing market power through keeping supply down. State control of the barrier on the other hand can be used either to prop up the economic position of those allowed through or to reduce their power (by a process of 'dilution'). The second aspect of the entry process involves defining what sort of actor is allowed through. The degree to which this definition is tight or loose (and again who controls the defining process) is also crucial. The definition may be based on qualifications (as with professional bodies), reputation (as with definitions of 'fit and proper persons' to run a bank or a company) or finance (certain level of assets). Entry control in effect acts as a licence to carry on as a particular sort of economic actor. It does not prescribe how to act; this is the sphere of performance control.

Performance control

The second dimension of regulation relates to the degree of performance control exercised over the collective economic actors. In a more general sense this is often described in terms of corporate governance, i.e. how principals are watching the behaviour of agents. The literature on this topic thus deals with the interplay between shareholders, corporate boards and executives. In addition, companies and other organizations are to an increasing extent controlled by auditors. These systems of corporate governance are built upon state legislation but still allow companies many degrees of freedom to choose the most appropriate solutions to meet the legal requirements. The purpose is principally to protect outside investors from inappropriate behaviour of insiders rather than for the state to define exactly what constitutes good performance. Ultimately, the market is left to 'regulate' performance on the basis that the state has ensured that appropriate information has been made available to stakeholders.

However, for professional groups, a different form of performance control may be insisted upon since market forces are deemed less relevant. For this purpose it is usual that special organizations are created in order to control their activities. In the case of professional groups, these are self-regulating bodies, such as the Law Society and the General Medical Council in the UK. Such organizations may either be direct arms of the state or hybrids – structurally independent from the sector being regulated and the state itself but in practice dependent on the knowledge and cooperation of insiders within the industry. Examples of such bodies are Financial Inspection Boards, Nuclear Power Inspection Boards and Civil Aviation Inspectorates. Performance control can be exercised through the market, through self-regulatory mechanisms or through the state. As with forms of entry control, performance control can be based on reputational/qualitative indicators, financial indicators or activity indicators (which may be either positive or negative).

Entry and performance control

To simplify our discussion, we can identify four ideal types in terms of entry and performance control (Table 5.1). The least constrained organization is here the private company, which has easy entry to the marketplace and which is subject to low outside performance control. As such companies search for outside finance and in particular launch themselves on stock markets, their ownership structure shifts and outside control increases substantially. Among organizations which are under high entry control, one group is constituted by self-governing professional organizations. Their field is subject to high entry control, but they decide themselves regarding performance evaluation. Other sectors, finally, are both subject to high entry and high performance control. This last category we refer to as 'government guild' since these sectors are highly dependent on the government for their existence and their modes of working.

Two points need emphasizing about our argument. First, the categories are not hermetically sealed. In particular, there are degrees of both entry

Table 5.1 Four types of entry and performance control

Entry control / *Performance control by external agents*	*Low*	*High*
Low	Private company	Self-regulating profession
High	Public company	Government guild

and performance control which means that sectors can move around both within and across these categories. Therefore, in any particular society there is likely to be a dynamic process as economic actors seek to shift their position according to their perception of the advantages to be gained from a certain form of entry and/or performance control. This may also be related to shifts in the form of control, for example from reputational/qualitative indicators towards quantitative indices of activity.

Second, and related to this, in any particular society one would expect a distinctive distribution of economic actors and sectors across these categories reflecting the specific nature of the national business system. Those national business systems which are based more on markets and self-regulation would be expected to have regulatory regimes with low entry and performance control, whereas those systems based on higher levels of state intervention would demonstrate regulatory regimes with high state involvement in entry and performance control. Not all regulatory regimes within a national business system would demonstrate the same sort of entry and performance controls. These are likely to be influenced by certain sectoral specificities, but looked at as a whole the distribution of types of regulatory regime in a particular society would reflect its underlying business system characteristics.

Regulatory regimes in action

In the following sections, we examine regulatory regimes in two sectors which are key to the provision of capital – human capital in the case of the universities and financial capital in the case of the banking system. We examine how different ways of regulating these institutions have become established in different countries. Initially, we look at the two sectors separately before considering the degree to which our discussion helps identify common elements in the regulatory regimes of specific countries.

Universities: variations in forms of state control

The universities as organizations appeared in the Middle Ages, many of them growing out of clerical schools. Early foundations occurred in Bologna (1088), Oxford (1167), Paris (1200), Cambridge (1209) and Padua (1222). At that time universities were subject to neither entry nor performance control. Rather they were basically customer-driven organizations, since students hired their professors themselves. Conflicts over curricula and the conditions offered by various cities made professors and students move elsewhere and start up new universities. Over time, as a result of competition between cities, various city governments felt a need to take over the university activities and became the employers of professors. In this way the foundations for universities as government guilds emerged. Some writers thus even compare the universities of the Middle Ages with merchant guilds, as in places like Paris the professors sought to protect their profession from unqualified intruders. It should also be kept in mind that 'universitas' was a designation for an association of professors and students in order to protect their interests in relation to clerical and worldly authorities (Kumlien 1933).

Many other Western European universities followed suit in the subsequent centuries. Entry control was operated through charters granted either by clerical or worldly leaders: the Pope, emperors, princes, etc. Among the European universities founded in the last century, the German research university, particularly Berlin University founded in 1810, came to play an important role model for other universities (Whitley 1984: 57–66). The German model of university–state relations with universities as independent institutions under the Minister of Education seems also to have provided inspiration for others (Kumlien 1933). In the United States, universities were founded in the seventeenth and eighteenth centuries: Harvard (1636), Yale (1701), Princeton (1746) and Columbia (1754) (Gates 1964). The motives behind the foundations varied: 'religious motives … the need for various kinds of professionals; state pride and local boosterism; philanthropy; idealism; educational reform; speculation in land, among others, and all in combination' (Trow 1989: 378). Central entry and performance control was limited, if existing at all. As a result, the growth of academic institutions in the New World was much faster than in the old one. Already by 1776 the United States had nine colleges, while Great Britain still had just Oxford and Cambridge, and by the late 1980s the number of US colleges and universities numbered 3,400 (Trow 1989: 376, 370).

The period after the Second World War led to an expansion of higher education all over the world. Particularly in Western Europe this development has meant that the earlier elite character of academic programmes has weakened. In addition, the variety within the field has increased. Many countries have developed a binary system through the expansion of professional academic schools, which are not universities (institutes of technology, business schools, medical schools, etc.). Another source of diversification has been the development of new institutions for higher education, which are not acknowledged as universities (polytechnics in Great Britain, Fachhochschulen in Germany and university colleges in Scandinavia). Not unexpectedly these institutions are eager to attain university status. In some countries this has already happened through the upgrading of existing institutions. In Great Britain the polytechnics gained university status in 1992 and in Turkey a uniform system in 1981 increased the number of universities from 19 to 57. In Sweden some of the university colleges are in the process of attaining university status (see Veld *et al.* 1996: 25, 55, 58, 65).

It is not unfair to say that quality control is the basic task of universities. Entry is generally limited to those with a certain minimum qualification (though in itself this does not guaranteee access either to the system itself or any particular institution). Students are assessed on a regular basis and in theory have to achieve a quality threshold if they are to be allowed to continue or graduate. However, the fact that universities have quality control as their basic task is no guarantee that they provide programmes living up to high external quality standards. The control is basically internal. This internal screening may be only loosely coupled with the requirements of the labour market where students are going to be employed. If we look at the quality of university education from this point of view, different issues arise. Higher education differs from most products, goods as well as services; the consumer cannot go through a trial-and-error process testing different alternatives thereby acquiring sufficient information for a long-term consumption choice. In this case, the customer by definition does not know much about the contents of the product. If this were not the case the consumption of the programme would be meaningless, because what is going to be learnt would be already known to the student. For the same reason consumption of a specific educational programme never occurs twice. In addition it is often unclear directly after the passage of an educational programme whether it was good or not, since the qualities do not tend to show up until after a number of years in practice (Hägg 1975, 1997). At that time a change in education may be too late.

These characteristics of educational programmes imply that reputation becomes very important. The quality of such programmes is associated with the success of alumni on the labour market. Obviously, this does not necessarily need to correlate with the quality of a programme. It can even be argued that success is a result of first-mover advantages, i.e. that old institutions will have a larger number of alumni on the labour market and that these together have better possibilities to hire students of their former Alma Mater than those of younger institutions. Some authors have argued that educational institutions provide filters for the employers in their selection process among job applicants (see further, Blaug 1976). However, in modern times with an expanded and more diversified system of higher education, some have questioned whether this filter theory of education still works (Veld *et al.* 1996: 29).

These problems which are common to the sector can be expected to be resolved differently according to the variations between different contexts in the ways in which university systems are regulated. Veld *et al.* (1996: 46–9) identified four educational policy traditions which identify particular national styles of managing universities. The first, French, Napoleonic tradition is characterized by high degrees of centralization, regulation and standardization. Universities are mainly one state bureaucracy among others. The second, German, tradition refers to the idea of Wilhem von Humboldt that basic research is the driving force of universities, and that teaching and research should go hand in hand. Universities are mainly self-governing bodies. The third, British, tradition is based on the idea of tutoring and non-standardized programmes as the most important means to prepare students for later life. The fourth, the American, implies that the society at large is the main stakeholder. Universities are parts of a market system for higher education. Clark (1983: 138) develops a similar schema which classifies six countries on a scale from 'unitary and unified state administration' at one end to 'market linkage' at the other. He then ranked them in the following order: Sweden, France, Britain, Canada, Japan and the United States. Again we find the Western Europeans at the state-governed end of the continuum and the United States at the market-governed end.

Both classifications thus point to major differences between the US and Western European traditions as regards quality control as well as differences within the Western European tradition. In terms of entry control the foundation of a university in the United States is not subject to any restrictions different from the foundation of any other private company. There is thus 'no central law or authority [that] governs or co-ordinates American higher education [and there is no] federal ministry of education with the power to charter new institutions' (Trow 1989: 370, 378). Two historical events seem particularly important for this state of affairs: the defeat in Congress of George Washington's idea of a national university, and the 1819 Supreme Court decision that a state cannot intervene in the activities of a private college or university (Trow 1989: 378–80). Needless to say, the general liberal market philosophy constitutes a fundamental reason for the conditions in the United States. As a result the North American system of higher education is characterized by a high degree of heterogeneity in terms of academic orientation and financing. Persons or organizations who have the resources can start up a new university without any entry or performance control. The issue is whether anybody will pay for the service, i.e. the market regulates through the operation of demand and supply.

However, the US model has become more complex as financing for the system is increasingly coming from public sources even though the language of the market remains central. At the present time North American colleges and universities obtain roughly half of their revenues from governments at different levels (Trow 1989: 387–8) and demands have grown for more control. Student-loan defaults, in particular, have created a concern among politicians. In 1992 Congress thus asked state post-secondary review entities to look into the problem and the Department of Education 'to impose standards for academic progress and accreditation' (Greenberg 1994: B1). Lying behind this is the notion that some universities are enrolling students (who thereby become eligible for loans) whilst not offering an adequate teaching and career advice service. Thus the students fail to complete their course and default on their loans. A possible response is only to offer loans to students at universities which have shown they have reached a certain quality level assessed by an external party. This in turn has led to a discussion of whether accreditation should be a matter for regional or for discipline-oriented accrediting associations. An example of such a discipline-oriented organization is the American Association of Collegiate Schools of Business (AACSB), founded already in 1916. It has, over time, established programme standards and is presently an accreditation body for business schools. It provides accreditation after self-evaluations and site visits, which particularly focus on aspects like 'curriculum and course content, faculty qualifications, research productivity of faculty, library and computer facilities, student admission and graduation standards, faculty utilisation and course coverage and instructional methods' (McKenna 1989: 44).

Thus, as soon as a university has any requests for public money it has, in the same way as the private company that goes public, to expose itself to performance control through organizations of accreditation. Or, in the words of a politician quoted by Veld *et al.* (1996: 45): 'Any university autonomy ends where the state subsidy is larger than zero.' We thus see tendencies also in the United States of increased performance control (see also Trow 1989: 395). However, it is important to note that this exposure to performance control is not directly controlled by the state but a complex amalgam of evaluation by peer groups, competitors, consumers, alumni, industry stakeholders and political appointees depending on the particular state (within the USA) and the particular subject area under review. Thus the limited strength of the federal state and its local counterparts compared with the collective social actors embedded within the US system is once again reinforced.

In Western Europe, on the other hand, there are a number of differences from the US model. Many of the oldest universities, as has been mentioned, were founded out of donations from benefactors and remained relatively independent well into the nineteenth century. Only as modernizing states sought to extend the reach of higher education through setting up new institutions did a more 'rational' system of university accreditation develop. In this environment, a new set of higher education institutions – sponsored financially and politically by the local bourgeoisie of the growing urban centres such as, in Britain, those in Manchester, Birmingham, Glasgow, Belfast and London – were established and a new set of nationally based rules governing their status and funding emerged. The result was that any new claimants to university status had to subject themselves to a process of approval before they could attain their own Charter to issue qualifications. Until the postwar period, this process remained very restrictive in most European countries as the universities continued to serve a very small elite within society. However, the establishment of these universities did require the development of a coordinated state response, particularly in terms of the degree of homogeneity which was to be expected. In some countries such as Britain there were major differences between the oldest institutions – which were often well endowed with their own funds – and those mainly dependent for their existence and funding on the actions of the modernizing state, a divide which became greater as the state authorized the expansion of higher education from the 1960s onwards. Thus, in spite of a shared funding system (which became linked with shared salaries and employment contracts), there was a high degree of differentiation and heterogeneity between universities. In other countries, homogenization of the universities enforced by the state went much further, reflected in the fact that university lecturers were quite clearly 'civil servants' (in terms of their employment conditions and status).

In spite of these differences, most Western European universities have been either directly or indirectly strongly influenced by government. Totally private universities (i.e. institutions with no state funding) are rare and even where there are supporters willing to sponsor and fund such an institution, their key requirement for survival (i.e. that they are able to issue degrees) cannot, unlike the US, be assumed; instead private institutions are subject to intense government scrutiny and may have to go into partnership with existing institutions in order to overcome this entry barrier (e.g. the link between IESE and the University of Navarra in Spain).

The high level of entry control to the status of university has been traditionally assumed to be one of the most important guarantors of high and common academic standards. Together with the limited numbers of places in such institutions (which were effectively rationed until the era of the welfare state by the combination of the cost of higher education itself and, earlier, the cost of a secondary education capable of meeting entry requirements), this meant that the universities were left relatively free to decide on their own performance criteria. They have been self-governing professional bodies. In the words of Trow (1989: 382): 'Europeans try very hard to reduce the influence of the incompetent mass on high cultural matters, and to preserve a realm of elite determination of cultural form and content.'

However, in times of mass education and marketization these traditions have been challenged. Budget constraints in welfare states, and the adoption of modern management techniques, have led to an increasing tendency to demand certain performance criteria with funding following more exactly an institution's perceived performance levels. One obvious move has been to switch funding away from a block grant system in which universities received a total amount to fund both teaching and research at historic levels towards a system based upon an exact allocation of funds depending on numbers of students at any particular time. University institutions are to an increasing extent remunerated for the throughput of students (Veld *et al.* 1996: 45, 78, 81). This in turn has also implied a need for new methods to control output quality, since a reward system directly linked to output numbers may lead to undesirable reductions in the requirements on students. Once European states moved from the relative generosity of university funding which characterized the 1960s (and was based essentially on keeping numbers small) and began to face more fiercely competing political and economic demands in the era of the 'fiscal crisis of the state', new mechanisms for managing the sector were sought.

This has been particularly the case in the United Kingdom, where, under the pressure of Thatcherite demands for 'value for money' from the public sector, the principles of resource allocation to universities have changed drastically over the last fifteen years. Initially the system provided a block grant to universities to cover teaching and research at certain expected levels of student throughput. This resource was first reduced – though the scale of reduction differed greatly between universities based as it was on some secret, reputational assessment of the value of different universities – whilst levels of throughput were expected to be maintained. The result was that class sizes were increased in many institutions whilst some had to lose large numbers of staff (mainly through early retirement schemes) to balance their financial accounts. Following this, the government shifted funding to a system based on numbers of students entering the university, though again the unit of resource per student was reduced and therefore expansion of student numbers could never be matched by a similar scale of expansion of lecturers or other resources. Finally, the government capped the numbers and split the funding between research and teaching. Using a peer-based review of research achievements within departments, the government gradually reduced the amount of funds available as of right to all universities and created a growing pool of discretionary funds to be allocated on the basis of peer review ranking. For many departments, the result is that they have to teach more students to earn the same amount of revenue to keep their jobs and time for research is reduced. Peer-based review of teaching has also been introduced though controversy has dogged its progress and, following an initial round of teaching quality assessments, there has been a hiatus. Consequently, the financial effects of the teaching assessments have mainly been indirect, in terms of their impact on student applications, especially those from the lucrative overseas market.

In the British case, the government has been able to use its power over funding to force significant changes, but the details of those changes remain administered by the universities and the academics themselves rather than directly by civil servants. This means that the universities can find their own way to deal with the context; some have clearly taken the opportunity to build on their strengths by seeking other funding sources whilst others have become enmeshed in internal politicking. These arrangements reflect a regulatory regime in which the power of the state is still limited to a degree by the power of long-established professional groups and corporate entities which are used to some degree of autonomy over their own activities. Although increased financial dependence on the state has legitimized increased involvement by the state, this is still within a broad expectation that universities do not 'belong' to the state but to those directly involved in their functioning. Traditionally the latter has meant the academics, rather than the students or potential employers or the more amorphous category of 'society in general' which is sometimes evoked in these discussions, though this also is increasingly changing.

This process of change is part of the broader process of restructuring the public sector in Western European economies. Some countries, like Sweden, have chosen less drastic methods than Britain and have launched systems for evaluating the work to improve quality in university activities (see e.g. Trow 1996; Brennan *et al.* 1997), whilst others like France are enmeshed in a political stalemate that means when university reforms (like other reforms to the welfare state such as pensions) are mooted, they are the signal for widespread demonstrations, resulting in the government backtracking and achieving little. In both of these countries, state control of the university sector is more accepted than in either the US or Britain, though the broader social context of the legitimacy of the state and its capacity for 'steering' civil society clearly differs. In general, the focus of the European governments on increasing throughput of students whilst holding steady the total budget has led to a process of decentralization in systems for higher education. Ministries in many countries are, to a lesser extent than before, deciding on the budgetary details but are instead delegating to the universities the issue of how to match resources with academic planning. The detailed resource allocation becomes a matter for lower levels in the administrative hierarchy, intermediate organizations between ministries and universities, university boards, faculty boards, etc. Needless to say the interaction between these different levels of university administration is a complicated game.

At the same time as quality issues are becoming more important on the agenda we can also see in some European countries a tendency of changes in governance structures towards a more American model. Sweden can here serve as an example. Since 1988 the boards of universities have had a

Table 5.2 Patterns of entry and performance control in university systems

Entry control / *Performance control by external agents*	*Low*	*High*
Low	Medieval Private US	Traditional Western European
High	Public US	Modern Western European

majority of representatives from the public at large. The present Social Democratic government has now proposed that from 1998 Vice Chancellors will no longer be the chair of the board. Instead, the Ministry of Education is going to appoint an external person. An earlier non-socialist government was more inclined to move the system towards the appointment of external persons (mainly from industry) to the posts of Vice Chancellor (a move mirrored in the appointment of business school deans from industry). Thus, although the means differ between the two major political camps, the goal seems to be the same: an increased linking of universities to the society at large.

Our analysis of university regulation (summarized in Table 5.2) indicates that there is a basic difference between the Western European and the US system for higher education in terms of entry control. While entry control and the keeping up of standards through exclusivity have characterized the Western European system, the US has been open to new establishments on a market model with little intervention from public authorities. In some parts of Western Europe, universities have mainly been treated as government guilds, for instance in France and Sweden, where control has been exercised through detailed resource allocation procedures. In Britain, on the other hand, there has been more self-regulation by participants in the university system, though the state has come to play an increasingly prominent role through its more detailed control of funding.

However, none of these systems are static and they are all undergoing a certain amount of change in terms of performance control as they respond to the twin pressures of the increased demand for higher education coupled with the seeming unwillingness of the public to support higher taxes (leading to a declining unit of resource per student with consequent fears for quality). Forms of state intervention in the university systems are becoming extended and more intrusive. Western Europeans are developing new institutions for higher education, which in turn means that the diversity is becoming larger within the system. In addition they are taking up new more output-related resource allocation procedures, which have led to increased needs to control what kind of output universities are offering. Similarly, North Americans are starting to ask questions of whether government support to higher education is spent in the right way. Even if the support is market-related by going to the students instead of directly to institutions, it has been found that the money spent is not efficiently used. This has led to calls for external evaluations and reform of the accreditation system.

Although regulatory regimes remain distinct, similar problems and responses are emerging. For this process to happen it is, of course, also very important that Western European countries to an increasing extent have taken on board both a similar definition of the problems (the crisis of educational spending in the context of the decreased willingness of the population to pay taxes) and similar proposed solutions, based on new forms of public sector management influenced by US management models (see e.g. Osborne and Gaebler 1992) and UK experiences of the introduction of quasi-markets into the public sector (on quasi-markets see Bartlett *et al.* 1994; on the new public management in the UK see Ferlie *et al.* 1996). Research on Nordic business studies also points to a heavy US influence (cf. Engwall 1992, Section 6.5, 1995, 1996, 1997). Obviously it has also been important that many of the evaluation exercises in Western Europe have included US evaluators. In this way we see tendencies for standardization in line with the reasoning of the new institutionalists (cf. Powell and DiMaggio 1991). These influences, coupled with the potential impact of new technologies of communication and learning which have led some authors to argue that universities may be seriously threatened by media industry conglomerates which may move into the education business (Veld *et al.* 1996: 31), may also imply that the diversification of the Western European system is increasing: 'The governance of universities in the next century will be characterised by hybridity and diversity' (Veld *et al.* 1996: 90).

In conclusion, our analysis of universities has identified three broad types of 'regulatory regimes':

- regulation of entry and performance left primarily to the market (US)
- regulation of entry controlled by the state; regulation of performance left primarily to the practitioners (UK)
- regulation of entry controlled by the state; regulation of performance and conduct partially controlled by the state (France, Sweden).

The discussion has also shown that whilst these systems have all faced similar pressure arising from increased numbers and higher costs, the way in which they have responded has been shaped by their existing regulatory regime.

Banking and regulation

Like universities, forms of banking can be traced far back into the past. However, a primary distinction which can be made is between those societies in which forms of banking were well established before the advent of industrialization and those in which banking evolved as part of the modernizing and industrializing project of the nation state. This has impacted on both entry and performance control.

In Britain, banking developed in the late seventeenth and eighteenth centuries as part of the establishment of the modern state rather than as part of the industrialization process. The Bank of England was brought into existence in 1694 in order to provide loans to the government which required funding for its war against the French; through the eighteenth century the Bank continued to fund the National Debt which grew as military adventures increased. Private banks, based on partnerships of individuals, operated in London and the provinces as means of siphoning funds into the system, at the centre of which stood the Bank of England. Weiss and Hobson (1995: 119) argue that 'the state intentionally formed a strong "organic" or "reciprocal" relationship with financial capitalists, where both parties cooperated and gained power in a positive-sum game' (see also Ingham 1984). Although this structure was partially altered by the process of industrialization and the growth of links between provincial banks and industrial companies, these changes were minimal, particularly once banks were allowed to move from private partnerships to a joint-stock company structure. From the mid-nineteenth century, the result was a speeding up of the process of amalgamation and merger, the disappearance of local banks and the consolidation of a small number of national commercial banks with their head offices in the City, where they linked in with merchant banks and the Bank of England to create financial markets dealing in international lending as well as national stocks and shares. The linkage between finance and the state was managed through the Bank of England which in turn was controlled until the early part of the twentieth century by the denizens of the City institutions; even leaders of the main clearing banks did not get on to the ruling body of the Bank, the Court, until the twentieth century.

In terms of entry control into banking, this was the province of the Bank of England and it occurred on an informal basis. Anybody could set up a bank, but only if the Bank of England itself approved were newcomers allowed access to the markets controlled by it. The result was an informal, social process of acceptance. This system was also coupled with a limited and informal system of performance control exercised by the Bank. Once inside the system, a bank was able to conduct certain sorts of business with other banks and the Bank of England. This was a privilege in two ways. First, it enabled the entrant to participate in the profitable business of funding the National Debt and gaining access to other safe and profitable areas of business. Second, in the event of potential collapse, the Bank of England would extend a helping hand. In return, banks were expected to cooperate with the Bank when it came to operating the monetary system. The state expected the Bank to organize its finances and to run the money supply system; so long as this was successful, it left it to run the financial system as it saw fit. Entry and performance control therefore operated informally through the Bank. Individual banks were responsible to their shareholders but this was in the context of keeping the Bank of England happy. It was accepted that bank managers did not have to reveal the 'true extent' of their profits since to do so would undermine the secret mechanisms whereby the Bank of England was able to manipulate the overall system (see Morgan and Quack 1999 for more details of this process).

This contrasts strongly to those continental systems where banking emerged as part of the nation state's project to modernize and industrialize its territory though this took different forms depending on the nature of the state–society relationship. In France, for example, finance in the nineteenth century was affected by the schizophrenic attitude of the state which saw the need for industrialization but was equally, if not more, concerned with its own aggrandizement. Trebilcock, for example, argued that

> the French state controlled the banks so that they could not properly serve the needs of industry. From Bonaparte's discovery that banks were useful engines of war finance and his consequent foundation of the Bank of France (1800), there developed an excessively tight relationship between finance and government.
>
> (Trebilcock 1981: 148)

The state sought to control entry into banking for fear that excessive competition would reduce its own potential funding; between 1815 and 1848, therefore, only a handful of provincial banks were opened. Even when banks deliberately designed to support industrial development were set up on the model of Crédit Mobilier under the sponsorship of the state, the overall structure remained under the control of the state. Trebilcock states that 'calculations of security, control by politicians rather than by capitalists, objectives set not in gold but in the coin of alliance and offensive – these, to an extent, unequalled in Europe, were the controlling guidelines of French investment' (Trebilcock 1981: 180–1). The structure of control established by the state was reaffirmed and modernized in the post-1945 period when the nationalization of the main banks was part of a broader strategy to enable the state 'to impose its will directly' or 'use indirect mechanisms of regulation and control to supplement its direct means of influencing the allocation of credit' (Zysman 1983: 111). In the post-1945 period, the state established a series of mechanisms and institutions in the banking sector which enabled it to direct credit and funds at favourable rates to those parts of the economy which the Planning Directorate had indicated as crucial for further industrial development. Unlike Britain, the French regulatory regime for banking left little role for the practitioners themselves. Instead, the key decisions were taken within the state. Not surprisingly, therefore, banking became dominated by institutions which were either state owned or strongly influenced by the state. Performance criteria reflected this: the main issue was whether banks were performing their function for the state rather than their depositors or shareholders. This reflected a continuity with the original formation of the French banking system (see Salomon's chapter in this volume for recent changes in the French context).

The continuity of the French and British systems contrasts somewhat with the US experience. During the nineteenth century, the issues of money and banking had frequently become highly political, representing as they did deeper social conflicts, for example, between the federal government and the rights of local states, and between the agricultural areas of the mid-West and the New York financial plutocracy. There was no single state structure that could control or shape the banking system either from above (as in France) or in consultation with the practitioners (as in Britain). The result was a lack of entry controls into the sector and a plethora of different forms ranging from local provincial banks through to national and international universal banks based in New York. The story of the collapse of the American banking system in the aftermath of the Wall Street Crash has been the subject of endless analysis (see e.g. Galbraith 1954). The way in which funds had been shifted from local banks into the large universal banks and then invested speculatively meant that the whole edifice was tightly connected. Collapse could not be confined to one part of the sector but ran remorselessly through all the institutions. It was this lesson which the US politicians and regulators took most to heart, introducing legislation which segregated commercial banking from wholesale banking and the banking systems of the different states from each other. Universal banking was no longer possible, thereby, in theory, insulating retail customers from direct contamination in the event of the collapse of industrial firms. Nor was national retail banking any longer possible, again insulating customers from prospective collapses in other parts of the country. From the perspective of the operations of the banks these were undoubtedly major changes, but from a broader perspective, the extent of the change in the 'regulatory regime' for banking, the changes are less dramatic. The state still remained at a distance from the banks and their functions; although market entry was more closely controlled, the formation of banks was still predominantly driven by market forces and not directly influenced either by the state or a central network of existing institutions (as happened in Britain).

As with universities, these patterns of regulatory regimes in banking have been placed under severe strain by the changes in the postwar period (for various studies of these changes in different European countries, see Morgan and Knights 1997). In Britain, the expansion of financial markets from the 1960s placed the Bank of England's system of informal control under severe stress. Outside its purview, the 'secondary banking' system grew up as a means of recirculating funds from the Euro-dollar offshore markets into Britain and elsewhere. These secondary banks needed no authorization and were able to win markets off the old-established institutions. However, their willingness to take risks led them into speculative investments which eventually collapsed and threatened to engulf the banking system more widely as some of the clearing banks and merchant banks had also got involved in lending to them. The Bank had argued that the secondary banks were not 'real banks' (i.e. within the Bank's circle of influence) and were therefore also not its responsibility. However, because of the potential contamination effect, it had to act to rescue the system as a whole. During the 1970s and 1980s, the Bank was forced to develop a more formal monitoring of the banking system. Until 1974, banking supervision had been undertaken within the Discount Office of the Bank (which also had responsibility for short-term money markets). Supervision had been based on the belief that 'it could be practised by a small number of people using chiefly their personal knowledge to form judgements about who could be trusted in the banking community' (Moran 1986: 115). At this time, the Discount Office as a whole employed only fifteen people. Following the crises of the early 1970s, a separate Banking Supervision Division was set up and the number of staff has grown steadily since then. The methods of supervision have also evolved, relying less on informal chats between the Bank and the top executives in the supervised banks and more on the analysis of quantitative indicators of banks' financial positions. Even here, however, there has remained controversy as the degree of monitoring has appeared variable with so-called 'safe' houses (determined again on the basis of informal reputation) being given a lighter touch than those on the social and economic periphery of the Bank. Coupled with the difficulties of monitoring liabilities in complex derivatives and futures markets (especially where firms are dealing out of other financial centres), this has led to a number of notable lapses in supervisory rigour (such as BCCI and Barings). These changes have led to both heightened control of entry and performance within the British banking sector.

The overall movement towards formalization has been speeded up by the demands of the Basle agreements on banking and the European Union's move towards a single European market. Both of these have required that banks and banking supervision be placed on a firm legislative footing and that monitoring against international standards be instituted. As with the developments in the US after the Wall Street Crash, this has necessitated an evolution of the regulatory regime but it is doubtful whether it constitutes a wholesale break. In the British case, there is still a high dependence on cooperation between the Bank and the banking system as a whole which is based on shared mores and expectations about how banks function. The state is still content to keep the financial system as far as possible at arms length, to organize its own self-regulation backed up and prodded on by legislation and public humiliation if necessary. Nevertheless, the system remains predominantly in the hands of the bankers and not the politicians or civil servants.

In the French case, the problem has been less about increasing control of the financial system but rather its opposite – towards a disentangling of the state and the financial institutions (and a consequent redefinition of performance criteria away from political objectives and more towards market indicators) and an opening up of the system to new entrants. As a number of authors have shown, this has been a highly complex and politically fraught process of transition (see Schmidt 1996; Coleman 1997; Salomon 1997), as attempts to deregulate the financial system have gone hand in hand with an unwillingness to leave processes of capital allocation to the market. In spite of changes, therefore, there remain elements of the schizophrenia identified in the nineteenth-century French state's attitude towards banking; the state wants to continue to use the banking system to achieve its broader industrial and diplomatic objectives whilst also allowing the banks some autonomy. The result has been that the extent of restructuring of the financial sector has been limited. French banking institutions have continued to feel pressured to achieve political objectives with consequent problems in terms of their market position, e.g. Crédit Lyonnais, which overstretched itself in France and abroad in its desire to support French financial expansionism in the late 1980s. Nevertheless, the need for reform continues to press in on the French system, not least as a result of the pressures arising from the single European currency project. Once again, French political and diplomatic objectives are driving changes in the banking structure. Overall, therefore, there remains a strong continuity in the French regulatory regime; in spite of some changes, the state is the central player and the banking practitioners and institutions have relatively limited autonomous influence on the nature of regulation.

In the American context, the regulatory regime which had developed from the aftermath of the Wall Street Crash can generally be described as fragmented. Cerny argues that 'the fragmented regulatory framework and policy process in the United States initially provided an impetus for internal deregulation by way of what economists call "competition in laxity" or "regulatory arbitrage" amongst competing agencies' (Cerny 1994: 426). As this process spread into the international arena, 'this competitive deregulation has generated pressures in the US for both further deregulation *and* more effective "re-regulation"' (Cerny 1994: 426). The problem is, however, that the very fragmentation which enabled deregulation and market forces to push through earliest and most effectively in the American context are also the forces which make it so difficult to achieve change in the formal structure of regulation. Cerny argues that attempts to legislate the system out of fragmentation, by, for example, allowing national banks and universal banking, have suffered from 'institutional gridlock' in which the various interests at local and federal level have proved incapable of creating an effective compromise. In his view, the result is that

> in a world where international market share is being lost to universal or quasi-universal banks favoured by centralised regulatory systems, it remains doubtful whether the United States – largely because of the domestic political structure – is capable of promoting this sort of financial competitiveness in any truly effective way.
>
> (Cerny 1994: 434)

Garten, on the other hand, is less pessimistic. She, too, recognizes that

> the legacy of fragmentation has kept US financial firms small relative to their non-US rivals [...] Further, fragmenting regulations prevented US institutions from operating as integrated universal banks in non-US markets forcing them to replicate their fragmented organisational structures overseas. Nevertheless, US firms have been able to exploit their principal strength at home, their ability to innovate in the development and marketing of specialised financial products, to compete successfully against their larger non-US rivals in a variety of national markets.
>
> (Garten 1997: 308)

Whichever of these two authors is correct, both seem agreed that the regulatory regime established in US banking shapes the capacities and capabilities of these firms in the current period. In spite of facing many competitive challenges, the trajectory of the banking industry is crucially affected by the nature of the regulatory regime.

In conclusion, we would argue that the regulatory regimes in banking in these three discussed countries (the United Kingdom, France and the United States) arose from distinctive historical conjunctures of state, civil society and the economy. These regimes differ in the role of the market, the sector itself and the state in controlling banking. In spite of facing similar challenges from competitive pressures in the internationalization of financial markets and the establishment of international banking rules, each regime is responding in a different way, depending on its initial trajectory. Regulatory regimes therefore operate as one further factor which maintains and even increases divergence between national business systems rather than enabling convergence to occur.

General conclusions

Bringing together our analysis of regulatory regimes in universities and banking, we would argue that there is a consistency at the level of the national business system in the type of regulatory regimes which have evolved. In France, the predominant role of the state means that developments in the regulation of economic actors are initiated and implemented within the state structure. Furthermore, the regulatory regime that develops is centrally concerned with the political objectives established by the state rather than emerging directly from the requirements of the sector and its participants. This is not to say that the state is capable of achieving its broader objectives against the interests and wishes of those involved. The strong French state is, in effect, mirrored by a strong 'civil society' which is capable of resistance as well as cooperation with the state. The result has been the construction of a broader system of societal regulation in the postwar period that is paradoxically capable both of being highly centralized and highly resistant to centralized change. In the US, on the other hand, regulatory regimes can be described as fragmentary, as can the economic actors themselves. The state is therefore incapable of delivering major change, whilst actors themselves rarely cooperate actively to achieve regulatory reforms. Instead, economic actors use market mechanisms and market imperfections to establish new innovations; as a result, some regulatory barriers may be effectively surmounted but by stealth rather than state action. The regulatory regime in the US case therefore further encourages the sort of individualistic opportunism amongst economic actors which is more generally a feature of the economic environment. The regulatory regime in Britain is more clearly a balance between the state and collective social actors which seek to use or cooperate with the state in the preservation of their own position and power. This is not so much 'regulatory capture' as the term is used in the US (where regulators become dependent on the industry and incapable of independent action) but rather a situation where a mutual dependency is recognized. Both sides can use their independent powers to a degree to shape the outcome of particular decisions but neither side can ultimately dictate.

The idea of a regulatory regime is by no means new (see e.g. the political science literature reviewed in Francis 1993, Chapter 2). Further research is clearly required to examine in more detail how these regimes emerge and change, as well as how international regimes develop and interact with the national level. In the case of the two sectors which we have examined, it is clear that the interest in establishing international regimes of regulation is most sustained in banking. In the sphere of universities, there is some international competition in certain sectors but this is mainly regulated by the market, e.g. in international league tables of business schools. Within more limited contexts, such as the European Union, there is some pressure to standardize higher education qualifications. This is currently beginning to impact on Germany where reforms are currently being introduced which may lead to the wider establishment and acceptance of Bachelor's and Master's degrees as reported in an article entitled 'German slouches beware' (*Economist* 1997). This is most acutely significant in the areas of professions like accountancy, medicine, law, management and engineering where the twin pressures of multinational companies and international labour mobility are generating the need for European-level skills and recognized qualifications. In the sphere of banking, internationalization has been long established and in the current period is becoming even more significant with financial markets and institutions spread around the world. Not surprisingly, efforts at international regulation have been proceeding for some time in the banking and securities industries (for discussions of these processes see Kapstein 1994; Underhill 1997). This makes for a more continuous and significant interaction between international and national regulators and, through them, with local banking institutions.

References

Bartlett, W., Propper, C., Wilson, D. and Le Grand, J. (eds) (1994) *Quasi Markets and Social Policy*, Bristol: SAUS Publications.

Berger, S. and Dore, R. (eds) (1996) *National Diversity and Global Capitalism*, Ithaca, NY: Cornell University Press.

Blaug, M. (1976) 'Human capital theory: a slightly jaundiced survey', *Journal of Economic Literature* 14: 827–55.

Boyer, R. and Drache, D. (eds) (1996) *States Against Markets: The Limits of Globalization*, London: Routledge.

Brennan, J., de Vries, P. and Williams, R. (eds) (1997) *Standards and Quality in Higher Education*, London: Jessica Kingsley.

Cerny, P. G. (1994) 'Gridlock and decline: financial internationalization, banking politics and the American political process', in R. Stubbs and G. D. Underhill (eds) *Political Economy and the Changing Global Order*, London: Macmillan.

Clark, B. (1983) *The Higher Education System. Academic Organization in Cross-National Perspective*, Berkeley, CA: University of California Press.

Coleman, W. D. (1997) 'The French state, dirigisme and changing global financial environment', in G. D. Underhill (ed.) *The New World Order in International Finance*, London: Macmillan.

Economist (1997) 'German slouches beware', 23 August: 29.

Engwall, L. (1992) *Mercury Meets Minerva*, Oxford: Pergamon Press.

—— (1995) 'Management studies: a fragmented adhocracy?', *Scandinavian Journal of Management* 11(3): 225–35.

—— (1996) 'The Vikings versus the world. An examination of Nordic business research', *Scandinavian Journal of Management* 12(4): 425–36.

—— (1997) 'Nordic business education: local arenas or Disneyland?', paper for the fourteenth Nordic Conference on Business Studies, 14–17 August (mimeo).

Ferlie, E., Ashburner, L., Fitzgerald, L. and Pettigrew, A. (1996) *The New Public Sector Management in Action*, Oxford: Oxford University Press.

Francis, J. (1993) *The Politics of Regulation: A Comparative Perspective*, Oxford: Blackwell.

Galbraith, J. K. (1954) *The Great Crash, 1929*, London: Penguin.

Garten, H. A. (1997) 'Financial reform, the United States and the New World Order in international finance', in G. D. Underhill (ed.) *The New World Order in International Finance*, London: Macmillan.

Gates, E. M. (1964) 'University', *Encyclopaedia International, Volume 18*, New York: Grolier.

Greenberg, M. (1994) 'A fresh look at accreditation', *Chronicle of Higher Education*, 7 September: B1–B2.

Hägg, I. (1975) 'Uppsala business students in working life – what they think about their education in business administration' ('Uppsalaekonomer i arbetslivet – vad anser de om sin utbildning i företagsekonomi'), Uppsala: Uppsala University, Unit for Educational Development.

—— (1997) 'Uppsala business students in working life – what they think about their education in business administration' ('Uppsalaekonomer i arbetslivet – vad anser de om sin utbildning i företagsekonomi'), paper presented to the conference 'Quality and Work for Improvement', 9–10 January, Uppsala.

Hirst, P. and Thompson, G. (1996) *Globalization in Question*, Cambridge: Polity Press.

Ingham, G. (1984) *Capitalism Divided: The City and Industry in British Social Development*, Cambridge: Polity Press.

Kapstein, E. B. (1994) *Governing the Global Economy*, Cambridge, MA: Harvard University Press.

Kumlien, K. (1933) 'University' ('Universitet'), *Nordic Family Encyclopaedia* (*Nordisk familjebok*), Stockholm: Familjebokens förlag.

McKenna, J. F. (1989) 'Management education in the United States', in W. Byrt (ed.) *Management Education. An International Survey*, London: Routledge.

Moran, M. (1986) *The Politics of Banking*, London: Macmillan.

Morgan, G. and Knights, D. (eds) (1997) *Regulation and Deregulation in European Financial Services*, London: Macmillan.

Morgan, G. and Quack S. (1999) 'Confidence and confidentiality: the social construction of performance standards in German and British banking', in S. Quack, G. Morgan and R. Whitley (eds) *National Capitalisms, Global Competition and Economic Performance*, Berlin: De Gruyter.

Osborne, D. and Gaebler, T. (1992) *Reinventing Government*, Reading, MA: Addison-Wesley.

Powell, W. W. and DiMaggio, P. J. (eds) (1991) *The New Institutionalism in Organizational Analysis*, Chicago, IL: University of Chicago Press.

Salomon, D. (1997) 'The problematic transformation of the banking sector in France', in G. Morgan and D. Knights (eds) *Regulation and Deregulation in European Financial Services*, London: Macmillan.

Schmidt, V. A. (1996) *From State to Market? The Transformation of French Business and Government*, Cambridge: Cambridge University Press.

Trebilcock, R. C. (1981) *The Industrialization of the Continental Powers 1780–1914*, London: Longman.

Trow, M. (1989) 'American higher education: past, present and future', in T. Nybom (ed.) *The University and Society. On Research Policy and the Role of Science in*

Society (*Universitet och Samhälle. Om Forskningspolitik och Vetenskapens Samhälleliga Roll*), Stockholm: Tiden.

—— (1996) 'Trust, markets and accountability in higher education: a comparative perspective', paper prepared for a seminar organized by the Society into Higher Education, 12 June, Oxford (mimeo).

Underhill, G. D. (ed.) (1997) *The New World Order in International Finance*, London: Macmillan.

Veld in't, R., Füssel, H.-P. and Neave, G. (1996) *Relations between State and Higher Education*, The Hague: Kluwer.

Weiss, L. and Hobson, J. M. (1995) *States and Economic Development*, Cambridge: Polity Press

Whitley, R. (1984) *The Intellectual and Social Organization of the Sciences*, Oxford: Oxford University Press.

Whitley, R. and Kristensen, P. H. (eds) (1996) *The Changing European Firm*, London: Routledge

—— (eds) (1997) *Governance at Work: The Social Regulation of Economic Relations*, Oxford: Oxford University Press

Zysman, J. (1983) *Governments, Markets and Growth*, Ithaca, NY: Cornell University Press.

6 Is the German model of corporate governance changing?

Nestor D'Alessio and Herbert Oberbeck

Introduction

Nowadays capitalism is written in the plural. There are capitalisms, national capitalisms, which, built up to models, are checked as to their economic efficiency within the structure of a 'globalized' world economy. This pluralization is not a new phenomenon; comparative surveys on the different functions and forms of organization of capitalistic national economies enjoy a long tradition in the social sciences (cf. e.g. Shonfield 1965). However, in the past, research was not as geared to test the development capabilities of national systems in the context of international competition as it is today. This type of questioning was more restricted to the systematic comparison between capitalism and communism. The situation changed after the collapse of the centrally steered economies of the East European countries. Today, the institutional variations of national capitalisms are compared with regard to their contribution to economic growth and increased productivity, employment and innovation, and not so much to their performance in the recent past – how adaptable they are in the light of a rapidly changing world economy (cf. e.g. Streeck 1995).

The current discussion about different capitalist systems and models of development is generally led with reference to individual social subsystems. There are comparative studies on concepts of industrial relations, work organization and vocational training and qualification. However, in the context of the question of financing enterprises, the different national forms of corporate governance are also the subject of comparative research (cf. e.g. Walter 1993).

Broadly defined, corporate governance refers to 'the whole set of legal, cultural, and institutional arrangements that determines what publicly traded corporations can do, who controls them, how that control is exercised, and how the risks and returns from the activities they undertake are allocated' (Blair 1995: 3). Thus defined, corporate governance concerns questions of ownership and control in stock corporations which in Germany have been traditionally associated with the rule of the banks over non-financial corporations (Hilferding 1981).

The classical exposition on ownership and control in modern large corporations is Berle and Means' *The Modern Corporation and Private Property*, which appeared in the US in 1932. The two authors discovered that in almost half the American stock corporations they investigated, the strong diversification of shareholding made it impossible to identify shareholders who, as groups or individuals, could be described as real controllers of the managers. In contrast to large corporations at the turn of the century, which were controlled by their owners, in the stock corporations investigated by Berle and Means ownership and control were separated, affecting the traditional notion of ownership.

Legally, shareholders continued to be owners of the corporations, although owners of a special kind. As is the case today, they were not held liable with their personal funds in the event of liquidation, they did not receive a fixed income from their investments in the corporation, and their claims on companies going into liquidation were only satisfied after the debts to banks, suppliers and employees had been settled. They did have the right of monitoring over management, however, but by not attending meetings of shareholders, where the performance of managers was scrutinized and supervisory boards were elected, they did not make use of this. Not only was it difficult to organize dispersed shareholders, but their relative ignorance about business affairs as well explained their behaviour. The consequence was that actual control lay in the hands of managers, who as agents of the shareholders were formally responsible to them, but who in fact could run the corporations independently without having to give an account of their actions.

However, as Berle and Means pointed out, shareholders had the 'exit' option to compensate for their weakness. So long as there was a liquid capital market, they could sell their stocks when they were not satisfied. However, this has not always been accepted as an efficient solution to the conflict of interests existing between principals (shareholders) and agents (managers). In this respect, uncontrolled managers are seen by different authors as people who have no long-term interest in firms and waste other people's money, an idea that goes back to Adam Smith:

> The directors of such companies, being the managers of other people's money than of their own, it cannot be well expected that they should watch over it with the same anxious vigilance with which the partners in a private copartnery frequently watch of their own. Like the stewards of a rich man, they are apt to consider attention to small matters as not for their master's honor, and very easily give themselves a dispensation for having it. Negligence and profusion, therefore, must always prevail, more or less, in the management of the affairs of such company.
>
> (Smith 1976, quoted in Henwood 1997: 256)

Since Berle and Means' discussions on corporate governance, there have been discussions on how to develop institutional arrangements and incentive structures which rule out opportunistic behaviour not only between shareholders and management but also between shareholders, lenders and management, since equity capital is not the only instrument corporations have to finance their investments. Bonds and bank credits also play a role in providing finance for investment and the interests of shareholders and lenders are not always the same. While shareholders may prefer high-risk investments with high returns and increasing stock prices, lenders are interested in the secure repayment of interest and principal, an expectation which does not necessarily fit well with high-risk investments. And managers may court capital markets when they need to raise equity capital, but otherwise will try to keep debts as low as possible and resort to internal funds in order to prevent external control.

In the context of these discussions, developments in Germany provide a distinctive model of how the relationship between ownership and control can be organized without confronting the problems described by Berle and Means, and how the conflicts between shareholders, lenders and management can be managed without extreme frictions. German banks – which are at the same time shareholders, depositaries of proxy owner rights and lenders – seem to different authors, as we shall see below, to offer an efficient solution to the problems and conflicts raised by the separation of ownership and control.[1]

In this chapter we shall first present the conventional description of the German model of corporate governance as well as the efficiency arguments as exposed by their supporters. We shall then deal with empirical data which, admittedly, do not radically question the model, but lead to a relativization of some of its aspects. Finally, we shall show how the model is being questioned and how German governance practices are changing.

The German model of corporate governance

The literature on the national systems of corporate governance characterizes Germany as a country in which 'firms invest more than they save from profits and get the rest of their funds from borrowing' (Zysman 1983: 193). In concrete terms this means that German firms, in contrast to British or American ones, finance the capital formation which exceeds their internally generated resources by borrowing long term from banks, rather than by the issue of shares (Carrington and Edwards 1979).

In addition to the credit dependence of German stock corporations, the literature lists two further characteristics which substantiate the distinctive features of the German governance structures. First, German banks are 'Universalbanken'; they not only act as commercial banks but also as investment banks. As commercial banks, the banks provide long-term loans to the firms, and as investment banks, they organize access for the enterprises to the capital market by issuing shares. Second, the banks have considerable blocks of shares, be it as shareholders or under proxy owner's right which, during general meetings of shareholders, gives them the opportunity to send bank representatives to the supervisory boards, whereby they are able to influence the election of the management.

Credit dependence of German stock corporations in the form of long-term bank loans and interlocking capital and personnel arrangements between companies and banks are structural components which are considered by some to be an ideal model of ownership, control and efficiency. In this respect, it is argued that financing of stock corporations with long-term bank loans makes long-term investment planning in companies possible and thereby helps to reduce business uncertainties. But how do banks reduce risks which are inherent in the granting of bank loans? Normally, banks aim at reducing credit risks by balance-sheet analyses, discussions with managers, supervision of money transactions by the borrowers and investigations of market developments. Despite this, an asymmetry of information between borrower and lender remains, because the former is better informed about risks and cash flow of the future investments than the latter (Leland and Pyle 1977; Diamond 1984). Supporters of the German model of corporate governance regard interlocking capital and personnel arrangements as additional control mechanisms which contribute to a further reduction of asymmetry of information between borrower and lender, and thereby to risk reduction. Further still, in contrast to dispersed and inattentive shareholders – as described by Berle and Means – who do not make use of their right of control of the management, banks – in their dual roles of long-term lenders and owners – are interested in this right. And the logical reversal is also plausible: the banks, as 'house banks', are prepared to extend long-term loans and to support further those enterprises in a difficult financial situation only because they are well informed about the business policy of companies (Cable and Turner 1983; Cable 1985; Fama 1985; Crafts 1992).

'Long term' is the key term here. As a macro- and micro-economic efficiency criterion it substantiates the alleged superiority of the incentive and control structures of the German system of corporate governance in comparison with other systems in which the finance of investment rests predominantly on the capital markets.

In the next section we investigate how this model-like presentation of the German system of corporate governance agrees with the empirical reality.

Are German stock corporations actually credit dependent?

Credit dependence is a relational term, the significance of which can only be determined in a comparative context. Authors such as Zysman, who refer to national differences for the sources of financing enterprises, base their statements on comparative statistics which apparently confirm the credit dependence of German enterprises. Such a comparative survey of the ratio equity/debt by British and German stock corporations at the beginning of the 1980s confirmed the greater bank credit dependence of German enterprises for capital formation in comparison with British ones (Friedman *et al.* 1984). However, it was overlooked that different institutional and accounting arrangements distorted the results. Once such differences are taken into account and the data are adjusted accordingly, British enterprises show a greater credit dependence than German enterprises (Edwards and Fischer 1994).[2]

Between 1971 and 1985 internally generated resources (retained profits in the form of risk provisions and depreciation) were the most important item for the physical capital formation of German stock corporations in the industrial sector, whereas the reserves for company pensions represented the second most important source of investment. Together these amounted to an average of 102 per cent of the net resources of the physical capital formation. In contrast to this, the proportion of long-term bank loans made up 1.7 per cent (Edwards and Fischer 1994: 128).

The compositions of the investment sources for the accumulation of physical capital of the German stock corporations point to the existence of a regulation system which greatly reduces the dependence of stock corporations on external financing. In this respect, German accounting and tax legislation and the pension system both play a role. While the former allows for the formation of generous risk provisions, the latter envisages the possibility of a company pension complementary to the state pension system, the financing of which is guaranteed by the formation of internal provisions.[3] As a deduction from profit, it reduces the tax burden of the firms (Welzk 1986; Kamppeter 1990).

Risk and pension provisions have not only advanced to the most important sources of investment in physical capital, but have also accelerated the debt reduction of German stock corporations which took place in the 1980s (Deutsche Bundesbank 1991). However, this does not mean that bank loans and debt do not play a role. Risk provisions and pension reserves have reduced the credit dependence of corporations for financing of investments, but bank loans and debt are still crucial in the event of liquidity crises and restructuring of corporations.

How the German model of corporate governance is being questioned

Two ways of questioning the German model of corporate governance can be discerned. One is of an empirical nature and hints at the fact that, due to the degree of independence reached by the stock corporations, we can no longer speak of such a model. The other assumes that the model continues to exist and its criticism is of a more normative character, directed against the power of the banks. We now discuss these positions.

For authors such as Sabel *et al.* (1993: 15), 'the German system of corporate governance is now in ruins'. On the one hand, they support their thesis by the decreasing importance of bank loans as a source of financing industrial investment, while on the other, they point out that the big banks (Deutsche Bank, Dresdner Bank and Commerzbank) are unloading part of their holdings in stock corporations as a further indicator of the dissolution of the traditional relationship between corporations and big banks.

In fact, one of the big banks, the Deutsche Bank, reduced its shareholdings in some corporations at the beginning of the 1990s (Sturm 1997). At the same time, however, the banks' own holdings as a share of the total nominal value of German shares increased from 5 per cent in 1964 to 9.7 per cent in 1992. While the share fell to 8.4 per cent in 1994, it rose to 10.3 per cent in 1997 (Deutsche Bundesbank 1996, 1997). Simultaneously, excluding insurance company shares, the proportion of shares deposited with banks amounted to 51.1 per cent in 1996 (53.5 per cent in 1988) (Deutsche Bundesbank 1989, 1996: 32, Table IV).

We have pointed out that German banks as shareholders, but also as users of proxy voting rights, are capable at the shareholders' meetings of influencing the election of shareholder representatives to the supervisory board, the body which appoints and dismisses the board of managers of a stock corporation.[4] In this respect, a study conducted in 1978 showed that, if one added up the bank's own votes plus those coming from the use of proxy voting rights, the three big banks – considered individually – in general did not have a clear majority in the shareholders' meetings of the largest German corporations, but through their combined votes they controlled, with few exceptions, the majority of votes (Monopolkommission 1978). Twenty-five years later, in 1992, banks controlled, on average, 88 per cent of the rights to vote in the shareholders' meetings of the twenty-four largest German corporations. The figures suggest that the banks' capability to influence decisions made at the shareholders' meetings remains intact. Taken together, the three big banks controlled, on average, 34 per cent of the rights to vote, far above the 25 per cent needed to block changes in the statutes of a corporation or propositions about increases or decreases in equity capital or merger and liquidation. Furthermore, the combined rights to vote of the five largest banks, which are stock corporations with a broad diversification of shareholders, guaranteed the majority in each bank (Baums 1996). Summing up, with all relativization of credit dependence, statistical evidence does not suggest that structural features of the German model of corporate governance such as the banks' own holdings or the use of proxy voting rights would recently have experienced a debilitation. In this sense, the idea of a dissolution of the model lacks empirical support.

A different kind of criticism addresses the control function of banks. With reference to the formation of provisions, the question arises why German banks, as holders of proxy voting rights, do not make use of their control function in favour of shareholders by allowing the formation of provisions to such an extent that they force the dividend amount down (Steinherr and Huveneers 1992). These authors claim that German universal banks are not interested in the development of the capital market; they even take advantage of its relative – by international standards – underdevelopment. The banks' policy of approval reduces the dividends for distribution and forces share prices down. As a result, the issue of shares becomes unattractive to enterprises and they are further dependent on bank loans. The banks take advantage of this dependence and raise the interest on loans, while the German capital market remains underdeveloped.

German universal banks are presented as ideal owners in the conventional wisdom of corporate governance, not only exercising their control functions competently, but also building up long-term financial relationships with corporations. In the opinion of Steinherr and Huveneers, however, the banks neglect the interests of shareholders and use their strong position as 'house banks' to collect quasi-rents through the credit business.

If Steinherr and Huveneers, with their criticisms of the way in which German banks look after the interests of shareholders, refer to a problematic side of the German system of corporate governance, their way of substantiating the position of the banks is not convincing. Neither credit dependence nor increase in credit costs, or retention of issue of shares, finds an empirical confirmation in reality. Competition between the banks for the loan business with large corporations has led to a drastic reduction of the interest margins (Oberbeck and D'Alessio 1997). Apart from this, in the 1980s the credit-based cost of capital was lower in Germany than in the US, the UK and Japan (MacCauley and Zimmer 1989) which, however, did not prevent large corporations from reducing their bank debts and building up their stock capital by issuing shares (Deutsche Bundesbank 1991).[5]

Nevertheless, the critical reference to the dividend payout policy of bank representatives cannot be ignored, even more so as in the past few years large losses in holdings such as the Metallgesellschaft or Daimler Benz have given rise to a new shareholder activism which attacks not only banks but also the management. Considered from this critical perspective, the problem is that, thanks to the banks' policy, German management has too much autonomy, is wasting resources, and thus damaging the shareholders' interests. Here, restrictions on the participation of banks and even the abolition of the proxy voting right are called for. According to the thesis, capital-market-based systems of corporate governance, like in the US where the management is exposed to hostile takeover, fulfil the control functions more efficiently. Before we can evaluate the questioning of banks as controllers, however, it is necessary to analyse other aspects of the German model of corporate governance which are normally overlooked in conventional presentations.

Taking into account the structure of interlocking capital arrangements in Germany, the German system can be described as an 'intrainsider' system (Walter 1993). This means two things. First, banks are relatively important as shareholders of stock corporations, and second, stock corporations are normally interlocked with each other within a *Konzern* so that the ownership of many firms is in the hands of other firms.[6] In this respect, German non-financial enterprises held around 42 per cent of the shares issued by German corporations in 1994 (Deutsche Bundesbank 1997).[7] At the same time, the shareholdings show a high degree of concentration: in 1992 around 70 per cent of the 290 shareholdings of German non-financial enterprises with the 500 largest enterprises amounted to 50 per cent or more of the equity capital in the hands of only one enterprise.[8] In contrast to these figures, only 3 per cent of the 89 banks' holdings represented more than 50 per cent of the equity capital in only one enterprise, whereas around 75 per cent of them amounted to less than 24.9 per cent, i.e. less than the 25 per cent needed to block modifications of the statutes of the corporations or propositions about increase or decrease of equity capital, mergers or liquidation (our own calculation on the basis of Windolf and Beyer 1995: 9, Table 1).

The figures on the banks' shareholdings suggest that the position of banks in terms of control of the equity capital of non-financial enterprises is not as strong as assumed. It is correct, as exposed above, that the influence of banks goes beyond their shareholdings due to the proxy voting rights. However, since around 44 per cent of the shareholdings of non-financial enterprises (around 50 per cent if shareholdings of insurance companies and investment funds are included) were deposited with banks in 1994 (Deutsche Bundesbank 1996: 32, Table IV), banks actually often represent the interests of owners whom they should theoretically control. This suggests that neither decisions about the provision and dividend payout policies, nor about the investment policies of corporations are taken alone by banks, and that the wide freedom of action management enjoys (management of banks included) is not necessarily a result of the intended leniency of banks before the management of non-financial firms, but rather a consequence of the structure of ownership itself.

All this means that German banks are part of *Konzerne* whose steering and control mechanisms cannot be adequately grasped with the conventional terms of ownership and control used to describe the German model of corporate governance. Within the framework of this web of interlocked enterprises, banks have contributed to screen off the *Konzerne* from the market of corporate control, making hostile takeovers difficult and thus creating the conditions for wide freedom of action by management. With this they have participated in the expansion of *Konzerne* but also in their restructuring when they encountered structural problems so that banks have often helped to coordinate the elimination of excess capacity in crisis sectors (Vitols 1995).[9] And even though sales or closures of firms and layoffs were inevitable, social and retraining plans have mitigated the negative consequences for the employees. At the same time, as mentioned above, strategic errors made by corporations such as Metallgesellschaft or Daimler Benz have led to an increasing questioning of banks and their indulgence towards a management too inclined to waste resources in pursuit of corporate expansion.

In actual fact, the combination of long-term loans, banks' shareholdings, proxy voting right and banks' representatives on the supervisory boards have transformed banks into favourite targets of attack. However, due to the ownership structure described above, doubts exist as to whether banks are capable of preventing the expansion of *Konzerne* and the errors management can make. They are part of the story, but only part. On the other hand, the question that cannot be answered conclusively at this point is whether the expansion pursued by management and the alleged waste of resources can be limited by a finance system with an open market for capital, with full disclosure of all material about the financial affairs of firms, and without linkages between firms and banks.[10]

For all the relativization of the German model of corporate governance and its alleged efficiency, one particularity is worth mentioning: none of the enterprise crises have left traces at banks (nor in the banking system). During the last four years, when the crises occurred, the profit situation of the banks has in part even improved, and the banking system has remained stable. Judged by macro-economic efficiency criteria, this is not a negligible performance if one considers that the financing of hostile takeovers in the US led to the local savings and loans crisis, the consequences of which today have to be paid by the tax payer. And a 'bubble' economy caused by overindulgence in real estate and stock market investment has not taken place so that banks (and the banking system) – despite crises in the real sector of the economy – have proved to be a reliable stabilizer.

Changes in the governance structures

Increasing attacks against banks have not remained without consequences; for this reason, the government approved a bill for a new law governing control in enterprises ('*Gesetz zur Kontrolle und Transparenz im Unternehmensbereich*') in November 1997. The reform provides that executive boards, supervisory boards and auditors should be made to discharge their duties. Executive boards are made responsible for adequate risk management within the enterprise. Furthermore, the executive board has to inform the supervisory board in more detail about the enterprise's planning than it has done up to now. This eliminates the possibility for supervisory boards to make excuses in the future about not having had crucial information, as has happened in the past. The original plan to limit the supervisory boards to a maximum of twelve members has been given up because of the unions' persistent resistance. Currently the rule remains in force that one person is allowed membership of a maximum of ten supervisory boards; however, membership as chair counts as two. In order to avoid conflicts of interests, shareholders in the future will have to be informed if a member of the supervisory board also has a membership of the supervisory board(s) of one or more competing enterprises.

As far as the proxy voting right is concerned, in the future, according to the plans of the German government, the banks will have to forfeit this right if, in a shareholders' meeting, they want to use votes from their own shareholding with the corporation of more than 5 per cent. In this case they are only allowed to vote for a deposit customer if this customer has assigned them power of attorney for the respective point of the agenda. However, this restriction will have only a limited effect because the banks' investment subsidiaries are not included in calculating the shareholdings. All this suggests that, in spite of the reform of the legislation, structural aspects of the German model of corporate governance will continue to be in force.

However, as mentioned above, corporate governance refers not only to laws and statutes but also to institutionalized practices. And it is at the level of restructuring practices that changes are taking place. *Konzerne* are being run as holdings within which the different firms have to be run autonomously. This means that the internal subsidy of less profitable firms, which was a common practice within *Konzerne*, disappears. Firms have to prove that they are profitable without the financial support of *Konzerne*. In the event of failing to realize the profit targets holdings fixed, firms are sold.[11] Along with new financial accounting methods introduced to improve the disclosure of financial issues, the new practices suggest that German *Konzerne* are reassessing the role of the capital market as arbiter who decides the market value of corporations.

Is there an explanation for this change? A tentative answer is that mergers and acquisitions which are accompanying the restructuring process of *Konzerne* – not least as a consequence of the increasing internationalization of the world economy – demand new money only the capital market can supply, and the market value of corporations is a relevant variable in order to fix the quotation of new shares.[12] Besides, an increased value of the *Konzerne*'s own shares is not a bad thing when they are given in pay by mergers or acquisitions.[13] However, an increasing role of the capital market as a financing source and arbiter of the market value of corporations is not incompatible with the screening off of *Konzerne* from the market of corporate control. Up to now, shareholdings which guaranteed the control over firms have remained in the hands of *Konzerne* and banks, and this means that German management continues to enjoy a wide freedom of action, although they have to pay more attention to the market value of the corporations they run. This is not a bad deal for banks.

Notes

1 Early in 1919 in *Industry and Trade*, Alfred Marshall pointed to the distinctive character of German banks which, in contrast to banks in the United Kingdom, were both investment and commercial banks and maintained close links to industry (Marshall 1919, according to Shonfield 1965: 293). Later, in his historical studies, Gerschenkron characterized the German '*Universalbanken*' as a 'powerful invention comparable in economic effect to that of the steam engine' (Gerschenkron 1968: 137).

2 In order to avoid the statistical distortions, Edwards and Fischer conducted their research on the basis of flow of funds and not of stocks of assets and liabilities: 'the flow of funds statement shows the sources of funds in a particular year, and the uses to which these funds were put in that year' (Edwards and Fischer 1994: 51).

3 Pension provisions represent claims to the enterprises so that although they are an important internal source of investment, they are actually borrowed capital. The pension regulation establishes that the pension rights are non-forfeitable after a given number of years worked in an enterprise, so that if an employee leaves the enterprise he/she retains her/his claims. A privately run mutual insurance fund takes over the pension claims in the event of bankruptcy of enterprises.

4 It is worth noting that in stock corporations with less than 2,000 employees, one-third of the supervisory board must be elected by its employees. In corporations with more than 2,000 employees, one-half of the supervisory board seats are reserved for the employee representatives. In this case the chair of the supervisory board has to be elected by a two-thirds majority of all members or by the shareholders' representatives if the necessary majority is not achieved. Chairs break the tie in supervisory boards.

5 It would have been more reasonable to substantiate the argument about the quasi-rents with the privileged role German banks as '*Hausbanken*' have in the issue of shares. However, the business practices of Anglo-Saxon investment banks do not seem to differ from those of German banks (*Economist* 1996).

6 *Konzern* means an institutional arrangement of interlocked enterprises which are under the rule of a dominant enterprise ('*herrschendes Unternehmen*'). There are different forms of *Konzern* whose relationships are regulated through the legislation. Enterprises are interlocked through shareholdings and personal links at the level of the supervisory boards. The aim of a *Konzern* is not the centralization of financial assets as in holding companies, but the rationalization of the production process within a branch of industry. Pools of profits or reciprocal dividend undertakings are the instruments used to increase the efficiency of the *Konzern* through internal redistribution of resources.

7 In contrast to Germany, American non-financial enterprises held only 15 per cent of the shares issued in the US in 1995. In the same year, the shareholdings of British non-financial enterprises amounted to only 4 per cent of the total of shares issued in Great Britain (Deutsche Bundesbank 1997).

8 It is worth noting that many of the controlled enterprises are unlisted stock corporations. In 1996 there were around 3,900 stock corporations in Germany; only about 17 per cent of them were listed corporations (Deutsche Bundesbank 1997)

9 Hostile takeovers are not impossible in Germany, although they are very difficult to organize, given the ownership structure described in the text. However, in 1997 the steel corporation Krupp Hoesch tried to organize with the support of the big banks a hostile takeover of the other large German steel corporation, Thyssen. The takeover failed because of an information leak which led to the public protest of the management of Thyssen accompanied by street demonstrations of the unions. However, the management of Thyssen was forced to negotiate the merger with Krupp Hoesch even though Thyssen is the more efficient company. It is worth noting that the rationalization of the German steel production through concentration was a request of the Deutsche Bank in the 1980s, when the chair of the Deutsche Bank invited the managers of the steel corporations to discuss the rationalization of the branch. The negotiations ended without concrete results. This case gives a partial insight on steering and decision-taking mechanisms within the system of corporate governance. Negotiations are at the centre of the system, but when they fail, an alliance between managers of banks and corporations can force the results pursued against the will of one of the participants in the deal. In contrast to people who claim that the failed takeover organized by Krupp Hoesch represented a break with the rules of the game which have traditionally governed the system of German corporate governance, one can say that the resistence of managers of Thyssen to negotiate the rationalization of the steel industry constituted the proper break with the tradition.

10 A recent empirical research conducted in the US shows that the control of the management through the capital market has not put limits to its autonomy in matters of corporation expansion (*Economist* 1997).

11 An interview in *Die Mitbestimmung* with the chair of the works council of Siemens AG gives an insight about the dynamic of the restructuring process some German corporations are currently experiencing and the consequences of abolishing the traditional subvention practice (*Die Mitbestimmung* 1997).

12 It is worth mentioning that the restructuring logics differ notably. While there are *Konzerne*, which through mergers and/or acquisitions as well as selling of firms are redefining their core business within their own branch, other *Konzerne* are expanding in business fields outside their traditional activities.

13 While there were 1,350 mergers and acquisitions in 1985, the number increased to 2,252 in 1996 with a peak of 2,839 in 1989 (*M&A Review Database*, April 1997).

References

Baums, T. (1996) 'Proxy voting right for the banks' ('Vollmachtstimmtrecht der Banken – Ja oder Nein'), *Die Aktiengesellschaft* 41: 11–26.

Berle, A. and Means, G. (1932) *The Modern Corporation and Private Property*, New York: Commerce. Clearing House, Inc.

Blair, M. M. (1995) *Ownership and Control. Rethinking Corporate Governance for the Twenty-First Century*, Washington, DC: The Brookings Institution.

Cable, J. (1985) 'Capital market information and industrial performance. The role of German banks', *Economic Journal* 95: 118–32.

Cable, J. and Turner, P. (1983) 'Asymmetric information and credit rationing. Another view of industrial bank lending and Britain's economic problem', Warwick Economic Research Papers No. 228, Department of Economics, University of Warwick.

Carrington, J. and Edwards, G. (1979) *Financing Industrial Investment*, London: Macmillan.

Crafts, N. (1992) 'Productivity growth reconsidered', *Economic Policy* 15: 387–414.

Deutsche Bundesbank (1989) *Statistische Beihefte zu den Monatsberichten der Deutschen Bundesbank*, Reihe 1. Bankenstatistik nach Bankengruppen, July, No. 7: 3.

—— (1991) 'Zur Bedeutung der Aktie als Finanzierungsinstrument', *Monatsberichte der Deutschen Bundesbank*, October, No. 10: 22–9.

—— (1996) 'Wertpapierdepots', *Statistische Sonderveröffentlichung*, August, No. 9: 32.

—— (1997) 'Die Aktie als Finanzierungs- und Anlageinstrument', *Monatsberichte der Deutschen Bundesbank*, January, No. 1: 27–41.

Diamond, D. (1984) 'Financial intermediation and delegated monitoring', *Review of Economic Studies* 51: 393–14.

Economist (1996) 'Corporate finance: rights at issue', 18 May: 75–6.

Economist (1997) 'Unintended consequences', 16 August: 55–6.

Edwards, J. and Fischer, K. (1994) *Banks, Finance and Investment in Germany*, Cambridge: Cambridge University Press.

Fama, G. (1985) 'What is different about banks', *Journal of Monetary Economies* 15: 29–40.

Friedman, W., Ingram, D. and Miles, D. (1984) 'Industrial investment in Great Britain and the Federal German Republic' ('Unternehmensfinanzierung in Großbritannien und in der Bundesrepublik Deutschland'), *Monatsbericht der Deutschen Bundesbank*, November, No. 11: 35–46.

Gerschenkron, A. (1968) *Continuity in History and Other Essays*, Cambridge, MA: Harvard University Press.

Henwood, D. (1997) *Wall Street*, London: Verso.

Hilferding, R. (1981) *Finance Capital* [1910], London: Routledge and Kegan Paul.

Kamppeter, W. (1990) *Capital and Currency Markets as a Challenge for Economic Policies* (*Kapital– und Devisenmärkte als Herausforderung der Wirtschaftspolitik*), Frankfurt am Main: Campus Verlag.

Leland, H. and Pyle, D. (1977) 'Information asymmetries, financial structures and financial intermediaries', *Journal of Finance* 2: 371–87.

M&A Review Database (1997), in *Handelsblatt*, 24 April: B2, Düsseldorf.

MacCauley, R. and Zimmer, S. (1989) 'Explaining international differences in the cost of capital', *Federal Reserve of New York, Quarterly Review*, Summer: 7–28.

Die Mitbestimmung (1997) 'Längerer Atem macht sich bezahlt', July/August: 40–2.

Monopolkommission (1978) *Hauptgutachten II. Fortschreitende Konzentration bei Großunternehmen*, Baden-Baden: Nomosverlag.

Oberbeck, H. and D'Alessio, N. (1997) 'The end of the German model? Developmental tendencies in the German banking industry', in G. Morgan and D. Knights (eds) *Regulation and Deregulation in European Financial Services*, London: Macmillan.

Sabel, Ch., Griffin, J. and Deeg, R. (1993) 'Making money talk: towards a new debtor-creditor relation in German banking', paper presented at the Conference of Law and Economic Studies, Columbia University School of Law and Economic Studies, 6–7 May, New York.

Shonfield, A. (1965) *Modern Capitalism: The Changing Balance of Public and Private Power*, London: Oxford University Press.

Smith, A. (1976) *An Inquiry into the Nature and Causes of the Wealth of Nations*, ed. R. H. Campbell and A. S. Skinner, Oxford: The Clarendon Press.

Steinherr, A. and Huveneers, Ch. (1992) 'Institutional competition and innovation', in A. Mullineaux (ed.) *European Banking*, Oxford: Blackwell.

Streeck, W. (1995) 'German capitalism: does it exist? Can it survive?', in C. Crouch and W. Streeck (eds) *Modern Capitalism or Modern Capitalisms?*, London: Francis Pinter.

Sturm, R. (1997) 'Banks as rulers of the German economy' ('Die Banken als Lenker der deutschen Wirtschaft'), *Der Bürger im Staat*, Landeszentrale für politische Bildung Baden-Württemberg: Heft 1: 53–7.

Vitols, S. (1995) 'Financial systems and industrial policy in Germany and Great Britain: the limits of convergence', Discussion Paper FS I 95–311. WZB. Berlin: Wissenschaftzentrum Berlin für Sozialforschung.

Walter, I. (1993) 'The battle of the systems: control of enterprises and the global economy', *Institut für Weltwitschaft an der Universität Kiel*, Kiel, Kieler Vorträge. N.F. 122.

Welzk, S. (1986) *Boom Without Employment* (*Boom ohne Arbeitsplätze*), Köln-Berlin: Kiepenheuer and Witsch.

Windolf, P. and Beyer, J. (1995) 'Cooperative capitalisms' ('Kooperativer kapitalismus'), *Kölner Zeitschrift für Soziologie und Sozialpsychologie* 47(1): 1–36.

Zysman, J. (1983) *Governments, Markets and Growth*, Oxford: Martin Robertson.

Part III

The evolution of regulatory processes

Formal and informal mechanisms of change

7 The regulation of price-sensitive information

John Holland

Introduction

The 1980s were marked by extensive deregulation in the UK financial system especially by the 'Big Bang' in 1987 in which many old City trading and control structures were dismantled and market forces allowed to flourish. However, in the early 1990s many problems of corporate governance, insider dealing and financial risks became apparent in the UK and other European financial markets. As a result, the deregulation trend was quickly followed by extensive reregulation in the financial system. More specifically, UK companies and financial institutions (FIs) were subject to many new regulations on insider dealing and on the release and receipt of price-sensitive information (PSI). These new regulations created new threats to the established City system for the self-regulation of private company and financial institution communications and for the avoidance of insider dealing.

This chapter begins by exploring how and why this new regulatory system has been constructed. Particular emphasis is laid on the emergence of the Stock Exchange (SE) guidance (1993–94) on the dissemination of PSI. The UK insider dealing and PSI regulatory control system can be seen as reflecting a broader UK tradition or environment of 'behind-the-scenes' governance as well as traditions of common law, case law, quasi-regulation and active financial markets. Institutionalism suggests that causality runs from the environmental templates for social organization down to specific (company–institutional) networks or interorganization forms (Scott and Meyer 1994). Another reflection of this social context lies in the need of City participants for proximity and sociability (Thrift 1995: 334). The major UK FIs, corporations and their representative bodies all have a heavy concentration of major offices and HQs in or near the City of London and use the physical proximity to maintain their influence on new regulation concerning the City.

Many of these corporate and institutional groups lobbied hard in 1993 to change the new insider-dealing law and exercised influence over the SE guidance on PSI. It is therefore no surprise to note that the guidance reflected a negotiated balance between the vested interests of these groups; this may explain why the committee stopped short of dealing with contentious matters such as inside, but non-price-sensitive, information collected by FIs during their regular contacts with companies. It also suggests why these connected groups (Scott 1993, 1997) seek to control the system for designing such rules, and why they have not sought radical change in this system.

Another manifestation of this social network lies in the observation that major UK companies and FIs were in regular contact as part of their normal transacting activity and this was based on the construction of 'close relationships' or networks based on trust and confidence. Companies and FIs valued the private exchange process and this created incentives to avoid illegal PSI release and internalize external regulation on this matter.

This somewhat cosy situation created major problems for UK and EU regulators concerned both with equity and with economic efficiency. The FIs were seen as having privileged access to information. As informed insiders they could trade before the rest of the market, made up of institutions and small investors. UK regulators therefore used 'good' practice as a basis for designing their guidance on corporate and institutional use of potentially price-sensitive information. This had the advantage of exploiting much experience from the City 'great and good', but also created problems of potential regulatory capture by the City. In addition, the regulators faced a major problem when trying to define 'price-sensitive information'. Their solution was to transfer the problem of definition to companies, FIs and others. This had the advantage of creating uncertainty in the minds of those intending to circumvent the regulation, but also created further opportunities for opportunistic adaption to the new regulatory regime by well-informed City participants.

Regulators faced an additional problem in encouraging the appropriate corporate governance structures for private information exchange. Regulators recognized that they faced a trade-off in avoiding insider dealing whilst at the same time maintaining efficient financial intermediation and informationally efficient markets. More specifically, the regulators had to control the private release of PSI whilst at the same time allowing FIs and companies to acquire a knowledge and understanding of each other's needs and activities. Too tough a regulatory regime could undermine these channels and drive them underground. This problem set a limit for formal 'self-regulation' as manifest in the SE guidance.

The chapter then turns to the empirical case data and reveals how companies and FIs have used their relationship contacts to develop similar and matched approaches to internalizing the external guidance and for self-regulating their information exchange activities. Companies and FIs responded to the new SE guidance by setting up quite specific procedures and functions to deal with the PSI problems. These included the adaption of existing decision processes, the use of technology and internal controls over PSI. They therefore sought to structure their private contacts so that they did not break the new SE rules and could continue with a fruitful private exchange.

The chapter therefore reveals how private self-regulation persists in the UK despite attempts to replace it with formal, more public regulation. The chapter also illustrates how private self-regulation has evolved with changes in the formal regulatory system and has survived as a central component of this system. Despite these formal changes we see how it still reflects the City social system and is deeply embedded in the wider City institutional setting. The self-regulation observed in this research reflects traditional solutions to control problems in the UK financial system.

Thus the private company and institutional exchange process and the associated self-regulation process can be seen as a consequence of several related factors. These include the benefits to the two parties of private exchange, of City–industry social preferences for implicit contracting, and of problems of failure in the market for information. The increasing concentration of institutional ownership (Gaved 1997) has also increased the incentives for private contracting and reduced the costs of regular private contact. These factors raise questions concerning the influence of the City social system and whether it will undermine the new regulatory system and eventually promote a return to a world of more sophisticated 'nods and winks'. In contrast to this pessimistic note, the absorption of the SE guidance within the existing City social control system has stimulated the development of 'good practice' relative to the guidance. However, much of this is hidden from public view and the chapter argues that transparency is required for public confidence to be established in this form of delegated and guided self-regulation. The chapter ends by discussing how the new self-regulatory process can be made more open and accountable to the public at large.

The chapter is based on case interviews with executives in twenty-seven large UK FIs, and twenty-seven large (twenty-two FTSE100, five FTSE 100–200) UK companies. The interviews were conducted in the period June 1993 to March 1994. The case FIs constituted twenty-seven out of the thirty-five largest UK FIs and included life insurance, pension fund, unit trust and investment trust institutions. The UK companies were sampled to cover a wide industrial and commercial spread and represented twenty FT sectors. The case-study method was adopted because of the limited prior work in the FI–company relations area. This research method allows rich insight into new research fields (for example see Hopwood 1983; Scapens 1990). Common patterns of response to the new guidance and of self-regulation methods have been identified from the full set of cases. However, generalizations should be restricted to the cases studied. Despite the coverage of the major UK FIs and major UK companies the chapter does not claim to be a representative study of all UK FIs and companies. Short cases and quotes are used to illustrate the self-regulatory process.

The evolution of regulation in the field of insider dealing and PSI

The insider-dealing law, the SE guidance, and club control are different but inter-related mechanisms to deal with the regulatory issues arising with PSI. The nature of the connections between these control mechanisms is illustrated in Table 7.1 by considering how the controls support each other. The mechanisms form a hierarchy of sanctions beginning with insider-trading law, followed by the SE's continuing obligations and then the guidance on PSI dissemination. Much corporate communication takes place through private channels with financial institutions, analysts and the media channels and this was the primary target of legal and guidance controls. The SE guidance performs a 'frontline' role or acts as the first layer of close, continuous control over the bulk of ongoing corporate communications to the City. It reflects 'good practice' at this level, as decided by the SE committee, and acts as a benchmark to assess if corporate behaviour was reasonable or deviant in some way. The sanctions from the SE guidance appear weak when viewed in isolation, but when placed in the broader control context they are formidable. If companies and institutions are discovered to have departed significantly from the guidance they could face a severe reprimand from the SE and the publicity could potentially trigger de-listing, or an inquiry by the SE insider-dealing surveillance unit, and possibly legal action. Reprimands and an inquiry are more likely since the SE has become more proactive in its regulatory role. The fact that case law has yet to establish the clear legal boundaries for company, analyst, fund manager and press communications increases this likelihood.

In addition, the stock market is a critical support to the formal regulatory mechanisms. The stock market, through its rapid assimilation of new information into prices, could alert regulators to unusual price changes and this could lead to regulatory investigation of corporate behaviour especially in the area of its relationship contacts with institutions, analysts, financial advisers and the media. The stock market, in the form of the 'market for votes' could be used directly to reprimand 'leaky' management teams at annual or extraordinary general meetings (AGMs/EGMs). The stock market acting as the 'market for corporate control' could be used to change management teams who selectively leaked PSI through private analyst and institutional channels to the detriment of existing shareholders. Table 7.1 makes it clear that the UK regulatory system and process goes beyond the idea of a system based solely on law and formal regulatory bodies. The broader control system reflects a long period of evolutionary development of UK laws, London-based financial markets and the City social system.

Coleman (1994) points out that 'social' or 'club' control at the level of informal City groups was the historic base for 'pure' self-regulation in the City, and has only recently been replaced in the 1980s with more formal self-regulation backed by government power and in some cases,

Table 7.1 Regulation of insider dealing and PSI

1 Law	1985 Company Securities (Insider Dealing) Act 1986 Sect. 47 of Financial Services Act 1989 EC directive (89/592/EEC) 1993 Criminal Justice Act (Part V)
2 Delegated self-regulatory system	SE listing rules SE surveillance unit SE guidance on dissemination of PSI (1994)
3 'Behind-the-scenes' self-regulation	Individual companies and institutions act as agents for SE and other City and corporate professionals to regulate PSI standards. They control information flows through public mechanisms and through their close links with each other. Analysts and media play supporting role
4 Social or 'club' control	Informal networks of corporate directors, CEs, FDs and institutional managers. Informal pressure on companies and on individuals (job market). Professional networks in the City, including legal, market and other social links

new legislation. Prior to 1985 the dominant UK mechanisms for control or regulation in the UK financial system lay in categories 3 and 4 in Table 7.1. This involved 'social' or 'club' control at the level of informal City groups ranging from social groups (organized around markets, professions and institutions) down to select core groups of FIs for a company, and eventually down to a particular FI–company relationship. Sir Adrian Cadbury (1993: 11–12) describes governance in the City as a social process as follows:

> The City's control over itself, so to speak, was largely exercised through peer pressure along the lines of a traditional English club. The rules of the club were unwritten and were set by example. They depended on a strong lead being given by individuals who commanded general respect and who set the standards of conduct within their own firms. The penalty for unbecoming behaviour was exclusion from the club, a powerful and effective sanction, which is in effect, the one used by the Takeover Panel today.

Cadbury outlines a series of problems which made it difficult for the City club to maintain itself as the dominant form of self-regulation. These included rapid expansion post 'Big Bang', deregulation and new entrants to the City. This created a governance gap which had to be filled by establishing formal standards of conduct within firms and partly through external regulation in the form of changes in the law and the setting up of the Securities and Investments Board Ltd (SIB) and self-regulatory organizations (SROs). Cadbury chaired the committee on corporate governance which recommended changes to UK board committees, financial reporting and also recommended a more active role for UK financial institutions in their investee companies (December 1992).

In parallel with this corporate governance development there was widespread concern that this City club system led to unfair and privileged access to PSI, and this was a spur to UK legislation throughout the 1980s. The major legislation on insider dealing and the misuse of PSI initially lay in the Company Securities (Insider Dealing) Act 1985. Section 47 of the Financial Services Act 1986 prohibits behaviour designed to mislead or manipulate the market. The 'continuing obligations' of the SE indicated events and situations in which companies must make full announcements to the market. Moran (1991: 81) characterizes this legislation as ending a period of ineffective enforcement and ushering in a period of dramatic change in which insider dealing was to be punished severely. Moran argued that this development revealed how inadequately the term 'deregulation' described what was going in financial markets.

However, a mixture of circumstances combined in 1993 and 1994 to stimulate an even tougher regulatory regime. First, the 13 November 1989 EU directive (89/592/EEC) on insider dealing had yet to be implemented in the UK. UK market participants and regulatory authorities had to defend the direct access to corporate information enjoyed by UK market makers and others, including FIs and analysts. The EU directive was instrumental in making the UK break with an informal tradition and formally to define and codify these practices. Second, the UK detection and prosecution record was poor (*Economist* 1993). Third, two cases, Shanks McEwan (Bain 1994), and London International Group (Marckus 1993), alerted the authorities to the continued existence of corporate steering of earnings forecasts and of private release of information to analysts. These three sets of circumstances made the UK government rethink its insider-dealing law, and the SE set up a committee to investigate the dissemination of PSI. As a result, Part V of the 1993 Criminal Justice Act came into effect on 1 March 1994. The London SE published a consultative document on 4 November 1993 and on 24 February 1994 published its final 'Guidance on the dissemination of price sensitive information'.

UK law was extended to cover a wider range of securities and derivatives, and by broadening the nature of the market, and the geographic spread in which illegal insider trading could occur. However, the definition of 'price sensitivity' remained as problematic as before. The 1994 SE report makes it clear that 'it is not feasible to define any theoretical percentage movement in a share price which will make a piece of information price sensitive' (London Stock Exchange 1994a: 2). Consequently, companies, fund managers and analysts faced difficulties and some uncertainty as to whether their contacts and information exchanges were within the law (see Rice 1994 or Keenan 1993). Similar problems exist with the 1984 and

1988 US Insider Trading Acts which prohibit insider trading. These Acts have established strong penalties but have not defined insider trading. In both the US and UK the use of the case-by-case approach reflects the iterative nature of learning by the courts and regulators in this field as they strive to find an operational working approach to regulating insider dealing. However, in the US, the Securities and Exchange Commission (SEC) as the first line regulator has a much tougher stance than UK regulators (the Financial Services Authority and the SE) on what is legitimate. Its ability to deal with insider dealing through civil law, where the burden of proof is less than criminal law, and its ability to impose punitive fines several times the size of the insider gain, makes the SEC a formidable regulator in this respect. The SE committee explicitly recognized the value to both companies and the market of a dialogue between analysts (broker and investing institution) and the company which builds up a view of a business's potential (1994a: 5). It sought to protect these private information channels by defining information which must be released into the public domain and must not be discussed privately with a small group of institutions or analysts. The 1994 guidance re-emphasised the corporate need to avoid a false market, to keep the public informed on the company position, to meet regulatory requirements and for the company to notify the Company Announcements Office in the SE of any potential PSI. It reminded companies that the SE listing rules identify many events which have to be announced to the market because they may trigger PSI, such as dividend announcements and board changes. Outside of these areas the company has to use its judgement to deal with PSI issues. The net result of this 1994 SE guidance and changes in insider-dealing law was that UK companies, as information releasers, and financial institutions and broker analysts, as receivers, must define 'significant effect' and thus PSI according to their own special circumstances.

Control over company and institutional information flows

Cooperative relationships between financial institutions and their investee companies involved complex economic exchanges. Invested equity capital was exchanged for a share of the company's residual cash flows. This primary economic exchange was characterized as follows:

> The basic nature of our relationship with companies we invest in is that we are consumers of dividends and growth and the company is the producer of these in return for the use of our capital. It is putting it a bit crudely but it's up to the company to produce the goods we want and these are dividends and growth.
>
> (FI case A)

This primary exchange was supported by many continuing exchanges of information and influence, and this led to desirable state changes in both partners. The sum of these changes in knowledge of partners, confidence in partners, and enhanced reputation of partners created the relationship environment for continuing transactions.

> The length of time we have been investing in a company is very important to the whole process. As the relationship matures we get to know and trust each other. This assumes continuity of personnel on both sides. If we don't get to trust each other the relationship will not last long basically because we do not invest in companies we do not know or trust. Knowledge and trust form an important background in which we can be more relaxed about the continuous stream of events and snippets of good and bad new s about companies. It is vital, when we are on the phone to each other that we know the person on the other end and can be confident that they are telling the truth ... We make it clear that trust, friendship and other emotional links will, at the end of the day, not form a barrier to us making rational decisions in the management of our funds or those of our clients.
>
> (FI case B)

The case FIs differed in their core company holdings in the FTSE 350. However, all of them had relatively stable stakeholding policies for a large number of UK companies. The case fund directors and managers operated in FIs that were all supplying some form of saving service for their clients. They all had a fiduciary duty to supply their clients with their preferred mix of return, diversification and liquidity (Pozen 1994). The case companies restricted relationship channels to core groups of twenty to thirty relationship FIs and this reflected corporate incentives to communicate in an efficient way (reduced management time, clear signal to informed parties, etc.) to the stock market. Relationships thus emerged in dynamic process, and were closely linked to communication processes designed to serve the funding and control needs of companies and investing needs of FIs. They involved complex networks between companies and shareholders. The relationships existed independently of a need for regulation. Their primary role in the cases was to serve as active transaction channels for extensive reciprocal exchanges of capital, information and influence between companies and FIs. These channels were a convenient and natural point for these parties to self-regulate each other on corporate information release and FI receipt of information. Thrift (1995: 335) argues that such relationship contact is a central feature of many forms of transacting in international financial centres such as London.

The case companies had proactive communication policies concerning their core institutions and analysts and the media. High-quality corporate communications to financial markets were seen as central to gaining support for strategic change undertaken by the company, for supporting financing decisions and to ensure support in hostile (often takeover or regulatory intervention) situations.

The broader strategic and financing significance of corporate communications is revealed by the following quote:

> We discovered the importance of investor relations in 1987 when a funding arrangement failed because of the stock market crash. The main reason for this problem was that no one other than our broker knew our business. By this I mean that the fund managers did not know us and as a result funds were not available for us in these tough times. We had to change our profile in the City. After 1987 we went out of our way to talk to brokers' analysts and to encourage fund managers to visit us and to make our investor relations much more receptive. We think this has worked because we had a very good reception to our recent rights issues and this must be down to good investor relations.
>
> (Company case Q)

The postwar concentration of share ownership in the hands of UK financial institutions has created a more concentrated form of institutional influence and control over UK companies. This reached the point in 1996 where up to 75 per cent of major UK companies' shares were held by institutions, with UK institutions owning about 60 per cent of shares in UK companies (Gaved 1997). Within this larger group of FIs is a further concentration of ownership. Gaved (1997) pointed out that in 1996 half of the UK equities in the UK stock market were owned by fifty FIs. The top twenty owned about a third of the market, the top ten about a quarter, with the largest, Mercury Asset Management, owning 4 per cent in 1996. The top fifty FIs dominated the shareholder bases of the case companies and constituted the bulk of their core FIs. This has concentrated company and FI minds on each other and increased the significance of their direct relationships and other forms of contact. This has also created a much clearer target for institutional research and corporate communications. Much of the case information-exchange practice has emerged in response to the growing institutional concentration of ownership. It has also become more dynamic and proactive in response to increasing takeover activity and, with it, increasing significance of the institutions in the change of management control. Michie (1992: 76) argues that such good communications alone will not solve the long-standing UK problem of the financial separation of City and industry. However, the case institutions and companies did see such sophisticated communication practice as a means partially to overcome problems of poor support in new financing issues, in takeover battles, and to ensure agreement during managerial changes.

The PSI management problem was seen as a constraint on this larger corporate communication process:

> Handling price-sensitive information is part of a bigger problem, which involves helping the financial community, the City, and the investing public to understand the company. The changes in the law and the Stock Exchange guidance have operated as a major new obstacle to our normal communications.
>
> (Company case R)

The case institutions had similar proactive communication concerning their investees' companies. This involved communication of their investment policies and their expectations for corporate financial performance and for satisfactory corporate governance behaviour. They therefore tried to ensure that companies took FIs' views into account before they made decisions. This preconditioning provided a continuous, 'live' context for FI influence in the company. They also used meetings to ask questions about these issues and see if the company understood the FIs' requirements. This behaviour was consistent with Scott (1997: 16). He pointed out that the core FI group of a company, as a 'constellation of interests', can exercise influence and constrain corporate power in subtle ways. This, and not managerial power, is the dominant form of corporate control in the UK and US.

> In general we are careful to only attempt to influence a firm on matters of principle such as the corporate governance issue of separation of chairman and CE roles. Our influence is boosted here by the social and political significance of the issues. Financial performance of the firm and financial management issues are areas where the financial institution can exercise influence based on its rights as an investor and its expertise in financial matters. In contrast, attempts to influence strategy involves the financial institution trying to second guess management in its own field of expertise. The financial institution should concentrate on listening and seeking clarification in these managerial domains.
>
> (FI case C)

There was no PSI constraint on FIs informing companies of their needs. However, if a company understood what its core institutions wanted and it pursued these aims, then this probably prevented unwelcome surprises for the institutions. Avoiding such surprises was a major aim of the FIs in the influencing process. If issues such as expectations of financial performance, succession of management and corporate governance changes were well understood by all parties, then surprises were thought less likely. As the core institutions were likely to be the major traders in the company's shares, the probability of company-sourced PSI was somewhat reduced by these shared understandings.

Company and institutional curbs over PSI

In the previous section we have explored the broader context in which both parties sought to control the corporate release and the institutional receipt of PSI. By setting up high-quality, two-way communication processes, both parties expected to lessen their PSI problems. However, they still faced major problems of managing PSI. They have responded by setting up quite specific procedures and responses to deal with the problems. Corporate responses to these market and regulatory pressures have involved the adaption of existing decision processes, the setting up of an investor relations function, the use of technology and internal controls over PSI. At the boundary with financial markets, the case companies have established a stable network of analyst, FI and press contacts. The City communications process and the PSI management process were conducted through extensive use of these internal and boundary structures.

Changes in the corporate strategic decision process are illustrated in Company case A:

> The strategy group, consisting of the executive directors, already meet two times per month. Now, every quarter [year] City communications policy is the sole item on the agenda. The questions are, what is the corporate communication policy, what are the key issues and what should we say as a company? As a result of this we get broad agreements at the top of the firm, at a strategic level, on information release and we also establish a commitment right at the top of the firm as to what the message is and how we go about getting that message over. The executive directors by being involved in the communications policy are accountable for their own policy and they own this policy and are committed to it.
>
> (Company case A)

Corporate finance directors and investor relations staff used new information technology to monitor events and share prices. These systems were often configured so that the observer could watch news flashes and share-price changes on the same or adjacent screens. They also used experience-based categories of PSI to help them to identify new PSI.

> Another way of looking at price sensitivity is to classify certain kinds of events that produce price-sensitive information in the insurance industry. These include a storm in the United Kingdom, fires in the United States, of price cutting in our US market, a strategic change such as implementing direct selling of insurance.
>
> (Company case F)

Advisers were also used to help companies assess how much a price change was 'sensitive', and to help the company script its response to the inevitable questions.

Despite these approaches, major problems remained for the case companies:

> Part of the problem is that we often cannot clarify a public message to reflect ever-changing events. We are often not in full possession of the information especially in a changing situation. This clearly gives us difficulty in articulating a sensible public announcement. In a way, the one-on-one meeting is more efficient in this situation in that fragments of information can be exchanged with analysts and financial institutions and we can together build up a picture to understand the changing situation. So in a way before the SE guidelines were issued it was easier to deal with those issues where there were darker shades of grey. However, there is now the danger they are going to be regarded as price-sensitive information and this may clam up this particular area of discussions.
>
> (Company case E)

In contrast to the case companies, the case institutions' primary strategic decision processes were to do with fund management. The institutions used their close links with companies to create a unique knowledge advantage by understanding corporate strategy and by directly assessing the quality of management, and the coherence of the top management team and succession policy. All of these qualitative and quantitative information sources were seen as essential ingredients in estimating expected corporate cash flows, income and their variances and hence in valuing the company. This valuation in turn played the central role in stock selection and asset allocation decisions. The receipt of PSI prevented FIs from trading until the PSI became public. Thus the FIs sought to avoid this and to retain their options to exploit their knowledge advantage.

Both the case company and FI interviewees found the formal regulatory concepts vague and difficult to implement. Specifically, they found it difficult to define 'significant effect' or 'price sensitivity' as employed in the law and the SE guidance. For example:

> Defining price-sensitive information arising in a meeting is very difficult. It depends on how much the information moves the price and how much a price movement is required for an investor to make a profit. A market trader might be able to cover trading costs on + or –1 per cent price movements. A FI might be able to benefit from + or –5 per cent changes, and a small investor might need + or –10 per cent change before they can make money.
>
> (FI case N)

Creating uncertainty at the level of the enterprise can be seen as an effective means for policy makers to ensure that companies and FIs expend considerable effort in avoiding PSI release and receipt misjudgements. However, this was not an explicit aim of policy makers and the law and guidance focused more on increasing individual corporate and FI responsibility. From the company and FI perspective this was another hidden regulatory cost for them and they argued it could have a negative aggregate impact in terms of impeding information flows to financial markets.

Both the corporate and institutional cases reveal that the emergence of extensive insider trading laws and of detailed guidance on the release of PSI in 1993 and 1994 have played a role in intensifying case corporate and FI activity to control their PSI dissemination and receipt practices. The emergence of a connected and clarified system of law and guidance appears to have increased the reputational costs for managers and companies of PSI errors and insider dealing. The possibility of a SE rebuke is now taken more seriously, and this is seen as potentially leading to a Department of Trade and Industry (DTI) investigation and prosecution. Any one of these interventions is problematic because it may reduce corporate credibility in the City and it may increase the cost of capital and market-maker spread penalties arising from a City perception of an enhanced informational asymmetry. Certainly, the case companies reported an increased investment in City communications, in controlling PSI release and in generally increasing voluntary disclosures during the 1993–94 'year of uncertainty'. The 1994 legislation and guidance appear to have played a major role in stimulating these decisions.

Internal controls and the PSI disclosure problem

Both the institutions and companies had established functions to control PSI problems. The case companies set up a corporate investors' relation function to implement policy towards FIs and analysts and to deal with PSI.

> External management of price-sensitive information is done through two related roles – one a semi-finance function in which you interpret a lot of accounting and finance figures. Competence here is absolutely essential. The second one is a semi-public affairs function or communications function in which you spend a lot of time promoting the image of the company in financial markets and ensuring that image is well understood and accurately reflects the underlying reality of the firm. Both kinds of skills are necessary to control the release of PSI.
>
> (Company case X)

The case companies also sought to establish tight internal control over PSI through a variety of methods, including the use of confidentiality contracts with staff, the use of an internal code of conduct and keeping all price-sensitive information within a sealed HQ.

> An important method of controlling price-sensitive information release is to make secretaries, middle managers, and directors sign confidentiality contracts. We only allow a small group of people to receive price-sensitive information. None of these individuals are allowed to buy or sell shares unless given permission by the Company Secretary ... In a way we have to be somewhat careful here because not trading by the insider shareholders is a signal to the market that something is up. The market is very quick to cotton on to such things and reads very subtle signals.
>
> (Company case G)

The case FIs did not have the equivalent of an investor relations function, but they had established internal procedures to analyse whether PSI had been received in a meeting with a company. If they thought they had received it they placed the share on an embargoed trading list. Once the information was made public the institution was in a position to act quickly and exploit any excess returns:

> Where do we draw the PSI line? A judgement is still required after the information is released by the company in a meeting. After the meeting our analysts and fund managers will ask me to clear their use of the information in fund management and market decisions. In some cases it is obvious that it is PSI or it is not. In other situations we have to assess the likely price changes if it were made public before we trade. If it is trivial then we can proceed as normal. If we think the company has given us significant price-sensitive information in the meeting then we tell them and ask them to disclose it as soon as possible. In the meantime we put it on our embargoed dealing list.
>
> (FI case Q)

The case companies also exercised extensive control over conversations and meetings by executives with the institutions and analysts:

> We will make it absolutely clear who the brokers' analysts and fund managers can talk to in our business. They can contact the Chairman, the Chief Executive, the Finance Director, the executive directors and the three members of the IR Group. This concentrates the brokers' analysts and fund managers on a specific internal audience who are well scripted. We have a diary in which we list all of our one-on-one meetings, our conferences, our employee contacts with brokers' analysts and brokers' analysts' site visits. We therefore keep a track of all IR activity and contact with fund managers and brokers' analysts.

> This diary is important because it is one of the Stock Exchange guidelines and therefore we make sure we note down everything that we do in all forms of contact.
>
> (Company case H)

The case companies probed their core institutions and analysts as well as traders. The purpose was to understand market expectations concerning the company. This improved their ability to assess whether event-specific information was already in the public domain or whether it was dramatically different to that held by the proxy market of core analysts and institutions. If the latter was the case then the strong presumption was that it was price sensitive:

> We must remember at the end of the day price-sensitive information is about expectations management. If we release information which is in line with what the market expects then we have not got a problem. The problem does arise when we are not too sure what these market expectations are.
>
> (Company case I)

The case FIs employed a variety of boundary techniques to control the receipt of PSI. They prewarned companies in meetings not to release PSI to them and they insisted that the company gave them the choice before the information was released. The institutions also asked companies to identify novel public-domain information sources on their company. This improved their information sources and allowed them to use public-domain information for a legal dialogue. Witnesses and written records were also employed as evidence of what was said in company meetings.

The case data suggest that self-regulation between the case companies and FIs may be an effective complement to legislation because it narrows both the internal and the 'relationship' opportunities for insider dealing and release of PSI. This is done by limiting internal corporate access to PSI and by restricting trading periods for internal staff. It is also achieved by the use of explicit corporate controls over the release of information to FIs and others. These internal corporate controls, their institutional equivalents, and the structured company–institutional contacts narrow the scope and timing of trading allowed by corporate insiders and by external relationship institutions. This makes it easier for external observers to monitor and pinpoint the illegal use of PSI. Companies and FIs are likely to be superior to external regulators in monitoring these possibilities. The complexity and flexibility of this private process suggest that any future legislative changes should build on a more open and transparent version of this process rather than be based on short-term reactions to highly public cases of error, fraud and criminality in the financial system.

Regulatory ambiguity, institutional knowledge and market efficiency

Insider-trading law and the SE guidance do not prevent institutions acquiring a company knowledge advantage through regular dialogue with companies. The law does prohibit the private release of event-specific information which could have a significant impact on the share price. The company–institutional parties sought to avoid this in their interactions and tried to boost the FI knowledge advantage. These legal circumstances explain why UK institutions could be relationship insiders and still be allowed to trade in highly liquid corporate securities at the same time. Thus the target of corporate communications to institutions was the improvement of the core institutions' understanding of the company:

> We focus on [explaining] the parts of the business that we think are not well known or understood by our investors. Our traditional products and business are well understood by most investors. We want our investors to be equally well informed about our newer businesses. If we can get them to go up a learning curve and acquire an in-depth understanding of both traditional and new businesses, we feel that they will be able to react well to unfounded rumours or to major events affecting us ... Their understanding of our business is essential to the relationship. It means that they are one step ahead of others who haven't bothered and it makes them more confident of our performance in an uncertain world.
>
> (Company case S)

The PSI dissemination and receipt problem was seen both as a threat to, and as a constraint on, this larger corporate–institutional communication process and to the development of the FI knowledge advantage. Given the benefits to both parties, extensive efforts were made to protect these communication channels.

If we look at the institutional side to the relationships, we find that the case FIs used their regular corporate contacts to acquire systematically a knowledge advantage that was central to their fund management function and had implications for their industry- and economy-wide knowledge.

> The whole aim of the exercise, to create a knowledge bank on many companies. We invest in over two-and-a-half thousand companies globally and learn a lot about individual companies, their industries, their FT sector and the national economies as well as the global economy. This extensive understanding of the corporate world is our major asset and a major source of value for us. The challenge to us is to capitalize on this knowledge asset.
>
> (FI case D)

Improving institutional knowledge was not seen as bound by the new regulations on insider dealing and PSI and was not seen as releasing PSI to the core institutions. The institution's knowledge advantage appeared from the case data to develop slowly through many corporate–institutional interactions. It also developed through cumulative analysis of many non-corporate sources. Thus an institution would not necessarily trade in the company shares immediately after a company meeting. To do so would invite accusations of insider trading. Despite this case view, there was some ambiguity about the acquisition of FI knowledge by direct corporate contact. This point has yet to be challenged in case law. Fragments of information may be used with other public sources over, say, a six-month period to build up a special understanding of a company. If an event occurs and the institution uses its special understanding to deduce PSI and trade on it, then how much of this can be attributed to the meeting?

Loomis described the mosaic approach. He explained the regulators view as follows:

> The [SEC] Commission's idea of highly specific information is a single concrete event or determination or fact, as opposed to a mosaic of general information, some of which is public some of which isn't. Skillful assembly of a mosaic may lead an analyst to a conclusion that the company's stock is going to go up or down a point. We are trying not to inhibit securities research. That's one of the reasons we refer to a specific event rather than the result of research.
>
> (Loomis 1972: 25)

This mosaic may be constructed from many fragmented data sources including regular contacts with management. Similar interpretations can be made concerning current UK regulation.

Neither UK nor US law has ever seriously challenged the right of fund managers and analysts to conduct research using public-domain sources and to combine these in some complex way with information acquired by direct contact with company management. If EU or US law did challenge direct corporate sources, it would be seen by companies and institutions as eroding an important economic function of investment financial intermediaries in which they use multiple sources of information to improve their management of asset risk and return in order to provide the required liability risk, return and liquidity. If this idea was seriously challenged it could also have ramifications for bank lenders and the economic gains they make for their shareholders from their insider position. We can therefore identify an implicit trade-off between regulation on financial intermediation and regulation on insider dealing, which is based on the perceived economic benefits of informed financial intermediation and seeks to minimize public disquiet on insider dealing.

Finally, we can note that these notions of institutional knowledge appear to go beyond conventional concepts of market efficiency. The case participants were, by implication, using ideas of informational efficiency by suggesting that PSI, once released, would immediately add to the public-domain information set and be rapidly reflected in share prices (semi-strong form). In contrast, the idea of institutional knowledge was an organizational state concept rather than an information flow or market capability concept. Knowledge created conditions whereby institutions and analysts, some time in the future, could interpret events and create their own PSI in a way that was expected to be superior to uninformed investors. It therefore refers to a capability of an informed section of the market to respond to new events based on their own resources. This is in contrast to an idea of market efficiency based on an ability to respond rapidly and in an unbiased way to new information arising outside of the market. These ideas of market efficiency and institutional knowledge may be connected in some way. For all of the case companies there existed an informed and knowledgeable institutional sector of the stock market. This may be part of the market capability to respond rapidly to new information about individual companies. Institutions with a specialist knowledge of a company will probably have been told by the company where difficult-to-find public-domain information is located, and will have collected together all other public-domain information in one corporate file. This will be added to insider-sourced information to form a unique mosaic picture of the company. Semi-strong market efficiency, in which the market fully reflects public-domain information, may, in part, be based on clusters of such 'informed core institutions' for each company and these may cover all the major sectors in the economy. If this is the case, then a legal threat to institutional acquisition of knowledge directly from companies threatens more than efficient financial intermediation. It could also pose a threat to market efficiency. Too tough a regulatory regime could undermine the private channels and their benefits for informed financial intermediation and efficient markets. It could also drive the channels underground. This problem set a limit for formal 'self-regulation' as manifest in the SE guidance. It also created a need for an active but private self-regulation process by companies and institutions.

Opportunities for reform

This chapter has shown that the new PSI regulation posed a threat to the private exchanges between companies and institutions, despite the guidance being devised by the City 'great and good'. The case companies and institutions recognized the threat of sanctions such as delisting or new legislation. They adapted quickly to the new circumstances and internalized the SE guidance into their private communication and research activities. As a result, the City traditions of private exchange and of self-regulation continued.

Despite this corporate and institutional reaction, questions will continue to be raised as to whether this regulatory system is working effectively. There is the possibility that companies and institutions could develop new ways of circumventing the guidance. For example, a company could provide information on key variables knowing that the FI could use the information to make PSI deductions. Companies could show FIs how to link up the financial statement numbers with the text in the Operating and Financial review, to deduce PSI. These practices would be more advanced forms of the 'nods and winks' prevalent before the new insider-dealing law and SE guidance. Before the publication of the SE guidance (4 November 1993) there were some indications that case companies interviewed by this stage were prepared to use meetings to steer profit forecasts produced by analysts. After the publication of the initial SE guidance, the case companies sought to avoid steering of forecasts and made no comment on next period results. In addition, no comment was made on research reports by analysts. Public-domain forecasts and facts were used to establish a legal dialogue on forecasts. However, steering now took more subtle forms.

> We do not release information on budget figures, or on new variables or factors we believe affect our profits. If our product costs suddenly became very sensitive this year to certain commodity prices, then we cannot tell anyone about this until we make our earnings announcements. If a well-known commodity price has changed over the year, and the impact on our kind of business is well known, we will steer analysts and investors in this direction. We will not tell them that this has happened to us, but we will say 'look what has happened to sugar prices this year' and leave them to make the rest of the deductions.
>
> (Company case K)

Policing this kind of behaviour will be very difficult given the private nature of the activity. 'Whistle-blowing' legislation may be required to encourage individuals to reveal that this practice has re-emerged. The possibility of traditional City mores encouraging a return to deviant behaviour, and the City control over the regulatory process itself, together reveal the problems faced by UK regulators. Too tough a legal regime could drive the private information exchange underground. The regulators require City help to define a working set of rules and to monitor their implementation at close quarters. They have to walk a fine line between discouraging insider dealing whilst encouraging informed financial intermediation and informationally efficient markets.

One way in which the regulatory system could be reformed would be to work from the existing relationship self-regulation process rather than from more formal legal changes. The following proposals may be the means to counteract a City tendency to undermine the existing regulation on PSI. First, relevant 'good practice' benchmarks could be developed further. The SE guidance on PSI could be extended to include much of what UK companies and institutions have learnt in the period 1992–98. This chapter and Holland and Stoner (1995) provide some insight into their responses to the regulatory changes and how they have developed their management systems to handle the PSI problem. A systematic study and identification of new ways of defining and disseminating PSI would be of considerable benefit to the UK corporate and institutional sector. It would also be of considerable use to those countries introducing new regulation in this area.

The problem with these benchmarks is that they are based on the narrower interests of the City and industry alone. However, they could form the basis of improved accountability and transparency by adopting existing City and business practices. Each company could release its own broad analysis of the questions asked by institutions over the past year. The case companies both 'spotted' questions before the meetings and documented the questions actually asked. They worked with their advisers (financial communications specialists, and corporate brokers) to prepare scripted answers for the 'spotted' questions and they documented their answers to questions posed in the meetings. The case companies thus had the information to report to the larger investing public on the general nature of this private dialogue and the key FI questions and corporate answers.

Second, the City regulatory body, the Financial Services Authority (FSA), set up in 1998 (or the SE, as its agent), could hire a professional City survey firm to survey company and FI attitudes relative to the improved PSI and communications benchmarks and thus establish the participants' views as to whether the broad communication and the PSI aims were being achieved. The results could include ranking of companies by institutions (and vice versa) relative to the benchmarks. Surveys on FI attitudes to companies and of company attitudes to analysts are already common practice in the City. For example, the UK Investors' Relations Society annually surveys about five hundred fund managers and analysts for their views of the quality of corporate communications by firms in the FT All-company listing. Regulator-sponsored surveys based on publicly agreed good practice benchmarks could be published in the same way in widely read public media such as *Euromoney*.

Third, the FSA or one of its constituent (self-regulatory) bodies such as the Accounting Standards Board (ASB) or the SE, could hire professional social audit companies to attend a representative sample of FI–company meetings and assess whether good practice was being implemented and whether good practice was satisfactory relative to other stakeholder needs such as small investors and employees. These results would also have to be published. In practice, as Table 7.1 indicates, the regulatory system is normally a mixture of informal and formal components. An explicit link is required between the new City regulatory system introduced in 1998 and the above proposals. One body, such as the FSA, must coordinate all elements. If the monitoring continues to be shared by the SE, various corporate governance committees and the ASB, then such reforms may face manipulation by a small minority of rogue corporate and institutional participants.

Fourth, we can note that in 1998 the Hampel Committee examined how to improve and formalize the UK corporate governance system (Committee on Corporate Governance 1998). The role of institutional shareholders was recognized as central to the corporate governance issue. More specifically, the Hampel Report emphasized its strong support for the Myners Report (1995) on how to improve company and institutional communications. It placed particular stress on improving business awareness on the part of fund managers (1995: 43–4). Thus the successors to the Hampel Committee, plus the SE and the ASB, could improve the transparency of the private disclosure process further by investigating best practice in private disclosure and the control over PSI. The above regulators could also strengthen insider-dealing law and exploit technological developments to improve transparency. For example, the times and dates of private FI–company meetings could be made public, as well as FI share trades in the company. This would place FIs, as quasi-insiders, on a level closer to director insiders and their trades.

The benefits of these proposals are fairly clear. They would work within the existing system, they would improve transparency and hopefully public confidence, the relatively small costs would be borne by City and industry participants, and together they would provide further impetus to embed generally accepted good practice or formal guidance in the private control process. Such a proposal would create a dynamic, learning regulatory system which reflects the evolutionary character of the City and of the wider UK financial system (see Michie 1992). It would reflect how participants in the UK system respond to new regulation and how they adapt or subvert it according to their local needs. This proposal would exploit the knowledge that FIs and companies acquire of each other through direct interaction. It would therefore capture the reflexivity of regulatees for the benefits of regulators and for the wider public and reflect the continuing change process occurring at the company–institutional interface.

Acknowledgements

Acknowledgements to the participants in research seminars at the Universities of Glasgow, Stirling, Bangor UCNW, Ulster, and Manchester Business School and to Lars Engwall and Glenn Morgan.

The author would like to express gratitude to the Chartered Association of Certified Accountants for funding the research project, and the case participants for their considerable contribution to the research. The normal caveats on the author's responsibility for the contents applies.

References

Bain, S. (1994) *Scotland on Sunday, Business Week*, 20 February: 2.

Cadbury, A. (1993) 'Reflections on corporate governance', The Ernest Sykes Memorial Lecture, The Chartered Institute of Bankers, 11 March, London.

Coleman, W. D. (1994) 'Keeping the shotgun behind the door', in J. R. Hollingsworth, P. C. Schmitter and W. Streeck (eds) *Governing Capitalist Economies*, Oxford: Oxford University Press.

Committee on Corporate Governance (1998) *The Hampel Report*, Final Report, January, London: Gee Publishing.

Economist (1993) 'Insider dealing: balancing act', 22 May: 100.

Gaved, M. (1997) *Closing the Communications Gap: Disclosure and Institutional Shareholders*, London: Institute of Chartered Accountants in England and Wales.

Holland, J. and Stoner, G. (1995) 'Corporate problems with the identification and dissemination of price sensitive information', paper presented at the BAA conference, April, Bristol (University of Glasgow working paper).

Hopwood, A. (1983) 'On trying to study accountancy in the contexts in which it operates', *Accounting, Organizations and Society* 8: 287–305.

Keenan, D. (1993) *Accountancy*, December: 139.

London Stock Exchange (1994a) *Guidance on the Dissemination of Price Sensitive Information*, London: London Stock Exchange.

—— (1994b) *Orderly Markets: Dealings Ahead of the Disclosure of Price Sensitive Information*, London: London Stock Exchange.

Loomis, P, (1972) 'Loomis on inside information', *Financial Analysts Journal* 28(3): 20–5, 82–8.

Marckus, M. (1993) 'Safe sex at the SE', *Observer*, 16 May: 26.

Michie, R. C. (1992) *The City of London, Continuity and Change, 1850–1990*, London: Macmillan.

Moran, M, (1991) *The Politics of the Financial Services Revolution, the USA, UK and Japan*, London: Macmillan.

Myners, P, (1995) 'Developing a winning partnership. How companies and institutional investors are working together', DTI report, February.

Pozen, R. C. (1994) 'Institutional investors: the reluctant activists', *Harvard Business Review*, Jan–Feb: 140–9.

Rice, R. (1994) 'Analysts wary of a tighter net', *Financial Times*, 22 March: 16.

Scapens, R. W. (1990) 'Researching management accounting practice: the role of case study methods', *British Accounting Review* 22: 259–81.

Scott, J. (1993) 'Corporate groups and network structures', in J. McCahery, S. Picciotto and C. Scott (eds) *Corporate Control and Accountability*, Oxford: The Clarendon Press.

—— (1997) *Corporate Business and Capitalist Classes*, Oxford: Oxford University Press.

Scott, W. R. and Meyer, J. W. (1994) *Institutional Environments and Organizations*, Thousand Oaks, CA: Sage.

Thrift, N. (1995) 'On the social and cultural determinants of international financial centres: the case of the City of London', in S. Corbridge, R. Martin and N. Thrift (eds) *Money, Power, and Space*, Oxford: Blackwell.

8 Regulation as a response to critical events

A century of struggle for the Swedish auditing profession

Eva Wallerstedt

Introduction

Around the middle of the nineteenth century most enterprises were small and managed by their owners. Partnership was the standard legal form, but even incorporated companies were run in a personal manner. Businesses were normally family affairs and businesspeople did not yet feel the need for any other legal form of enterprise. Entrepreneurs thus owned and controlled their own enterprises. The first modern business enterprises which required a large number of full-time employed managers were the railroad and telegraph companies in the US in the 1860s and, as the size of these and other companies grew, general principles and management procedures were developed. Managerial hierarchies were created, and enterprises were defined in organizational manuals and charts. Internally generated data began to be used as a management tool, but in the interests of controlling and disciplining the workers rather than the control of other managers. So long as the enterprises were financed internally from the cash flow generated by high-volume production and distribution, the founders rarely had to raise capital by issuing stock. Increasingly, however, companies became dependent on the supply of outside capital. Investors, in turn, required assurance of the proper management of the capital invested (Chandler 1977: 36–146, 381).

These corporate entities, in which ownership and management were separated, provided the stimulus for financial auditing. Power (1997: 1), addressing the question of trust and monitoring, points to the fact that trust 'releases us from the need for checking'. He points out that people have always checked up on each other, and that we need to decide 'as individuals, organizations, and societies' (1997: 16) how to combine checking and monitoring behaviour with trusting others. Where principals do not 'trust' agents, they either have to check themselves or institute mechanisms which they can 'trust' which involve others doing the monitoring and checking. Auditing is one such mechanism whereby investors (principals) assure themselves that their agents are being appropriately checked. However, this in turn requires that there is some mechanism for trusting the auditors. An audit is supposed to reduce the risk of unreliable economic information, but who should be responsible for ensuring that auditors and their procedures are trustworthy?

Auditing has a crucial role in a developed industrial economy, yet the manner in which it is regulated is not predefined. As the following study shows, there are a large number of stakeholders involved in the process of regulation, including those claiming the right to act as auditors, the principals requiring the audit, the agents undergoing the audit and the state monitoring the stability of the financial and industrial systems.

In this chapter, the main focus is on the inter-relationship between the state and those groups claiming professional expertise and professional monopoly over the process of regulating the audit procedure. As many authors have noted, the state is a key player when it comes to regulation of accounting and auditing (Watts and Zimmerman 1978; McCann and Galbraith 1981; Scott 1981, 1995; Willmott 1986; Puxty *et al.* 1987; Chua and Poullaos 1993; Powell 1996; Power 1997). Through debates within the state and outside, the process of regulation becomes a political process in which proponents and opponents deliver arguments for the positions that they support (Watts and Zimmerman 1978; Morgan 1986: 141–99). Political debates may lead to state control or they may provide the framework for devolving responsibilities to other parties who can be 'trusted' to act properly. Thus regulatory regimes emerge which combine elements of formal and public regulation with elements of private and informal control (see Grandori *et al.*'s chapter in this volume). Claims to professional status are the mechanisms through which occupational groups seek to assure the state and other interested parties that they can be entrusted with such responsibilities, thus formalizing and legitimating a type of private regulation.

These relationships between the state, the professional associations and other stakeholders can be conceived as constituting an organizational field which develops and evolves its own governance mechanisms 'ranging from market-like, competitive controls to self-regulating mechanisms to the development of hierarchical, centralized control centres' (DiMaggio and Powell 1983: 147). An organizational field will thus be composed of a set of firms in the same industry and of related organizations. Governance mechanisms will develop over time as a product of interorganizational struggle, of actions taken by parties inside or outside the field who are concerned in one way or another. Within a field, critical events will occasionally occur which cannot be managed within the existing governance mechanisms. These events lead to changes within the field.

This chapter uses this framework to understand the evolution of the regulatory process in Swedish auditing over the last century. At the beginning of the 1900s there were no formalized instructions or requirements as to how the work should be done or what qualifications were needed for auditing. Lay people interpreted the auditing assignment according to their own traditions or cultural beliefs. The lack of clear rules for disclosure and authorization created unacceptable levels of risk for potential investors. Gradually, over the years, the situation changed and today a great number of regulations exist, regarding the profession itself and the qualifications for auditors. The material will reveal that the auditing profession has passed through all the stages whereby the other established professions have become established (Wilensky 1964: 142–6). In sequence these steps are: full-time occupation; professional training and pressure from early recruits for the establishment of a training school; the establishment of professional associations; political agitation to win the support of a law to protect the professional territory; and a formal code of ethics.

The role of professional organizations has been particularly important for the process of auditing regulation in Sweden. This role can be described from three perspectives (Willmott 1986: 557–8). The functionalist approach emphasizes attributes such as esoteric knowledge, independence and altruism, and the enjoyment of prestige and other rewards are regarded as a fair exchange for the services rendered to society. The interactionist approach sees a profession as an interest group seeking to convince others of its legitimate claim to professional recognition. This approach also reveals the presence of competing interests within individual professional organizations. In the third approach, applying a critical perspective, 'the emergence of professional bodies is seen as a means of achieving collective social mobility by securing control over a niche within the market for skilled labour' (Willmott 1986: 558). The establishment of professional organizations is thus seen as a strategy of control. It is easy to agree with Willmott's conclusion that in an analysis of the auditing profession insights from these different approaches can be advantageous.

The chapter is arranged chronologically, starting in 1895 and ending in 1995. The empirical material is organized in four periods: 1895–1921, 1922–31, 1932–69 and 1970–95. The rationale behind the choice of periods was that in each one some critical event or events should have promoted the development of the profession in a significant way. Besides critical events, the analysis of the periods concentrates on what happened in the field as regards laws and rules affecting the auditing profession and the organization of various interest groups. The gradual unfolding of the process of regulation will be related to the development of limited companies in Sweden and to the turnover on the Swedish stock market.

The auditing field in Sweden 1895–1921

The first time any law stipulated that limited companies should have auditors was the Companies Act of 1895. However, this had been a tradition since the first half of the nineteenth century. From that time most limited companies had included stipulations about auditing in their articles of association. In a way, then, this law can be seen as the confirmation of a long-established practice, as pointed out by Watts and Zimmerman (1978). These authors found that company practice preceded the debates noted in the accounting literature as well as the regulations introduced by the legislative authorities. Jönsson (1985: 85) also observed that the passing of a law is often preceded by good and accepted practice. 'The law is no experimenter. Laws should be passed subsequent to and in confirmation of what is accepted as a good way forward according to public opinion, but should not include details that block further development' (Jönsson 1985: 85, my translation).

In the 1910 revision of the Companies Act, the legal rights and obligations of the auditors were better expressed, but there were still no formal stipulations about the qualifications of the auditors. The first distinctive mark of the emergence of a profession came in 1899 when the Swedish Society of Accountants (SSA) was founded as the first society of auditors in Sweden (see Table 8.1). The Institute of Chartered Accountants in London and their organization served as a model for the SSA (SSA archive, minutes, 001029, 3). Although the call for members to join the society went out to 'professional auditors and accountants', those who joined were not full-time professional auditors. In fact they were a very mixed group of people from many different professions. From the very beginning the society endeavoured to obtain some kind of recognition for the profession through governmental authorization of its members. By submitting several motions to the Riksdag, the Swedish parliament, they tried to convince the elected representatives that auditing conducted by appropriately qualified auditors was a societal necessity. In view of the fact that most members of SSA were people without any professional education, their actions at this time can be interpreted as a strategy of control in accordance with the critical approach, rather than a question of esoteric knowledge and altruism as the functionalist approach would argue (Sarfatti Larson 1977; Willmott 1986; Collins 1990).

In 1905, as a result of setbacks in the authorization campaign, the SSA appointed a committee of its own to investigate the need for official auditors. The society argued that to ensure public confidence, accountants needed some kind of Royal Charter. The committee declared that a governmental authority should stipulate the kind of knowledge that an official auditor needed, and that it was also the duty of the government to see that adequate procedures were instituted to test this knowledge (Sjöström 1994: 54–5). The committee completed its assignment by early 1908, and waited for a reaction from the authorities. However, the timing of the proposals seems to have been wrong. The Riksdag did not support the SSA's ideas. Instead they were probably waiting for the pending establishment of the Stockholm School of Economics and the opportunities that this new institution would create for auditors. It thus appears that certain influential members of the Riksdag saw other desirable directions for the development of the profession, and that these differed from the

Table 8.1 A chronological overview of market situation, organizations, critical events and major legislation in the development of the auditing profession in Sweden, 1895–1921

	1890s	*1900s*	*1910s*	*1920s*
No. of limited companies		700	4,000	10,000
Stockmarket turnover (mill. SEK)		6	87	328
Organizations	The Swedish Society of Accountants (SSA) (1899)		Central Board of Auditing (1919)	
Critical events		The Stockholm School of Economics opens (1909)	The Stockholm Chamber of Commerce began certifying authorized auditors (1912)	
Legislation	Companies Act (1895)		Companies Act (1910)	

SSA's ideas. The process that was to lead to the founding of the Stockholm School of Economics had been ongoing since 1903, and once the school was established in 1909 it became central to discussions on the regulation of auditing.

When the chamber of commerce in Stockholm decided to authorize its first auditors in 1912, the timing of the decision was connected with the establishment of the school. It was also of relevance that Denmark (1909) and Norway (1910) had already begun to authorize auditors (Föreningen Auktoriserade Revisorer 1962: 42). Although an application by the chamber of commerce in the middle of 1912 to have an auditing exam established at the school was turned down, the chamber still made attendance at the school a prerequisite for being an authorized public accountant in Sweden. This authorization procedure endowed public accountants with one of the important characteristics of being 'a profession', namely the monopolization of its particular knowledge (Wilensky 1964: 144; Collins 1990: 11–23). However, the consequence was that most members of the SSA found themselves excluded from the group of authorized auditors since they had not attended the school. The decision of the chamber of commerce thus prevented the SSA from being members of the official 'guild' and set up the basis for continuing conflicts between groups seeking to monopolize the role of auditor.

Besides having a degree in business studies from the Stockholm School of Economics an authorized public accountant was required to have had three years of documented practical service with an authorized public accountant. It was also stipulated that an authorized public accountant should not have a business of his own, should not be allowed to audit companies in which he had an interest of his own, and could not have either private or public employment (Stockholm Chamber of Commerce 1912). Further, the auditor should keep a record of his clients and maintain professional secrecy. In this first established regulation it was stipulated that an authorized public accountant should renew his certificate each year.

The Central Board of Auditing was created in 1919. Thenceforth authorization procedures changed, in that each chamber of commerce submitted a list of applicants from its own region, whom it judged to be competent for authorization, and the Central Board of Auditing then made the decision (Sjöström 1994: 63).

Key to the growing perception of the need for auditors who could be trusted was the growth in the Swedish stock market. Although there were major fluctuations in the turnover on the market, as more investors placed their money in firms which they did not know in any detail, the requirement for 'objective' reports on the state of the health of these companies grew. By 1921 there were twenty-three authorized public accountants and seventy accountants belonging to the SSA.

One of the main tasks of these individuals was to spread knowledge about the new profession and to seek to persuade others that auditing could only be done by them. They sent information to business people and urged them to turn to authorized auditors with their accounting problems. In the following years, many attempts were made to increase the demand for auditing services. The Central Board of Auditing distributed catalogues containing lists of authorized auditors and worked persistently to make listed companies be obliged by law to use authorized auditors. There were now about 10,000 limited companies, as against 700 at the beginning of the century. All this meant that the potential market for auditing services had grown. The number of authorized public accountants was not very high, however, and it is doubtful whether these auditors would have been enough if there had been a real demand for auditors with such qualifications.

As can be seen in Table 8.1, several organizations had emerged in the auditing field by 1921. All of those mentioned above were in some way connected with each other. Their members all belonged to the same network of business people in Sweden. Some of them were members of more than one of the organizations, which meant they could persistently bring up questions concerning company auditing along congruent lines. This is probably why, despite putting forward many reasonable proposals, the SSA never managed to get any of them through the Riksdag.

A critical event was the foundation of the Stockholm School of Economics. This school could provide auditors with an education appropriate to their auditing task. The authorization procedure was in fact the first real barrier to entry into the profession. There was thenceforth a group of auditors who could lay claim to esoteric knowledge in the field of auditing. Over the following years SSA members consistently tried various tactics either to erase that barrier or to break through it themselves. Their interaction thus very clearly exposed competing interests. The field was neither homogeneous nor integrated; rather, it consisted of two coalitions, each of which was pursuing its own interests. This division weakened the ability of those concerned to create a professional monopoly and persuade the state to force companies to use their services.

1922–31: the extension of auditing regulation

Although the first authorized public accountants were appointed in 1912, the Swedish Institute of Authorized Public Accountants (APA) was not set up until 1923 (see Table 8.2). In 1923 the authorized accountants in Kristiania (now Oslo) in Norway called for a Scandinavian meeting for professional accountants. It was felt that this was an appropriate time to launch the APA. As soon as they had formed an institute of their own, the public accountants began to work out ethical norms for their profession (Sillén 1949; Wallerstedt 1988: 321).

Membership in the SSA had been gradually falling off since the establishment of the Stockholm School of Economics. None the less, those who remained had not given up their aspirations to establish some kind of Royal Charter. In the early 1920s the members of SSA decided to appoint yet another committee to try to reactivate the society. Their proposal that they should authorize auditors themselves was certainly a radical one, and the chair of the APA spoke of a 'war' between the two groups of auditors. In 1922, in confirmation of their decision, the SSA sent an official letter to the government wherein they announced their intention to authorize auditors themselves, but also requesting that the government should take over the authorization procedure. They pointed out that the auditing process, which according to the 1910 Companies Act was to be conducted in companies, was not working as intended. They urged the government to make it mandatory on limited companies to have at least one authorized accountant. Their proposal was sent in the form of an exposure draft to the Patent and Registration Office, where it was thought that the issue called for 'serious consideration'. The office suggested, however, that their authorization procedure should be postponed until there had been a revision of the Companies Act (Svensson 1924: 12–13).

The Central Board of Auditing agreed that auditors were not being used to a desirable extent. They also argued that, because of its bureaucratic nature, governmental authorization of auditors would make it difficult to examine adequately the qualifications of auditors applying for authorization. They pointed out that the institution of authorized public accountants was still very new, and they appealed to the authorities to promote the profession by using authorized public accountants when appointing auditors for authorities, or in cases where savings banks and public authorities were to be examined.

At the first inter-Scandinavian auditing congress in Norway in 1924, the authorization procedure was discussed and it was clearly stated that the dissociation of the authorized public accountants from any authorization procedure provided by the state was 'a matter of principle' (*First Inter-Scandinavian Auditing Congress* 1924: 123). What the APA auditors were afraid of was that the state would impose certain extra obligations (like acting as tax spies) on the auditors. It was argued that no development in such a direction would occur as long as the authorization procedures were dealt with by organizations representing industry and commerce. The auditors definitely did not want any intervention by the state.

In 1928, in an attempt to solve the conflict between the APA and the SSA auditors, the chair of the APA, Oskar Sillén, submitted an unofficial proposal to the Stockholm Chamber of Commerce about reforming the regulations on authorization procedures. Sillén suggested that an opening should be made for auditors who had not graduated from the Stockholm School of Economics. In order to handle this idea the Central Board of Auditing set up a committee, which in 1930 presented a proposal whereby some kind of official recognition should be established for accountants or auditors with lower qualifications than the authorized auditors (*Swedish Chambers of Commerce, 18th Meeting* 1930: 5–7). Discussions in the SSA led to a decision to remove the authorization issue from the agenda, provided the Central Board of Auditing decided in accordance with the proposal. The Central Board of Auditing decided in favour of this, and from then on there were two kinds of auditor appointed by the chambers of commerce: authorized public accountants and registered accountants (see Table 8.2). The difference between the two groups was that the theoretical and practical requirements for the registered accountants were lower. The only requirement for a registered accountant was to have a good knowledge of accounting and several years' practical experience. There was no stipulation that this experience should have been acquired with an authorized auditor. Another difference was that registered accountants were allowed to conduct audits as a sideline to another occupation.

Most applications for the rank of registered accountant came from bank clerks and people employed in business. Of the 215 people who applied in 1931, 88 were referred to the Central Board of Auditing for evaluation. Of these, 77 were accepted as registered accountants. Accordingly, about one-third of the applicants were accepted into the new profession. From the Central Board of Auditing's point of view, the system involving two kinds of auditor was not ideal. It was felt that the two classifications would create

Table 8.2 A chronological overview of market situation, organizations, critical events and major legislation in the development of the auditing profession in Sweden, 1922–31

	1920s	*1930s*
No. of limited companies	10,000	16,000
Stockmarket turnover (mill. SEK)	328	638
Organizations	The Swedish Institute of Authorized Public Accountants (APA) (1923)	
Critical events		A new kind of auditor – the registered accountant – was instituted (1931) A special auditing examination is introduced (1931)

confusion between the groups on the one hand, and between the auditors and their clients on the other (Rosman 1932: 2–3; *SOU* 1993:69: 119–20; Sjöström 1994: 72).

In 1931 a special auditing exam was introduced as a new opening for those who had not attended the Stockholm School of Economics, but who wished to become authorized auditors in Sweden. This step did something to lessen the barrier to entry into the authorized auditor group, but it was probably mainly motivated by the fact that an equivalent exam had already been introduced in almost all other countries. The conditions for becoming an authorized public accountant according to this system were that the applicant should be at least thirty years old and should have completed an upper secondary school education. The first entrance exam was held in 1932, when thirty-six people were accepted to take it. The pass rate is unclear, however. It was in any case a very difficult exam, and by 1963 only 3–4 per cent of all authorized auditors had entered the profession by this door.

In 1930 there were 16,000 limited companies and around 120 authorized public accountants and registered accountants. At the same time, two contradictory claims were being made about the auditing profession. People in industry complained that there were too few qualified auditors, and the auditors themselves complained of having too few clients. One solution to the first problem was the introduction of registered accountants, but there were no quick solutions to the problem of the low number of authorized auditors. Students fulfilling the theoretical qualifications complained that there were not enough opportunities for acquiring experience with an authorized auditor. The situation was that there were too few authorized auditors relative to the number of young people wanting to work their way into the profession. This issue was also connected with the fact that the demand for authorized auditors among companies was not as high as had been hoped. H. Rosman, the secretary of the Central Board of Auditing, pointed out that when the chambers of commerce had set up their authorization procedures, they had been sure of the support of their members, but in fact business people had not turned to the authorized public accountants to the extent desired. Of 300 auditors appointed by the stock-exchange listed companies, only thirty-six were authorized (Rosman 1932: 3).

An investigation carried out in 1931 (Rosman 1932) showed that it was unreasonable to expect registered accountants to be able to support themselves from their auditing work. With one exception, none of them had received more than six to fifteen assignments. Their auditing was thus a sideline to other occupations. The situation was a little better for a limited number of the authorized accountants: eighteen accountants had more than thirty assignments in 1931. It is obvious, however, that many of them did have a hard time supporting themselves from this profession.

The number of auditors receiving their authorization from chambers of commerce outside Stockholm gradually rose. At the end of this period there were fifty-seven authorized public accountants in Sweden as a whole. Stockholm had 68 per cent of all authorized auditors, but authorization was gradually spreading across Sweden. Relations between the SSA and the APA were somewhat ambiguous during the period 1922–31. At certain times they negotiated for cooperation, and at others they dissociated themselves from one another. The recognition of registered accountants and the special audit exam were critical events which eased the tension between SSA and APA auditors for a time. SSA's decision to authorize their own auditors was then postponed.

1932–69: the Kreuger crash of 1932 and the Companies Act 1944

The registered auditors founded the Society of Registered Accountants (SRA) in 1932 (see Table 8.3). Thenceforth there were three societies in the auditing profession in Sweden – the SSA, the APA and the SRA – and two kinds of auditor enjoying the recognition of the Central Board of Auditing. These various auditors offered their services in a context where business remained relatively indifferent. This situation changed in the early 1930s with the collapse of the Swedish Match company run by Ivar Kreuger. This showed the weaknesses of the existing system.

Ivar Kreuger was the owner of Swedish Match, which in 1921 controlled all the important match markets in Europe. This dominant position was attained with the help of long-term loans provided by the company to

Table 8.3 A chronological overview of market situation, organizations, critical events and major legislation in the development of the auditing profession in Sweden, 1932–69

	1930s	*1940s*	*1950s*	*1960s*
No. of limited companies	16,000	22,000	31,000	44,000
Stockmarket turnover (mill. SEK)	638	129	318	317
Organizations	Society of Registered Accountants (SRA) (1932)			
Critical events	The Kreuger crash (1932)			
Legislation		Companies Act (1944)		

various countries in exchange for a monopoly on their markets. Kreuger, who lent money to the international market at rates lower then even the French government, was regarded accordingly as a very prominent businessman. The strategy consisted of long-term lending of money financed by short-term borrowing. The lenders were supposed to renew their loans continuously. Because of the stock market crash in New York in 1929, however, bankruptcy had begun to hit many banks, which consequently called in their short-term loans. This led to the collapse of the Kreuger consortium and to personal devastation for all those who had invested money in the Kreuger companies. Many Swedish banks had made big loans to Kreuger, and the Swedish government was forced to come to the rescue. In the investigations that followed, criticism was directed at the way in which the auditors of the Kreuger company had done their auditing. Step by step the shortcomings of the company's accounting system were unmasked. The auditing report was described as 'the most nondescript ever seen'. It also became clear that the auditor of the company, Anton Wendler, was not independent of Ivar Kreuger. Wendler was a public accountant authorized by the Stockholm Chamber of Commerce, and a member of the APA (Wallerstedt 1988: 245; Sjöström 1994: 79–81).

On many counts the Kreuger crash supported the SSA in their former criticism of the auditing system. The society's members argued that the root of this disaster in the Swedish financial system was to be found in the poorly organized auditing system, and that the official authorization of auditors would mean greater independence *vis-à-vis* private-capital interests. The SSA also argued that by lowering the requirements regarding theoretical education, the number of competent auditors could be raised to an acceptable level. As expected, their conclusion was that only the state authorization of auditors would guarantee objective auditing procedures (Rosman 1932: 1–2).

It was not only the SSA that took action when the crash occurred. In fact, all those who in one way or another had an interest in the auditing system, reacted to what had happened. The APA began to investigate third-party liability insurance, and reviewed its statutes and tightened up its entrance requirements. After this, to become a member of the APA, applicants had to have had one year's practical experience as an authorized public accountant (Sjöström 1994: 72). The Central Board of Auditing initiated a debate over the authorization procedures and stressed the importance of the independence of auditors *vis-à-vis* their clients. An auditor could on no account be employed by a client, and nor should the impartiality of an auditor ever be in question. The board of the stock exchange reacted to the long-felt desire of the APA and the Central Board of Auditing that regulations obligating listed companies to have at least one authorized public accountant should be inaugurated. The legislative authorities suggested stricter rules regarding auditing procedures in companies, and in 1932 the Ministry of Justice issued a memorandum in which they proposed an amendment to the Companies Act. Here it was stipulated for the first time that auditors should be 'well acquainted with business'. It was also suggested that auditors for companies with share capital exceeding 500,000 SEK or a balance-sheet total exceeding one million SEK should be appointed by the County Administration. According to this proposal the County Administration would collaborate with the chamber of commerce in appointing an auditor. At the same time auditors in companies took measures themselves to improve the auditing procedures, especially in the case of consolidated accounts, where consolidated balance sheets were now introduced (Wallerstedt 1988: 245, 283).

In 1934 the SSA sent an official letter to the Central Board of Auditors in which it suggested extending the period of practical experience required of authorized public auditors and registered accountants from three to five years. The APA agreed to this, suggesting also that only authorized public accountants could appoint other authorized public accountants. An upper age limit of fifty-five for becoming an accountant was also suggested, to avoid people entering the profession as a last resort upon retirement or after failure in other areas (Sjöström 1994: 73). The Central Board of Auditing accepted the suggestions, and revised the existing rules to encompass them.

The new Companies Act which came into effect in 1944 was preceded by several years of committee work, from 1933 to 1941 (Wallerstedt 1988: 238). The APA found it 'the most important manifestation' ever of their importance in Sweden (Sillén 1949: 77). The reason for their satisfaction was that they felt the stipulations in the Act now gave them satisfactory protection for their title of 'authorized public accountant'. It was now mandatory, for instance, that an authorized public accountant be appointed by a chamber of commerce. Thenceforth no other authority could authorize public accountants. Another reason for satisfaction was that authorized public accountants now became compulsory in all listed companies. The lawmakers pointed out, however, that there was no possibility at this time of enforcing limited companies to have a qualified auditor (authorized public accountant or registered accountant), because there were still were too few of these to go round (*SOU* 1941:9: 456). Only in the case of companies whose share capital exceeded two million SEK should one of the auditors at least be authorized. There was now also a better chance of being able to engage an authorized public accountant or a registered accountant, should a group of shareholders wish to do so. The only specification about the qualifications of auditors for limited companies was that besides having Swedish citizenship and having come of age, they should have relevant experience of accounting and some acquaintance with the economic circumstances of the companies under audit (*SOU* 1941:9: 446).

Many of the stipulations in the new Act can be traced back to the earlier reactions to the Kreuger crash. In the proposal of the law-drafting board, the importance of the auditors' independence *vis-à-vis* their client was stressed. The content of the audit report was now more elaborate and the auditor was required to sign the balance sheet and the profit and loss statements, verifying that they were in accordance with the company's books. The comments attached to the Act included detailed discussions about the growing importance of company groups and the importance of proper auditing of such groups. The auditor was permitted to use assistants (*SOU* 1941:9: 363–74). From 1949 onwards, APA published accounting recommendations to provide guidance for the annual accounts of limited liability companies, and continued to be very active in rule-making activities (Artsberg 1992; *Swedish Annual Accounts Act with FAR's Guidelines* 1997). Since that time, according to Jönsson and Marton (1994: 191), they have also been very active in setting standards in Sweden.

The regulations regarding the auditing profession included in the 1944 Companies Act seem to have worked quite well, and it was about twenty years before demands to modernize the law began to be heard (Sjöström 1994: 135). In 1964 the old question of the relevance of the authorization procedures of the chambers of commerce was again raised in the Riksdag. According to the chambers of commerce, an authorized public accountant was not to be in anyone's employ. This meant that auditors who held appointments with the local or national government had to forfeit their authorization. Consequently it had been difficult to recruit qualified auditors for public service. Another view was that because statements issued by the Central Board of Auditing were not official, the person submitting the motion could not rule out the possibility of some kind of monopoly on the part of the chambers of commerce. It was also argued that the authorized public accountants had been privileged as a result of the 1944 Companies Act, and that the state should thus have some control over the procedures (Sjöström 1994: 99–100). No action was taken, however, and once again the authorization system survived the attack.

The Kreuger crash worked in many ways to propel the development of the auditing profession. Never before had any single event been so important to the promotion of the profession. All those with an interest in auditing reacted to what had happened by tightening the regulations concerning auditors and auditing. All the above-mentioned actions following the crash thus paved the way for the new 1944 Companies Act, which implied a genuine advance for the authorized public accountants. The stipulations in the Act had been much influenced by Oskar Sillén, founder and chairman of the APA and one of its most prominent members. With this law the authorized public accountants acquired real protection for their title for the first time. It was now stipulated by law that the chambers of commerce were the only bodies that could grant the title of authorized public accountant to an auditor. And, with this law the legislation referring to auditors and auditing obviously made real progress. It seems likely that if there had been enough qualified auditors in Sweden at the time, it would also have been made mandatory on all limited companies to use them. However, this was destined to wait until the 1983 Companies Act.

1970–95: the state and the authorization procedure

By 1970 the SSA's frequent urgent requests over a period of seventy years on the question of the public authorization of auditors finally seem to have ceased. The head of the Ministry of Commerce had at last ordered an investigation of the procedures for the authorization of auditors. The directives stated that the investigators should focus on an authorization procedure in which the state would bear the main responsibility (Sjöström 1994: 96). There is no doubt that it was the discussions in the Riksdag during the 1960s that had paved the way for this investigation.

The committee submitted two proposals. According to one, the National Board of Trade was to be responsible for the authorization and supervision of auditors. According to the second, the chambers of commerce still handled authorization, but in accordance with state regulations. Appeals were be made to the National Board of Trade. The investigators themselves favoured the first alternative, which they believed would create more homogeneity and consistency in the application of the regulations. This proposal was referred to various interested parties for comment. As expected, there was little enthusiasm for the proposal on the part of the APA, the chambers of commerce, the Federation of Swedish Industries or the Swedish Bankers' Association, whereas other bodies – among them

Table 8.4 A chronological overview of market situation, organizations, critical events and major legislation in the development of the auditing profession in Sweden, 1970–95

	1970s	*1980s*	*1990s*
No. of limited companies	100,000	126,000	262,000
Stockmarket turnover (mill. SEK)	708	8,000	94,000
Organizations	The Accounting Standards Board (ASB) (1976)	The Swedish Financial Accounting Standards Council (SFAS) (1989)	The Supervisory Board of Public Accountants replaces the National Board of Trade as the the authorizing authority (1995)
Critical events	The Swedish government takes over the certification of auditors and the National Board of Trade becomes the authorizing authority (1973)		Sweden agrees to join the European Economic Area (1992)
Legislation	Companies Act (1975) Accounting Act (1976)		Auditing Act (1995) Accounting Act (1995)

the SSA – were positive. Thus, in 1973, the system of authorization through the chambers of commerce that had been in operation for more than sixty years was brought to an end. The state, in the shape of the National Board of Trade, was thenceforward the new authorization authority (see Table 8.4).

Since there had now been many changes and additions to the 1944 Companies Act, it was felt that the old arrangements needed modernizing (Sjöström 1994: 119). In 1975 a new Companies Act was introduced, and the auditing profession advanced another step towards securing its status. Thenceforth companies of a certain size, i.e. with at least one million SEK restricted equity, were to have a qualified auditor (authorized or registered). What was most important about this Act, however, was that from now on auditors were to examine the annual reports of the companies according to certain Generally Accepted Auditing Standards (GAAS). These standards were to be interpreted according to the recommendations of the profession and statements issued by the National Board of

Trade (Sjöström 1994: 134–6). This meant that the APA were even more involved than before in making accounting recommendations.

In a new Accounting Act in 1976, yet another important set of principles came into operation, namely Generally Accepted Accounting Principles (GAAP). In connection with the introduction of the Accounting Act, a governmental organization called the Accounting Standards Board (ASB) was created to promote the development of GAAP and to consider how best to apply the new accounting law in practice. Part of their job was now to set standards for accounting. The government appointed the members of the ASB, who included representatives of the auditing profession, business, the tax authorities, the stock exchange, academia and the trade unions. Thus, besides having its own standard-setting body, the APA was represented in the ASB. It was intended at its initiation that the ASB was to be neutral, and not to represent any single group. But, as Jönsson and Marton point out, from the start APA was 'in practice, the dominant participant' (1994: 187, 193).

The 1975 Companies Act and the 1976 Accounting Act thus refer to GAAS and GAAP as representing the accepted auditing and accounting principles. The Acts provide a framework for standards, and accepted principles and standards are referred to for specific rules. The GAAS and GAAP are thus legally binding. 'In this sense, accounting differs from most legal areas in that in accounting, the distinction between law and practice is not as clear' (Jönsson and Marton 1994: 198). However, it soon became evident that there were too many interests to be attended to in the ASB, and few recommendations were subsequently issued (Jönsson and Marton 1994: 188). In 1989 some members of the business community and of APA felt that they were losing control over Swedish accounting practice, and accordingly yet another body – the Swedish Financial Accounting Standards Board (SFAS) – was created jointly by the government, business and the APA. 'The purpose was to gather all standard-setting functions for public companies in one organization ... The board can decide where new recommendations are needed. This can be based on a reconsideration of previous recommendations issued by [APA], international accounting rules, legal and tax developments in Sweden, and corporate practice' (Jönsson and Marton 1994: 195).

Around 1980 the National Board of Trade considered that the supply of authorized and approved auditors was expected to be sufficient for the future. By 1983 an important modification was accordingly made in the 1975 Companies Act, namely that at least one auditor in a limited company should be authorized or approved (Sjöström 1994: 149).

When Sweden signed the European Economic Area agreement (EEA) and later joined the European Union this meant adjusting the country's legal practice to the European statutory requirements. In view of this, a committee was appointed in 1992 to investigate the requirements that would apply to the auditing profession (*SOU* 1993:69). Earlier, in 1989, the

National Board of Trade had asked the Riksdag for a review of the twenty-year-old Regulation of Auditors. Now their request for such a review could be combined with the investigation of the necessary adjustments in the legal practices to comply with European statutory requirements. The investigation proposed that an auditing board should be set up and should take over the duties of the National Board of Trade on auditing matters. The qualified auditors should be on this board. The review also led to the enactment of a new law, and in 1995 a separate law for auditors and auditing was introduced in Sweden for the first time. The harmonization of the Swedish auditing regulations with the EU auditing directives provided the impetus for the Auditing Act.

During this period there was a good deal of activity in the field. In 1973 the state thus finally became the authorization authority, something that SSA had been pleading for since the beginning of the twentieth century. In this light the decision must be regarded as a critical event. The APA had been resisting the role of the state as authorization authority over the years as a matter of 'principle', but an examination of the development of the profession since 1973 suggests that the authorized auditors had in fact strengthened their position as a standard-setting body. The fact that the state is now the authorization authority has not so far been to the disadvantage of the authorized public accountants. Joining the EU in 1992 must also be seen as a critical event, as it provoked the Auditing and Accounting Acts of 1995.

In 1982 the auditing corps consisted of 997 authorized and 1,183 registered auditors, compared with 581 authorized and 1,035 registered auditors in 1975. These numbers finally made it possible to adjust the Companies Act in 1983, such that at least one auditor in a limited company should be authorized or approved – something that had been on the agenda ever since the beginning of the century.

Conclusions

In this chapter it has been shown how, in a direct or indirect way, interaction between market conditions, various actors (organizations) and certain critical events have influenced the evolution of regulatory regimes in the auditing field. In the earliest period, between 1895 and 1921, the first two important actors evolved, namely the SSA and the APA auditors. Two critical events occurred: the establishment of the Stockholm School of Economics in 1909, and the certification by the Stockholm Chamber of Commerce of the first authorized auditors in 1912. The foundation of the Stockholm School of Economics was a prerequisite for the emergence of authorized auditors, and it has been shown above that the second of these critical events is closely connected to the first. The main mission of the two auditing groups during this period turned out to be the regulation of the auditing field, with each one pursuing a model that benefited their own interests. The APA members' subsequent struggle to protect their status as authorized public accountants can be said to illustrate a strategy of control, in other words approaching the argumentation of the critical perspective. The actions of the SSA auditors seem to have had more of the functionalist and interactionist approach, as they sought to convince others both inside and outside the profession of their legitimate claim to professional recognition (Willmott 1986: 558).

In the 1922–31 period a new kind of auditor began to appear, namely the registered accountants, and for some years this eased the tension between the APA and SSA auditors. The fact that the SSA auditors had now received recognition and had a niche of their own to protect, and that a special auditing exam was invented for those who wanted to become authorized auditors without attending the Stockholm School of Economics, must be considered as critical events. From now on the field was changing in character. But the market conditions were confused: industry complained that there were too few auditors, and the auditors complained that they had too few clients.

The most important critical event of the whole hundred years was the Kreuger crash in 1932, the beginning of our third period. This event had an effect on every stakeholder in the field, as well as – and most importantly – on the 1944 Companies Act. If there had been a sufficient number of qualified auditors in Sweden at that time, this would probably have included a stipulation that all limited companies should employ qualified accountants. The next critical event occurred in 1973 when the state finally took over the authorization procedures from the chambers of commerce, thus inaugurating a fourth period in the evolution of the profession. This move was made despite opposition from the APA and the chambers of commerce. However, by now the position of the APA accountants was very strong, and this change in the source of authorization hardly diminished the importance they had acquired within their profession. As a result of the 1975 Companies Act and the 1976 Accounting Act the position of the auditors was strengthened by the creation of two more bodies, the Accounting Standards Board and the Swedish Financial Accounting Standards Board. Auditors were now ensured by law of an important role in the development of accepted auditing and accounting principles (GAAS and GAAP), the application of which is binding. This meant that the profession now exercised great influence over the standards and principles to be applied in the Swedish companies as regards accounting matters.

When Sweden signed the European Economic Area agreement and later joined the EU, it also agreed to adjust its legal practice to the European statutory requirements – these two events must also be regarded as critical. The Auditing and the Accounting Acts of 1995 were strongly influenced by the adjustment to EU standards. The 1995 Auditing Act embodies the final acknowledgement of the importance of the profession today. It is thus not surprising that the general secretary of the APA, Björn Markland, declared that auditors had now acquired a key position in the development of the profession (Föreningen Auktoriserade Revisorer 1995: 6).

The changes in the Companies Acts between 1895 and 1995 were closely related to market conditions, i.e. the supply of auditors and the demand for their services. At the beginning of the twentieth century, when the profession was quite new, auditors complained that companies did not employ them as much as they would have liked, and later when more auditing facilities were required by society, the population did not match the demand. It was not until the 1980s that the market conditions could support a law whereby every limited company was to have at least one qualified auditor. The auditing profession is now well established in Sweden. The story told here shows how it has passed through all of the stages in the development of a profession identified by Wilensky (1964: 142–6). Many researchers in the field have stressed the importance of establishing an association or society in the process of professionalization. In describing the professionalization of railroad managers in America in the 1880s, Chandler (1977: 130–3) pointed out that at a relatively early stage in the development of their profession this group 'had their societies and their journals'. Sarfatti Larson (1977: 5) claims that the existence of professional associations 'indicates the maturity' of the process, while the present study has identified the foundation of a professional society as the very first step in the professionalization process. It seems that in the case presented here the professional organizations were not able to direct developments in any substantial way. On the other hand they initiated discussions about the jurisdiction appropriate to their field, and have been useful to the legislative authorities by providing models for regulatory mechanisms when these authorities have felt that the time was ripe for some kind of coercive change to be embodied in law. The law provides the framework, but the standard-setting bodies – the ASB and the SFAS – in which APA's auditors are considered to be the most influential actors, are referred to when it comes to defining specific rules. But these rules have the same status as law, and in this way the 'distinction between law and practice is not ... clear' (Jönsson and Marton 1994: 198).

The establishment of limited companies was an important factor in the genesis of full-time auditing. This accords with Sarfatti Larson's conclusion in *The Rise of Professionalism* (1977: 6), that the professionalization of 'modern' professions is probably connected with the rise of industrial capitalism and the related evolution of the large corporations. The emergence of bigger companies created a presumptive market for the new auditing profession. According to Sarfatti Larson, one of their first tasks was 'not exploiting already existing markets but ... to create them' (1997: 10). The first auditors to support themselves entirely on auditing were the APA auditors, since they were not in fact allowed to do auditing as a sideline to another occupation. It was not until the 1930s that there were more than fifty APA auditors in Sweden. The SRA auditors, on the other hand, usually conducted audits as a sideline to another occupation. The claim to esoteric knowledge was given concrete form with the establishment of the Stockholm School of Economics in 1909, to be reinforced later when the 1944 Companies Act gave legal protection to the title of authorized public accountant. The empirical description above has shown that the regulation of the auditing field has been a long process. Important actors in this process have been the auditors themselves in their professional organizations, and the legislative authorities. But what has emerged most clearly is just how important certain critical events have been as catalysts in the process. Thus, in conclusion, the regulation process in the auditing profession can be said to have been influenced by the interaction of market conditions, professional bodies and critical events. It is not a question of self-regulation *or* state control, but of state control built upon and in close association with self-regulation.

References

Artsberg, K. (1992) *Policy Making and Accounting Change – Considerations Behind the Choice of Measurement Principles in Swedish Accounting* (*Normbildning och redovisningsförändring. Värderingar vid val av mätprinciper inom svensk redovisning*), Lund: Lund University Press.

Chandler, A. D. (1977) *The Visible Hand. The Managerial Revolution in American Business,* Cambridge, MA: Harvard University Press.

Chua, W. F. and Poullaos, C. (1993) 'Rethinking the profession – state dynamic', *Accounting, Organizations and Society* 18(7/8): 691–728.

Collins, R. (1990) 'Changing conceptions in the sociology of the professions', in R. Torstendahl and M. Burrage (eds) *The Formation of Professions,* London: Sage.

DiMaggio, P. J. and Powell, W. (1983) 'The iron cage revisited', *American Sociological Review* 48: 147–60.

First Inter-Scandinavian Auditing Congress (*Den Förste interskandinaviste revisorskongress*) (1924) Oslo: S. and Jul. Sorensens boktrykkert.

Föreningen Auktoriserade Revisorer (1962) *Authorization of Auditors 50 years* (*Auktorisation av revisorer 50 år*), Stockholm: FAR.

—— (1995) *New Auditing Act* (*Den nya revisorslagstiftningen*), Stockholm: FAR.

Jönsson, S. (1985) *The Elite and the Accounting Standards. Impulses Behind the Development of Accounting Praxis* (*Eliten och normerna. Drivkrafter i utvecklingen av redovisningspraxis*), Lund: Doxa Ekonomi.

Jönsson, S. and Marton, J. (1994) 'Sweden', in J. Flower (ed.) *The Regulation of Financial Reporting in the Nordic Countries,* Stockholm: Fritzes.

McCann, J. and Galbraith, J. (1981) 'Interdepartmental relations', in P. C. Nystrom and W. H. Starbuck (eds) *Handbook of Organizational Design 2,* Oxford: Oxford University Press.

Morgan, G. (1986) *Images of Organization,* Beverly Hills, CA: Sage.

Powell, W. W. (1996) 'Fields of practice: connections between law and organizations', *Journal of the American Bar Foundation* 21(4): 959–66.

Power, M. (1997) *The Audit Society,* Oxford: Oxford University Press.

Puxty, A. G., Willmott, H. C., Cooper, D. J. and Lowe, T. (1987), 'Modes of regulation in advanced capitalism: locating accountancy in four countries', *Accounting, Organizations and Society* 12(3): 273–91.

Rosman, H. (1932) 'Comments on the auditing system of the chambers of commerce' ('Några synpunkter på handelskamrarnas revisorsauktorisation'), *Central Board of Auditing*, archive.

Sarfatti Larson, M. (1977) *The Rise of Professionalism. A Sociological Analysis*, Berkeley, CA: University of California Press.

—— (1981) *Organizations. Rational, Natural, and Open Systems*, Englewood Cliffs, NJ: Prentice-Hall.

Scott, W. R. (1995) *Institutions and Organizations*, Thousand Oaks, CA: Sage.

Sillén, O. (1949) 'Authorized public accountants – yesterday, today and tomorrow' ('Auktoriserade revisorer förr, nu och framdeles'), *Tidskrift for Revisjon og Regnskapsvesen* 6: 73–87.

Sjöström, C. (1994) *Stipulations in Auditing – a Historical Perspective* (*Revision och lagreglering – ett historiskt perspektiv*), Linköping Studies in Science and Technology, Thesis No 417.

SOU (1941:9) 'Proposals concerning a new Companies Act' ('Lagberedningens förslag till Lag om Aktiebolag mm Motiv'), Stockholm.

SOU (1993:69) 'The auditors and EG' ('Revisorerna och EG'), Stockholm.

Stockholm Chamber of Commerce (1912) 'Stipulations from the Stockholm Chamber of Commerce Concerning the Authorization of Auditors' ('Stockholms Handelskammares bestämmelser ang. auktorisation af revisorer'), enclosed to *Stockholms handelskammarens årsberättelse* 1912.

Svensson, S. (1924) 'A report on auditing in Sweden', *The First Inter-Scandinavian Auditing Congress* (*Redogjörelse för revisorsförhållanden i Sverige, Den förste interskandinaviske revisorskongress*), Oslo: S. and Jul. Sorensens boktrykkert.

Swedish Annual Accounts Act with FAR's Guidelines (1997), Stockholm: Föreningen Auktoriserade Revisorer FAR.

Swedish Chambers of Commerce, 18th Meeting (*Handlingar till 18:e Svenska Handelskammarmötet*) (1930), Stockholm.

Wallerstedt, E. (1988) *Oskar Sillén, Professor and Practitioner – Business Administration at the Stockholm School of Economics* (*Oskar Sillén – Professor och Praktiker. Några drag i företagsekonomiämnets tidiga utveckling vid Handelshögskolan i Stockholm*), Acta Universitatis Upsaliensis, Studia Oeconomiae Negotiorum 30, Uppsala: Almquist and Wiksell (diss.).

Watts, R. L. and Zimmerman, J. L. (1978) 'Towards a positive theory of the determination of accounting standards', *The Accouning Review*, January: 112–33

Wilensky, H. (1964) 'The professionalization of everyone?', *The American Journal of Sociology* LXX(2): 137–58.

Willmott, H. (1986) 'Organising the profession: a theoretical and historical examination of the development of the major accountancy bodies in the U.K.', *Accounting, Organizations and Society* 11(6): 555–80.

Archives

Central Board of Auditing, CBA (Centrala Revisorsnämnden), Stockholm.

Swedish Institute of Authorized Public Accountants, APA (Föreningen Auktoriserade Revisorer), Stockholm.

Swedish Society of Accountants, SSA (Svenska Revisorsamfundet), Stockholm.

9 Regulatory compliance

Glenn Morgan and Kim Soin

Introduction

Analyses of regulatory systems tend to follow two main approaches. The first is dominated by economists and seeks to build models of the economic impact of varying forms of regulatory intervention: we term this the cost-benefit approach to regulation. The second approach tends to be the preserve of political scientists examining the degree to which regulatory systems are 'captured' by those whom they are supposed to be regulating – this can be termed the regulatory-capture approach. In this chapter, we suggest that a third approach is necessary which takes seriously the complexities of the internal organizational features of both the regulators and the regulated companies – we term this the organizational approach to regulation. The organizational approach emphasizes that both the regulatory bodies and the regulated companies are complex social spaces within which actors construct meanings that make sense of their roles and activities in changing contexts. At a simple level, this notion emphasizes the need to consider the range of perspectives on and interests in regulation based on the structural position of actors within organizations. Certain actors are more powerful than others in articulating a set of values and practices for the organization as a whole; this is revealed in conflicts and arguments within organizations over the nature of regulation. Similarly, certain organizations play a more influential role than others in constructing the system of regulation. Hancher and Moran (1989) use the idea of the 'regulatory space' to describe the complex field of actors and interests that participate in the construction of a regulatory system; our argument is that this concept needs to be extended to emphasize the internal dynamics of the organizations within the 'regulatory space'.

In this chapter, we develop our argument by reference to the evolution of regulation in the context of UK financial services. We concentrate in particular on the regulation of personal financial services, i.e. life insurances, unit trusts, pensions and other forms of personal investment sold through retail banks, building societies, insurance companies and brokers.

Within this regulatory space, there have been four main categories of organizational actors – the government, the regulatory authorities, the financial services companies and the consumer lobby groups – that have been influential in constructing the regulatory system. In this particular study, however, we concentrate on the regulators and the regulated companies, referring to government and consumer lobbies only occasionally, though we certainly do not wish to downplay the significance of the latter. Our focus is on how the organizational structure of the regulators and the regulated companies affected the emergence of the regulatory system. In brief, the complex and fragmented structure of the regulators in the period up to the formation of the Financial Services Authority by the Labour government in 1997 created confusion and uncertainty about how it was to work. Similarly, the internal structure of the regulated companies meant that adaptation to regulatory changes was slow and variable between and within companies. From an organizational perspective, therefore, the regulatory system emerges as an example neither of 'efficient regulation' nor 'regulatory capture'. Instead, we argue that it is necessary to examine the processes within and between organizations that shape the evolution of regulatory systems.

The chapter is organized into the following three sections. The first briefly outlines the key elements of the regulatory structure, focusing specifically on the regulatory bodies for personal financial services. In this section, we emphasize the uncertainties which arose from the organizational fragmentation of the regulatory authorities. This was partly a result of the uncertain division of function and authority between the regulatory bodies which was exacerbated by the differing types of relationship between the regulators, the companies and the government. These problems are illustrated by reference to the particular problem of legitimating the role of the regulatory bodies. In the second section, we report on a series of studies which have been conducted on attitudes towards regulation and compliance within financial services companies. These studies reveal a range of differences within and between companies in their responses to regulation. The concluding section elaborates on the importance of the organizational approach to regulation.

The Financial Services Act: structure and function

The Financial Services Act 1986 (FSA) was the first comprehensive attempt to create a unified, statutorily based system of regulation within the financial sector (see Clarke 1986 for the background; also Moran 1991 and Clarke in this volume). Regulation of securities and investments under the Act was delegated to the Securities and Investments Board Ltd (SIB), a private company whose members were appointed jointly by the Secretary of State for Trade and Industry and the Governor of the Bank of England. The SIB had four main tasks. The first was responsibility for devising 'model rules'. This meant developing the principles articulated in the Act into a set of rules for financial services companies; as will be described, this led to long debates about the relationship between principles and rules and the role of the lower-tier regulators (the self-regulatory organizations – hereafter, SROs) in modifying/implementing principles and rules. The second role of the SIB was a policing role in respect to a range of offences against the Act. The third responsibility was for the licensing and supervision of individual businesses (although in general, it encouraged businesses to join the lower-tier regulators, the SROs). Finally, it was responsible for authorizing the 'self-regulatory organizations' which in practice were responsible for the licensing and supervision of individual businesses.

SROs, like the SIB, had a legally private character; they were limited companies, funded by the subscriptions of their members. Unlike the SIB, they were able in the first instance to choose their own staff and governing bodies. The SROs are central to the regulatory process. An individual firm effectively acquires a licence to operate by being accepted into membership of the appropriate SRO. Membership of a SRO is conditional on acceptance of its body of rules and its system of monitoring and discipline, as well as the payment of fees. No firm can provide investment advice unless it is a member of a SRO (or the SIB). A SRO can fine a member for breach of rules and in certain circumstances can order it to cease business, either entirely or until certain procedures are put in place. SROs have the right to visit member companies at any time and have full access to their records and procedures. Although the dates and timing of monitoring visits to companies are usually negotiated in advance, the degree of notice given can vary. Once inside the company, the monitoring teams can visit any particular branch or individual to assure themselves that the company is operating according to the rules. FIMBRA (the Financial Intermediaries, Managers and Brokers Regulatory Association) and LAUTRO (the Life Assurance and Unit Trust Regulatory Organisation) were the SROs largely responsible for ensuring the protection of investors in the market for retail investment products. In 1992 they combined to form the Personal Investment Authority (PIA). The Association of Futures Brokers and Dealers (AFBD) licenses and supervises firms in commodities and futures. The Securities Association (TSA) was formed from the old regulatory arm of the Stock Exchange. In 1991 the AFBD and the TSA combined to form the Securities and Futures Authority (SFA). The last SRO was the Investment Management Regulatory Organisation (IMRO) which specialized in the regulation of investment fund managers. This chapter is mainly concerned with the relationships around the regulation of retail financial services, i.e. between the SIB, LAUTRO and FIMBRA (and the PIA as the latter two became in 1992) and their member companies (banks, building societies, insurance companies and brokers).

The system of regulation under the FSA (1986) was described by its first chairman, Sir Kenneth Berrill, as being 'practitioner-based, statute-backed regulation'. The SIB was funded by a levy on the markets and its governing body was made up of leading figures from financial services firms. The financial services sector had a significant input into the recruitment of SIB personnel – largely because it is the industry itself which is the most important source of qualified people (Moran 1991). Many commentators argued that the closeness of the financial community and the regulatory bodies was so strong that the contract of its founding chairman was not renewed because powerful groups in the City felt that his approach to regulation was too 'legalistic' and 'inflexible' (*Financial Times*, 29 March 1988: *The Sunday Times* 21 February 1988).

From its inception, there was uncertainty about the purpose and nature of the regulatory process. On the one hand, there was an emphasis on the need for practitioner involvement. Without such involvement, it was argued that the regulators would not be able to understand the markets; it was a case of turning 'poachers into gamekeepers'. On the other hand, it was not clear where the practitioners, who had presumably been happily involved in the game up to the moment of their appointment (and many of those on the governing bodies and advisory committees – unlike those who actually became employed to regulate – continued to be involved), would draw the line between what was acceptable and what was not. Attempts to formalize this line by insisting that everybody demonstrate their adherence to certain rules ran against long-standing feelings within the sector that the institutions were trustworthy and the problem was only with a few 'cowboys', usually individual operators. Many practitioners believed that rules were counterproductive, increasing costs for companies (and, by implication, consumers as well) whilst being ineffective in stopping anybody who really wanted to break them. They argued for a form of flexibility, which in effect meant changing things very little from past practice, whilst giving regulators power to rid the industry of 'cowboys'. Quite how this might be accomplished was unclear.

Establishing the system: the SIB, the SROs and rule books

These debates were reflected in the evolution of the regulatory system in the period from 1988 into the early 1990s. At SIB level, there was an initial attempt under Berrill's leadership to produce comprehensive rule books. SROs were supposed to adapt these to the circumstances of their own sector. Members of SROs were then to adapt them again into a 'compliance manual' for their organization. SRO monitoring would consist of ensuring that companies had properly incorporated these rules into their policies and practices. What this led to was a veritable merry-go-round of 'practical hermeneutics' between the companies, the SROs and the SIB. What did a certain rule mean? Was a particular practical interpretation of the rule acceptable, etc., etc.? The initial attempt to dictate a rule book which covered all aspects of regulated business was condemned by practitioners as too legalistic and bureaucratic. Berrill's successor at the SIB, David Walker, sought to move away from this approach towards a set of overarching principles; SROs and companies had to show compliance with the principles rather than en bloc incorporation of SIB rules into their own practices.

Within the retail sector, discussion focused on the implementation of two key principles: 'know your customer' and 'best advice'. Together these two principles had a simple objective, which was to ensure that the seller of the product had gathered sufficient information about the current and expected future financial position of the client to enable him/her to advise on the best product (and premium level) out of the portfolio of products which they were authorized to sell. However, beneath this simple objective lay a wealth of complexities which have continued to plague the sector (see Clarke in this volume). The complexities arose from uncertainty about how to implement these principles. Some aspects were relatively simple and involved little more than extending principles implemented elsewhere. For example, the regulators sought to reduce the use of misleading adverts which had become endemic in the industry. More difficult, however, was the issue of 'know your customer'. The principle implied not only that the salesperson 'knew the customer', but that a third-party monitor could agree that sufficient information had been taken down to support this claim. Companies faced two uncertainties – did the salesperson in fact know the customer *and* could this be demonstrated? The paradox was that companies gave the second question the priority, devising ever-growing 'fact-finds' which were designed to cover every possible aspect of the customer's life. For many salespeople used to the previous informal system, this fundamentally changed their job, extending discussions with customers from thirty minutes into perhaps two sixty- to ninety-minute interviews, in the process, of course, reducing the number of contacts and consequently the number of sales (and commission earnings). Completing a fact-find was seen as a regulatory necessity, only tangentially related to the sale itself (Knights and Morgan 1990).

The sale itself was covered by the best advice principle, but what did this mean? One thing it meant was that advice was not supposed to be determined by commission earnings – in other words, the salesperson (as had often been the case previously) would persuade the client to buy the product that offered the best commission. However, best advice remained a subjective phenomenon with some outer limits on which there was general agreement that a sale would be inappropriate, but for the great bulk of products, there was little way of telling if they were best advice or not until some years down the line when investment returns might be compared. Again, the industry tended to act as though anything it did was generally to be trusted because the companies themselves were trustworthy. For example, it occurred to very few people within the industry in the late 1980s and early 1990s that they would later be criticized for overselling pensions – after all they were only doing what the government wanted them to do.

The result was that in this period from 1988 to 1992, rules on 'know your customer' and 'best advice' were seen as the intrusion of formal regulations into areas where they were not needed. From the industry point of view, the rules increased costs and reduced productivity, which in turn had a negative impact on customers. The regulators had to continually justify what they were doing in the light of these claims from practitioners that the industry was basically working well and it was only a 'few cowboys' who were the problem. The SIB, LAUTRO and FIMBRA engaged in a series of negotiations about the status of the rule books and how they could be made less restrictive.

Delegitimation: evolving rules, regulations and regulatory bodies

Gradually, however, the context was beginning to change in ways which undermined the claims of the industry that regulation was basically unnecessary. As these changes occurred, the regulatory bodies began to respond and their relationships with each other and their member companies changed. First indications emerged following an early report on training in the industry. In effect, this found that there was little or no training for salespeople in most companies. As their earnings were usually based on commissions, they were only paid when they sold. Companies therefore took on more and more salespeople to whom they gave minimal training – perhaps a couple of days. The salespeople then either sank or swam! Either way, it cost the companies very little because of the commission system. The implications of the report were devastating, if widely unacknowledged. The notion that people with a couple of days' training could even come close to meeting 'know your customer' and 'best advice' requirements was untenable. In effect, these principles were simply a fig leaf which covered up the fact that the industry was taking very little care to train and employ people who could offer such advice. This argument shifted relations between the regulators and the companies on to a new plane since it exposed the companies' claim that there was really nothing to be concerned about in most of the industry.

In effect, what now began to occur was a differentiation process. On the one side were the regulators, gradually but slowly being supported by some of the largest companies in the industry. For this group, a system of rules and regulations which insisted on higher levels of training and competence would increase the costs of entry into the sector whilst at the same time pushing out those firms which lacked the capital to implement the new system. On the other side, therefore, stood those individuals who had worked in the industry for some time and considered themselves competent without the sort of formal training and assessment which was being proposed. Also on this side were those companies which had relied on the low cost of creating large sales forces in order to bring in business.

LAUTRO's high water mark: the training and competence scheme

Out of this process came what was termed the Training and Competence Initiative (TCI) led mainly by LAUTRO, though FIMBRA also had to develop its own version of this. The TCI was LAUTRO's most significant contribution to the evolving regulatory space. It was developed over a number of years through extensive consultations with selected groups in the industry. As previously described, a number of the largest companies were enthusiastic about the scheme as a way of reducing the number of competitors in the industry. It also received widescale support from training and development specialists both inside the firms and in the various management consultancies which had grown up round the sector during the 1980s. Secondments into LAUTRO from these outside supporters solidified an alliance which was articulated in terms of 'professionalizing' the industry. Opponents were left looking like reactionary conservatives, though it was obvious to all concerned that the real importance of the TCI was going to be in terms of shaping new recruits into the industry and not changing the 'minds' of those already in it. Some companies understood this quickly and began raising their entry standards and assessment procedures in the hope of creating a new ethos of 'professionalism'; others sought to graft the TCI on to their existing sales force which created much more difficulty.

Every member of LAUTRO had to produce a scheme which showed how they were going to train and develop their sales force and its management. Minimum knowledge standards were created as were minimum expectations of what this training consisted. Companies had to show how all their sales force were going to be trained and how they were going to be assessed. Even people who had been working in the industry for some time were going to have to demonstrate their competence. The hoped for consequence was to raise the standard of advice; the economic consequence was that the cost of maintaining a sales force was significantly increased. Companies could no longer afford to treat training as an optional luxury; instead they had to develop detailed procedures which implied in many cases a massive increase in costs. This changed the economics of the sales forces. High levels of turnover which had been common in an environment driven by commission was no longer a viable option as up-front training costs were so high. Companies sought to reduce their turnover by shifting in part away from straight commission payment to commission plus salary. For banks and building societies (the bancassurers who were expanding in this period, see Morgan 1994), this was a perfect solution. They already carried high costs of training because of their traditional structure; now their potential competitors were going to be forced to carry a similar cost or get out of the business altogether (which happened to a number of marginal companies). On the negative side, all this provided greater encouragement for new types of entrants – those who did not offer advice but simply sold over the phone based on their reputation as trustworthy, such as Marks and Spencer, Virgin and so on.

LAUTRO's failures, the SIB and the politics of regulation

LAUTRO's training and competence scheme brought it prestige and authority amongst the regulators and some of the companies after its initial years of controversy. However, on another important issue it continued to delay and procrastinate. Right from the start of the regulatory process, there had been concern about the way in which firms and individuals were remunerated. The problem was the commission-based reward system which pervaded the industry at all levels. How could the customer trust that they were being sold a product because it was suited to him/her as opposed to the fact that it made a big commission for the salesperson? The argument that the seller had a duty of 'best advice' was at best feeble and at worst a legitimation for whatever the seller chose to sell the client. Various solutions were offered. One early suggestion was to revive the Maximum Commissions Agreement (MCA) which had operated amongst some companies in the industry earlier. The MCA would limit the amount of commission, thereby supposedly reducing the temptation. However, the MCA had never been universally accepted and with the industry becoming more variegated had little chance of success in the 1990s. Also, this could be interpreted as a restraint of trade and competition, again unpopular in this period of free-market dominance. Instead, the regulators set up what were referred to as LAUTRO rates and firms expressed their commission as a percentage of these rates.

This solution, however, revealed the essential vacuity of what was being proposed. No customer knew what LAUTRO rates were, or was interested in them (see Morgan and Knights 1991). Once again, the industry had come up with a fig leaf attempting to conceal the real problem. LAUTRO's failures to resolve this question were a growing embarrassment to SIB and the government. Practitioners within LAUTRO continued to insist that the issue was basically irrelevant to the customer who neither knew nor cared about commissions. The regulator seemed incapable of cracking this problem. Unfortunately the scale of the problem was becoming increasingly visible, mainly as a result of a series of devastating and extremely carefully researched critiques of the industry launched by the Office of Fair Trading (OFT 1993a; 1993b). A number of reports and discussion papers gradually revealed the full extent of the problem, of which commission was the tip of the iceberg. In essence, these reports revealed that the industry structured its products so that they were front-end loaded. This meant that a large amount of a customer's premium in the first few years went to pay the commission of the seller, leaving the actual amount credited to the client as small. In some cases of regular premium products, it could take up to seven years before the amount invested equalled the amount credited to the customer, investment gains having filled the gap left by the removal of large sums to pay commission. As many policies were surrendered early (i.e. before seven years), many policyholders actually made a loss. Furthermore, many companies end-loaded their payment policies by giving a large final bonus to the few policyholders who actually lasted out to the end of the term of their product. The mass of people who surrendered before this point were in effect subsidizing those who maintained their policies, allowing companies to advertise huge final surrender values that were likely to prove irrelevant in practice to most clients. The OFT emphasized not just the fundamental injustice of this system but the fact that it was concealed from the public. They argued in favour of clear statement of surrender values based on the real cost of commissions and other expenses.

LAUTRO's inability to take on this issue was a growing source of embarrassment to the SIB. This was further exacerbated by the growing awareness within the SIB and more generally that pension selling in the late 1980s and early 1990s (supposedly when LAUTRO was in action, regulating sales) had been deeply flawed. As the lead regulator, the SIB was being pressured to take a more active role on all these fronts. On the pensions issue, it instituted an investigation into the pensions-selling practices of the companies. What was of concern was the way in which many people had been persuaded to leave perfectly respectable occupational pension schemes and invest the lump sum withdrawn into a personal pension. The SIB investigation revealed quite easily that for most people, the result was that they were almost certainly likely to be worse off when they came to pensionable age than they would have been if they had stayed in the occupational pension scheme. For a while, some of the larger companies argued against this verdict, claiming that their sales of such products were not in this category. The Chief Executive of the Prudential, Mick Newmarch, was amongst the most vociferous complainants, arguing that not all companies could be tarred with the same brush and the Prudential would never act in this manner. As events and investigations progressed, it became clear that there was hardly a company in the land which was immune from these charges. LAUTRO and its successor, the Personal Investment Authority (PIA), were told by the SIB to clear the mess up by identifying its extent in every company and ensuring that each company investigated each sale again and offered compensation to clients who were potentially losing out.

The pension issue was not unrelated to the question of commissions. The companies had been given a clear run at the public by the Conservative government's espousal of private pensions in ideological and practical terms (see Knights 1997 for the broad sociopolitical background to this process). Salespeople saw an easy opportunity to maximize their commission income through sales of pension products. Whether they sold these products through incompetence or with full knowledge of what they were doing will never be clear; what is certain is that they knew it would be to their own financial advantage no matter what it did for the client. The OFT's assault on the commissions and surrender system (which was supported by groups such as the Consumers Association) added further embarrassment to the SIB's position on pensions. The SIB commissioned a well-known economic consultancy service to consider the impact on the industry and consumers of disclosing more information about costs, commissions and surrender values. The National Economic Research Associates (NERA) study on Disclosure was unequivocal in its recommendation. Disclosure would increase competitive pressure in the industry and enable consumers to make a better informed choice about products.

Relegitimating regulation and the financial services industry

In these years, the tensions between LAUTRO and the SIB were increasing. Both had started from the position of more or less accepting the industry's argument that most institutions were trustworthy. Their implementation of 'know your customer' and 'best advice' was therefore ridden with contradictions. They constructed bodies of rules and monitoring procedures which forced companies to take notice of them and yet they provided very little evidence that all this was worth the effort. They were left apologizing for themselves and looking for ways to cut down the regulatory structure. As the evidence emerged that they had been gullible and had swallowed wholesale the industry's legitimatory explanations, wider questions about the nature and purpose of regulation and the regulatory bodies were raised. The SIB, which was closer to the political machine of government than LAUTRO, found itself forced to act on controversies as they emerged but it could only act through the SROs which remained more dominated by industry interests and therefore procrastinated and stalled. In some areas, such as the TCI, LAUTRO was able to take up the gauntlet, at least partly because it had some crucial allies amongst large companies in the industry. In others, most notably commissions and disclosure, it stalled. Perhaps most fatally of all, it appeared to have failed in some fundamental way by not stopping the pensions mis-selling.

These problems in turn left the SIB looking inept and vulnerable to political criticism. Efforts were made to re-establish the purpose and function of the SIB through the Large Report in 1993. Produced by Walker's replacement, Andrew Large, this report emphasized that the SIB should increasingly take a strategic overview of the regulatory system, disengage itself from operational questions (including ceasing to allow firms to regulate direct with the SIB) and provide leadership to the system as a whole including the future role of British financial institutions in European and worldwide regulatory efforts. The Large Report also began to articulate a new view of regulation which used the language of the market in two key respects. First, the report explicitly linked regulation to the notion of making a proper market. The rhetoric of regulation was shifting from that of 'protection' to that of 'competition'. By implication, the argument was being conceded that the secrecy with which the companies concealed their commissions and expenses from consumers meant that there could be no proper 'choice' and therefore no proper market in which competitive pressures could operate. The role of regulation was to act in order to ensure that such a market came into being. Therefore, the SIB was moving irrevocably towards disclosure as central to choice, markets and competition, whilst LAUTRO continued to hesitate. This language linked into a number of other features of the period. The idea of regulation as 'market-making' was, for example, central to the regulatory process in the privatized utilities where potential monopoly powers had to be undermined by creating in various political ways a process of competition (see Waddams Price's chapter in this volume). The language of 'choice' also chimed in much more with broader notions of markets and individualism than did the language of 'investor protection' with its paternalistic overtones of the regulators 'knowing better' than the consumers. Moreover, this language of the market and choice also resonated with that of the companies themselves. It made it harder for them to resist the logic of the regulators, reducing them to the claim that customers did not want to know these sort of details.

What however did help to make this language appealing to the companies was the second way in which Large discussed market-based regulation. In effect, he turned the language back on to the SIB itself by arguing that the SIB had to show that regulation was efficient and cost effective. If not, regulation could and should be abandoned. This was translated into the idea that regulatory changes needed to be subjected to a cost-benefit analysis. This strategy had emerged in the US in what were termed Regulatory Impact Assessments which the Federal government had to conduct in certain areas if it wanted to introduce new regulations (Office of Management and Budget 1991). As an approach, it had been partially incorporated into the UK governmental system by Michael Heseltine and his Deregulation Task Force set up to tackle 'red-tape' (DTI 1992, 1994; Deregulation Initiative 1996a, 1996b, 1996c). The Large review indicated that future moves in regulation would be subjected to much stronger scrutiny to identify their costs and benefits. In a section on the SIB and cost efficiency, the following action points were stated:

- SIB to generate information about the cost effect of regulation
- SIB to commission an independent study of cost-benefit techniques
- SIB to establish a Cost of Compliance Unit.

In 1994 this led to the SIB contracting NERA to do a cost-benefit analysis of its disclosure proposals. In 1995 it established its own cost-benefit department, with its main role being to develop ways of examining the costs and benefits of particular elements of regulation.

The SIB's espousal of a market approach to regulation offered it the chance to raise itself above the immediate difficulties in LAUTRO. It gave it a language which could in theory connect the regulators, the companies and the Conservative government as all of them claimed to espouse the market and competition in one way or another. This was reinforced when the Conservative chancellor, Kenneth Clarke, finally came down on the side of full and open disclosure of commission and expenses and told the regulators to come up with ways of implementing it as soon as possible.

LAUTRO, on the other hand, was becoming increasingly enmeshed in a series of operational and strategic battles between itself and some of its members. Disclosure would not go away, but nor would company opposition. The pensions mis-selling was bubbling to the surface and blame was starting to attach itself to LAUTRO for lax monitoring procedures. Partly to protect itself against these accusations, LAUTRO seemed to become fiercer in its sanctions over recalcitrant members, shutting down some sales forces until company management instituted proper training and monitoring as well as fining companies increasingly large sums for failure to abide by the rules. Finally, the vexed relationship between the companies and the independent brokers organized in FIMBRA was coming to the boil (see Clarke in this volume for a discussion of this).

Restructuring regulation: SIB and the PIA

Whilst it was the problems with fees to FIMBRA that precipitated the merger of LAUTRO, FIMBRA and parts of IMRO into a new regulatory authority, the PIA, it is also clear that this enabled the regulators and the politicians to try to sweep under the carpet the failings of LAUTRO. The PIA was to be a new start, symbolized in the first instance by the dominance on its governing body of non-industry representatives; academics, consumer lobbyists and others of the 'great and the good' were numerically dominant on its board. The PIA became far more open than either its predecessor, LAUTRO, or its lead regulator, the SIB, to voices beyond the industry and the emerging market-regulation consensus amongst powerful actors in this group. The result was that, for a number of years, the SIB and the PIA seemed in competition with each other for leadership of the regulatory process with the SIB continuing to develop its market-led approach whilst the PIA was more cautious.

The PIA's approach leant more towards continued protection of the consumer rather than wholesale espousal of a market-led approach. This was revealed in the fact that rather than examining its own activities from a cost-benefit point of view, it developed the idea of 'regulatory effectiveness'. This was to be measured in a range of ways, most of which were not financial at all but rather indicators of the quality of selling, for example, the persistency ratio (how many policies were surrendered within the first one or two years, generally considered a key indicator of whether a sale had been based on 'know your customer' and 'best advice'), early surrender measures more generally, turnover of staf,f etc. The issue was not just that different languages and measures were being used, but also that the PIA was setting itself up as a source of power and knowledge on regulation separate from the SIB. The PIA explicitly developed a strategy involving consumer representatives and consumer opinions. It created a special 'consumer panel' whose responsibility it was to devise ways in which the voice of the consumer could be brought into the regulatory debate and to bring to the attention of the PIA's committees any issue which they thought was being ignored. Members of the panel were chosen from outside the PIA's other committees, representing a further drawing on expertise from consumer lobby groups and the wider 'great and good' of British society. One of the main things which the consumer panel did was to set up a longitudinal study of attitudes amongst the British public to financial services products, the industry as a whole and the regulatory process itself. An annual survey was to be conducted by a market research firm on how these attitudes were evolving (PIA 1996).

The PIA's approach to regulation was different from that of the SIB. The SIB had constructed a discourse within which markets and competition could, in theory, at least sit happily alongside a certain form of regulation. A possible implication of this was that as the market began to work 'properly', detailed regulations could be dismantled. Indeed, there was discussion of what was termed the 'disclosure dividend'; if the industry accepted disclosure and thereby allowed the emergence of more consumer knowledge and choice, it might be possible to reduce the amount of detailed regulation. Although this was highly speculative, it seemed to hold out to companies the possibility that in the short to medium term, the rigours of regulatory monitoring and so on might be removed. In this environment, discussions also emerged around the theme of 'compliance culture' and the notion that some firms (because of their higher level of internalization of the regulatory principles) could hope for a 'lighter' regulatory touch than others.

Although the PIA was involved in these discussions, the logic of its own notion of 'regulatory effectiveness' and the reports of its consumer panel implied a much more long-term process of change. The PIA approach as laid out in its regulatory plan was to check 'that we are actually achieving our long-term aim of making a difference to what happens in the marketplace' (PIA 1995: 6). This implied an indeterminate process of long-term change assessed in a whole range of ways. As well as measuring what it termed 'key performance indicators' (i.e. persistency ratios, etc. as described earlier), the PIA intended to use its consumer panel survey and *ad hoc* surveys on topics such as disclosure to assess its contribution to regulatory effectiveness. This is not to imply that the PIA was not also trying, like the SIB, to create a common discourse that could unite its various constituents. It instituted what was known as the Evolution Project to discuss with a wide range of stakeholders, including companies, the future direction of regulation, including the possible selective elimination and/or reduction of certain regulatory requirements.

Like LAUTRO, however, the PIA found that its success in certain fields was compromised by its failure in others. In particular, the PIA found itself enmeshed in the pensions-selling debacle. It took over responsibility from LAUTRO for ensuring that companies identified all potential losers from the scandal. Companies were supposed to identify all individuals concerned, write to them about the issue and then negotiate compensation with each individual where it proved necessary. Companies took varying attitudes towards the urgency of the process and progress reports revealed that only very small numbers were being compensated. From outside, journalists, consumer lobbyists and politicians found it easier to blame both the companies and the PIA for the delays. Failure to resolve the problem undermined the PIA's reputation in other areas.

The Labour opposition had made its dissatisfaction with the existing system clear from the early 1990s. As the 1997 election approached, it made clear its intention to do away with the fragmentation of regulation and supervision in the financial services industry. Soon after it became the government, it announced the creation of a single super-regulator, to be known as the Financial Services Authority, which was to take over the functions of the SIB and the SROs and the work of a number of other regulators, including part of the function of the Bank of England. What remains unclear (in 1998) is the way in which the authority sees its role. The Labour government is likely to look for increased consumer protection, perhaps along the lines of the PIA's regulatory effectiveness concepts, but it is also going to want to distance itself from old-style paternalism, making some adherence to market-based regulation likely. Commitment to greater education on financial issues is one way which has been discussed to link long-term change to 'informed choice' and competitive markets. Another has been to ring-fence certain types of products and make them 'fire proof' from bad selling by giving government approval to them so long as they follow a strictly defined set of government criteria. This is being considered for certain types of pensions, particularly amongst those with lower incomes and irregular patterns of labour market participation.

Regulatory bodies as organizations: concluding comments

The previous sections have examined how regulation has evolved. Our main argument is that this process can best be understood from the point of view of a range of organizations seeking to develop a role for themselves in a complex and changing environment where competition over jurisdictions and legitimations plays a central part. For the first few years, the regulatory bodies had a function but lacked a clear legitimation in the face of the claims of the industry to be trustworthy and regulation to be unnecessary. In the period following 1992, however, their freedom of action extended due to the delegitimation of the companies' accounts of the industry. LAUTRO, in conjunction with a number of industry insiders, was able to launch the TCI which has had a profound impact on the whole practice of selling and sales-force management. LAUTRO's freedom, however, remained constrained and especially on the issue of commissions, it could not release itself from the stifling embrace of its members. The SIB, on the other hand, used the freedom to construct a market-based view of regulation which offered the possibility of recreating a broad coalition amongst regulators, the government and the companies. The setting up of the PIA, however, muddied the waters again as the PIA itself articulated a vision of regulation which was more cautious and less market oriented than the SIB. Competition between the two emerged but the PIA's advocacy of more consumer involvement was undermined by its inability to solve the pension problem. The Labour opposition, frustrated by the organizational fragmentation and associated failures, advocated a single superregulator which in government it has now put in place. Quite how this will function is unclear at present (1998).

Company responses to regulation

At various points in the previous section, we have referred to the responses which companies have made to regulation and how this has shaped the regulatory space. In this section, we wish to extend this analysis by drawing on evidence collected at various times over the last ten years concerning the responses of companies to this process. Our discussion is based on three sources; first, a questionnaire survey plus a range of interviews conducted by one of the authors in the period 1988–90 (full details in Morgan and Knights 1990); second, a series of interviews conducted during 1995 on the Training and Competence Initiative and regulation more generally (reported in Morgan 1995b; Morgan 1996); and finally a questionnaire survey plus a range of interviews conducted by the present authors (Morgan and Soin 1997).

From denial to provisional acceptance

In the 1990 survey of companies regulated by LAUTRO, Morgan and Knights (1990) found that the way the FSA had been dealt with by the companies was negative from the beginning. Company responses to regulation were reflected, and indeed reproduced, by the structural location of compliance away from the major strategic functions of the organization. In over a quarter of the companies surveyed, responsibility for implementation was given to *one* person whose job it was to report to senior management. In many cases, it seems that this meant that one person was faced with keeping track of all the rules and changes of rules coming from LAUTRO and the SIB, interpreting their significance for the company and incorporating them into a compliance manual. Less than half the companies instituted decision-making structures that involved people from all parts of the company. Morgan and Knights (1990) stated that:

> People were involved on a 'need to know' basis derived from how much it was anticipated that a person's work would be affected by the LAUTRO rule book. This it was believed would 'minimise disruption' to the organization. In truth, what it did was to place the FSA outside the range of environmental forces that positively contribute to the construction of corporate strategy. Instead, FSA became part of an external set of constraining rules to which the company would comply through establishing administrative systems and internal policing procedures. Like other legal enactments, it was primarily a technical matter which the 'experts' (in this case Compliance Officers) had to make sure the rest of the organization did not transgress. Thus the enabling aspects of FSA were lost in a mire of regulatory detail.
>
> (Morgan and Knights 1990: 135)

Consequently, the compliance department was simply perceived as another tier of 'unproductive labour' – which was a cost on the rest of the workforce (in straight monetary terms). The results of this survey suggested that the FSA was treated mainly as an operational issue rather than a strategic one and its main importance was for those people who would have to operate its rules in detail. The FSA was seen as a constraint upon company operations. This reflected the way in which the debate on regulation was framed in the period 1988–92. As discussed previously, the companies argued that there was no need for the rules. Insofar as they had to comply, it was seen as unnecessary imposition.

As regulation moved beyond simple rule fixing towards more active involvement in key areas of company strategies, attitudes began to evolve. This was revealed in Morgan's (1995a) study on 'The costs and benefits of the Training and Competence Scheme (TCI)' in which managers in nine companies were interviewed with regard to the costs and benefits of the TCI. The findings showed that most companies had not undertaken any internal cost-benefit analysis of the TCI, arguing that assessing costs or benefits was not relevant because the TCI regulation was mandatory. Few companies considered the TCI regulation in a strategic light from the outset by assessing how it could be properly incorporated with their overall objectives. By the end of the implementation process, however, most companies did see that it was having a powerful impact on their overall strategy and structure through its cost impact on the economics of sales-force management.

A more general point which arose out of this research was the sense of a growing differentiation between and within companies as they responded in distinct ways to the challenges of regulation. Some company managements became more willing and able to articulate the advantages of the new regulations. In the sphere of training, some companies linked it clearly to ideas of professionalism amongst their workforce and the attempt to establish brand identity and brand differentiation as a highly compliant company. The broad delegitimation of the industry and the companies (which has been described earlier) became a potential means whereby some felt they could raise their own status and reputation. By aligning themselves closely with the ideal of a professionalized industry, these companies hoped to renew bonds of trust and reputation with customers as well as cultivating more consultative and cooperative relations with the regulators. Other companies were either unwilling or unable to make this transition and instead made a pragmatic adjustment to the immediate demands of the regulators without fundamentally overhauling their structures and cultures.

These arguments linked to the idea of 'compliance culture' referred to earlier – that is, the values and beliefs about the purpose and significance of regulation which have developed inside companies and how these are communicated and reinforced. The compliance culture acts as a framework through which decisions about operational processes are conducted. Interviews conducted during 1996 revealed an increasing differentiation between those companies explicitly espousing a 'positive compliance culture' and those which lacked managerial direction (Morgan 1996). The study illustrated that some firms are attempting to build regulation into the overall strategic and decision-making process and have moved away from treating regulation as just an operational issue. Two alternative models of compliance culture were identified. The first model was 'good compliance/good business', which emphasized high compliance standards in the long-term belief this will create better business performance. The second was a 'pragmatic adjustment model', which posited a fundamental gap between everyday business activity and compliance behaviour. Emphasis was placed on minimizing cost and disruption to existing business practice.

The perspective underlying the 'good compliance/good business' model was that the regulatory structure is seen as mirroring what good business should be like anyway. Training of representatives, disclosure of information and cooling-off periods, for example, are all considered part of good business practice. Therefore compliance should be integrated as part of the business as a whole. It is a part of the business concerned with good practice and quality; its role lies in providing advice on how this can be achieved in the light of the regulatory constraints. In the 'pragmatic adjustment model', the over-riding responsibility of the compliance department is to make sure that the company does not get into trouble with the regulators. It therefore primarily acts as a check on what the business part of the organization is doing. Compliance is an 'overhead' and a burden imposed by an external body. Expenditure on compliance is therefore directly taking away from 'the bottom line'. In such a culture it is generally the case that management will be involved in a 'damage-limitation' exercise, reducing to an acceptable minimum the impact of compliance constraints on their business strategy, goals and performance. The compliance department may relate to this culture in a number of ways. It may itself be thoroughly imbued with the same ideas or it may resist and demand that the company go further than some of its managers may want. These two models were treated as extreme positions and it was expected that most companies would be situated on a continuum somewhere between these two.

These studies showed that there were changes occurring in companies which reflected and reacted upon the regulatory context itself. The industry was becoming more differentiated in its responses to regulation. However, even this underestimates the range of diversity as shown in the results to a survey conducted of sixteen companies during 1997 (full details are available in Morgan and Soin 1997). This showed that within each company there were a range of different responses to regulation affected particularly by the degree of involvement in the sales process. Those involved in sales were least likely to be sympathetic to regulation whilst those in other functions (such as compliance, marketing or administration) were more willing to be positive about the purpose and impact of regulation.

In terms of the system as a whole, there is no doubt that the industry is now highly committed to the principles that underlie it: 97 per cent either agreed or strongly agreed with the statement that 'The FSA was necessary to provide investors with greater confidence in the financial services industry'; 91 per cent disagreed with the statement that 'the FSA has failed to provide any benefits to consumers'; 88 per cent also agreed that 'the FSA has made the industry much more professional'; and 96 per cent agreed that 'the FSA has led to improved training for people in the industry'. There are, however, concerns about the impact of the FSA both for the survey as a whole and for the different categories of employees. Overall, 38 per cent disagreed with the statement that 'the FSA has succeeded in improving the image and reputation of the financial services industry'. A similar number responded to the statement that 'the FSA has succeeded in cleaning up the industry'; 37 per cent disagreed with this statement. The results showed that the sales managers in the independent financial advice (IFA) companies are significantly less confident about the FSA's success in this respect than are company sales forces. Only 40 per cent of the IFA sales managers agreed with this statement compared to 58 per cent of sales people. Concern about the impact of the FSA was also related to the respondents' feelings about their own status and careers. For example, 35 per cent agreed with the following statement that 'the FSA treats us all like potential fraudsters and crooks'. Again for the individual categories of employees 50 per cent of both sales managers in IFA offices and FSA-authorised sales staff agreed. Significantly only 22 per cent of head office staff agreed with this statement reflecting the argument referred to previously that throughout the survey the head office staff were generally much more positive and supportive of the regulatory system than any of the other groupings.

In response to the statement 'the FSA has led to improved career prospects for people in the industry', 44 per cent of respondents disagreed whilst 21 per cent also agreed with the view that 'the FSA has made it more difficult to earn a decent living from selling regulated products'; 62 per cent supported the view that 'the FSA has led to increased costs which are passed on to the consumers'. These responses indicate that although our respondents accepted the broad principles of the FSA, there was a substantial minority who felt that it was failing in some of its main tasks. This dissatisfaction was reflected in concerns about the impact which the Act has had on the status, career prospects and earnings potential of people in the industry and is most visible in the responses of the IFA sales managers and the sales people. When it came to assessing how the regulators themselves worked, there were again a number of areas of concern. The most positive attitudes to the workings of the PIA occurred in response to two general queries: 76 per cent agreed that 'the PIA is basically doing a good job', whilst 80 per cent agreed that 'the PIA's monitoring system is fair'. In other areas, however, there was more implied criticism of the PIA and the way in which it was working: 30 per cent agreed with the statement that 'membership of the PIA pushes up our costs unnecessarily and therefore adversely affects our customers'; 36 per cent disagreed with the statement that 'the PIA's monitoring system is effective'; 32 per cent also disagreed with the statement that 'the PIA has helped everybody to reach professional standards of training and competence'. This criticism was most powerfully expressed by the IFA manager responses, with almost 50 per cent agreeing with the above three questions. When it came to assessing the relative rigidity of the PIA and how it operated, responses were almost evenly split on the relevant two questions: 43 per cent agreed that 'the PIA involves itself in too much internal company detail' and 52 per cent agreed that 'the PIA is too rigid in its interpretation of rules' – 66 per cent of IFA sales managers agreed with this compared with just 44 per cent of head office staff. It is clear that the IFA sales managers are more critical of the impact of the PIA on costs and bureaucratic rigidity. These analyses also generally point to a gap in perception between sales forces and the people who manage them. For example, 59 per cent of appointed representatives' (AR) sales managers agree that 'the PIA monitoring system is effective' compared with 67 per cent of salespeople. Similarly, 58 per cent of sales managers agree that 'the FSA has succeeded in cleaning up the industry', whilst 68 per cent of the people they manage agree.

Support for the statement that 'good compliance is good business' was very high and varies only between 96 per cent (for the salespeople and the head office staff) and 100 per cent (for the IFA sales managers). There was also a generally high level of agreement with the statement that 'the compliance department is an essential part of the team when it comes to any significant decision-making in our organization'. Responses varied from 86 per cent agreement amongst sales managers to 93 per cent agreement amongst head office staff. However, when presented with more specific questions, variation began to be revealed. For example, in response to the statement that 'the compliance department does all it can to ensure that we get on with our business within the rules', 88 per cent of head office staff agreed but only 65 per cent of sales managers. There was also a wide degree of variation in response to the statement that 'the compliance department is more concerned to make sure that they keep on the right side of the PIA than to help us to develop our business'; this statement was supported by 69 per cent of sales managers and 68 per cent of the sales force. This indicates that the difficult task of creating a unified compliance culture was not yet achieved, reflected further in the fact that, overall, head office staff disagreed with this statement.

There were also differences in response to the statement that 'the compliance department is approachable and willing to help if there are any regulatory issues'; 90 per cent of head office staff and 89 per cent of IFA sales managers agreed, compared with only 80 per cent of sales managers in other companies and 81 per cent of the salespeople in the sample. Sales managers were also the most likely to be satisfied with communications from compliance. In response to the statement that 'compliance communicates with us in legalistic and obscure documents which are impossible to understand', 76 per cent of sales people and 80 per cent of sales managers disagreed. When asked whether they agreed that 'compliance is essentially a business prevention unit', 97 per cent of IFA sales managers disagreed, compared with 81 per cent of sales managers in other companies. The role of the compliance department was also considered in relation to the nature of the business being undertaken. Two questions revealed some interesting differences between the groups. When presented with the statement 'compliance is concerned to help us as individuals improve the quality of our business', only 72 per cent of sales managers agreed compared with 84 per cent of head office staff. There were also small differences between these two groups in response to the statement that 'compliance requirements make it almost impossible to meet our individual sales performance targets'; whereas 88 per cent of sales managers disagreed, 92 per cent of head office staff and 95 per cent of IFA sales managers disagreed.

In response to the statement 'our sales training emphasizes the positive aspects of the regulatory system for improving sales performance', 78 per cent of sales people agreed, whilst only 67 per cent of sales managers did so. We also asked 'how often have people from the compliance function been in attendance at your training sessions?': 75 per cent of sales managers reported that people from compliance have rarely been in attendance; 43 per cent of the sales force reported that they had sometimes been in attendance. On the question of whether regulatory issues have been significant in their training sessions, 60 per cent of sales managers reported that they had, compared with 77 per cent of salespeople. Finally, there was an interesting response to the statement 'in our training, compliance issues are dealt with separately from selling skills'. Again, this question was designed to tap the notion of integration; the more the two are dealt with as part of the same process, the more likely that there will be overall integration between business and compliance, thus creating a mutually reinforcing positive compliance culture. However, the results indicate that this did not accord with how the respondents saw their experience, as only 49 per cent of sales managers agreed with this statement, whilst 71 per cent of sales force respondents agreed. The degree of integration is further revealed by responses to questions on feedback from fact-finds during the training period. Sales managers, for example, were asked their views on the statement 'feedback on fact-finds is always presented in a constructive and helpful manner'. Whilst 57 per cent of them did agree with the statement, 43 per cent disagreed, indicating a high level of concern with the sort of feedback which was being given to people on training programmes: 90 per cent of sales people agreed that they had received constructive feedback from their sales managers compared with only 49 per cent who agreed that they had received constructive feedback from the compliance department.

The survey also examined attitudes towards disclosure. This can be considered under a number of headings. With regard to status disclosure, there was a high level of agreement with the statement that 'status disclosure is an essential part of the regulatory system' (95 per cent of sales managers and 93 per cent of salespeople agreed) and an even higher rate of agreement with the statement that 'it is important that the client knows exactly whom we represent and what we are authorized to sell' (99 per cent of sales managers and salespeople). In response to the statement 'nobody really understands the difference between being an IFA and an appointed representative', 75 per cent of sales managers and 79 per cent of sales people disagreed. This shows a rather surprising level of confidence in the knowledge and understanding of the general public, particularly since it is generally agreed that there is 'public confusion over "polarisation"' as the PIA's Consumer Panel Report in 1996 noted and reinforced in 1997 when its survey found that 33 per cent of the sample thought that 'a bank is the best place to get independent financial advice'. If the respondents were confident that the distinction between an IFA and an appointed representative was clear to people, they were less so about the PIA itself. In response to the statement that 'most people have never heard of the PIA', 70 per cent of sales managers and 52 per cent of sales people agreed.

With regard to the disclosure of information more generally, there was a great deal of concern. For example, when confronted with the statement that 'people do not understand all the information which we have to give them now: it just confuses them', 71 per cent of sales managers, 75 per cent of the salespeople and 96 per cent of IFA sales managers agreed. Criticism of the disclosure system is also reflected in responses to the statement 'full disclosure of expenses and their impact on projected values is a positive benefit to the consumer': 56 per cent of sales managers, IFA sales managers and salespeople agreed with the statement, meaning that a substantial minority in each case disagreed. The concern with full disclosure was also reflected in the response to the statement 'I do not understand why we have to give clients so much technical information which they will not read': 36 per cent of sales managers and 37 per cent of sales people agreed with this statement.

Regulation and companies: differentiation, legitimation and compliance

The results indicate that in spite of the regulatory system being in operation for nearly ten years and the efforts of the PIA to get closer to the industry through means such as the Evolution Project, there is still some way to go to get the practitioners who face the day-to-day reality of regulation entirely behind the system. There are substantial minorities who are critical of the way the system works and the regulators who operate it. On the positive side, there is on almost every issue a majority of respondents who are supportive of the system and the regulators. The results show that the IFA sales managers and the salespeople appeared to be more sensitive to potential criticism, whilst the head office staff are more supportive of the FSA and the PIA. It may be argued that this is the group which is least affected by the actual operation of the system and therefore are naturally likely to be least critical. However, this raises an interesting issue inside particular companies about the range of attitudes which may exist. In an extreme case, it may be that the views of the two groups may be directly in conflict with consequent problems for managing the organization as a whole. A similar problem arises from the gap in perception between sales forces and their management, though this gap is not as wide as that between the IFA sales managers and the other groups. In some areas, there is a definite difference between sales managers and their sales forces. These findings show the difficulty of defining a unified industry attitude towards regulation. They are even more crucial when considered in the context of particular companies where differences of perception may contribute to the difficulty of creating and sustaining a unified compliance culture, should management want to do so. There is clearly a substantial minority who are critical of aspects of the system's operation.

Conclusion: regulation and organizations

This chapter has presented what we termed the organizational approach to regulation. Within the regulatory space of personal financial services, a process of evolution has occurred. In our view, this cannot be understood from an economic point of view (i.e. towards a more efficient system) or from a 'regulatory capture' point of view. The regulatory space is inhabited by organizations. Some of them, such as the regulatory bodies, are new; others, such as the companies, are old. We have sought to show that the organizational dynamics within and between organizations affects the direction of regulation.

With regard to dynamics between organizations, we have concentrated on the inter-relationships between the regulatory bodies themselves and also their relationship with member companies. Uncertainties about the nature and process of regulation have led to differing responses from these organizations. We have emphasized in particular that the different positions of SIB, LAUTRO and the PIA were reflected in the ideas and practices about regulation that became dominant within those organizations. These practices interacted with those of the companies and led to attempts to legitimate a certain approach to regulation and its function. In the early stages of these debates, the regulatory bodies were on the defensive against the companies and were caught between on the one hand appeasing the companies by reducing regulatory overload and, on the other hand, satisfying government and the general public that they were delivering on regulation. The gradual delegitimation of the industry's views opened a space in which the regulators could construct their own discourse of regulation. The SIB moved towards a market-based model, whilst PIA was more open to consumer interests. Various concepts of regulation were put forward in order to solidify a legitimate regulatory space. In the end, all of these foundered because of the intransigence of the industry and its rapid fall in reputation and esteem as a result of mounting scandals, most particularly the pensions mis-selling. This made it easy for the Labour government to implement its plan for a single super-regulator with no dissent, though it remains unclear actually how this will work.

This intransigence was further revealed in the second part of the chapter which illustrated the extent of disinterest in regulation from its origin. Disinterest gradually turned to involvement as some companies saw the advantages which they might gain from certain forms of regulation. Thus a process of differentiation occurred in the industry, providing the regulators with well-placed supporters at particular moments. This differentiation has occurred between companies and within companies. Some companies have sought to build close links with the regulators as part of a strategy to re-establish respect and reputation. Within all companies, however, there remains resistance to regulation.

What lessons does this have for the wider study of regulation? Our argument at this point is relatively simple. Regulation is delivered through organizations and involves the compliance of other organizations. The study of organizations generally emphasizes that they are arenas of conflict and competition. In order to understand the evolution of regulatory regimes and systems, therefore, it is necessary to understand how these organizational processes are impacting. By looking at regulatory systems from an organizational point of view, we see that the impact and outcome of regulation are uncertain and ambiguous. They evolve as actors (both individual and organizational) and compete within the regulatory space for power and resources. The study of regulation is therefore inevitably a study of how organizations within that space work.

References

Clarke, M. (1986) *Regulating the City*, Milton Keynes: Open University Press.

Department of Trade and Industry (1992) *Checking the Cost to Business: A Guide to Compliance Cost Assessment*, London: DTI.

—— (1994) *Thinking About Regulating: A Guide to Good Regulation*, London: DTI

Deregulation Initiative (1996a) *Checking the Cost to Business: A Guide to Compliance Cost Assessment*, London: HMSO.

—— (1996b) *Good Regulation: A Checklist*, London: HMSO.

—— (1996c) *Regulation in the Balance: A Guide to Regulatory Appraisal Incorporating Risk Assessment*, London: HMSO.

Hancher, L. and Moran, M. (1989) 'Organizing regulatory space', in L. Hancher and M. Moran (eds) *Capitalism, Culture and Economic Regulation*, Oxford: The Clarendon Press.

Knights, D. (1997) 'Governmentality and financial services: welfare crises and the financially self-disciplined subject', in G. Morgan and D. Knights (eds) *Regulation and De-regulation in European Financial Services*, London: Macmillan.

Knights, D. and Morgan, G. (1990) 'Management control in sales forces: a case study from the labour process of life insurance', *Work, Employment and Society* 4(3): 369–89.

Moran, M. (1991) *The Politics of Financial Service Revolution*, London: Macmillan.

Morgan, G. (1994) 'Problems of integration in bancassurance', *Service Industries Journal* 14(2): 153–69.

—— (1995a) 'The costs and benefits of the Training and Competence Scheme', report prepared for the Financial Services Forum, UMIST, May.

—— (1995b) 'The costs and benefits of regulation', report prepared for the Financial Services Forum, UMIST, November.

—— (1996) 'Compliance culture and effectiveness', report prepared for the Financial Services Forum, UMIST, April.

Morgan, G. and Knights, D. (1990) 'The Financial Services Act: the origins, development and future of a regulatory regime', final report presented to TSB/UMIST Joint Board, November.

—— (1991) 'Constructing consumers and consumer protection: the case of the life insurance industry in the UK', in R. Burrows and C. Marsh (eds) *Consumption and Class,* London: Macmillan.

Morgan, G. and Soin, K. (1997) 'Attitudes to regulation and compliance', report prepared for the Financial Services Forum, UMIST, November.

Office of Fair Trading (1993a) *The Marketing and Sale of Investment Linked Insurance Products,* London: OFT.

—— (1993b) *Fair Trading and Life Assurance Products,* London: OFT.

Office of Management and Budget (1991) *Guidelines for Regulatory Impact Analysis,* Washington, DC: Executive Office of the President.

Personal Investment Authority (1995) *Regulatory Plan: First Year,* London: PIA.

—— (1996) *Consumer Panel Report,* London: PIA.

10 Regulation in network industries

Staffan Hultén and Claes-Frederik Helgesson

Introduction

Over the last decade, network industries in most industrial countries have been subjected to processes of regulation and change. Sectors such as telecommunications, transport, electricity, gas and water share the characteristic that they involve the establishment of a single network. To lay two electricity or telephone cables to the same house may be competitive but it is expensive. In the past, network industries tended to be perceived as 'natural monopolies', i.e. there could be only one network owner and manager. Since they were 'natural monopolies', they were also inevitably highly regulated and often state owned. In the last decade, however, these 'natural monopolies' have been dismantled in many countries by a combination of privatization and deregulation designed to bring the competitive forces of the market into the sector. Why has this occurred? Explanations can be divided into two categories. The first category, which we refer to as the 'technological determinist approach', points to the emergence of new technologies which remove certain key characteristics that explained the natural monopoly of a network industry. This explanation has perhaps been most widely offered to explain and justify changes in telecommunications where the advance of mobile phones, digital technology and fibre-optic cable systems have challenged the traditional technological bases of the state-owned telecom operators. The second category, which we refer to as the 'political voluntarist' approach, focuses on the advantages of market-mediated transactions as opposed to firm internal transactions. Thus 'natural monopolies' have been seen as inefficient and unresponsive to their customers' requirements. Devising ways of breaking them into parts has therefore become the stock-in-trade of the purveyors of free-market liberalism in politics, the media and the banking system.

In this paper, we examine these two approaches to regulatory change in more detail. We argue that neither is adequate to understanding the processes of change in network industries. We illustrate our argument by reference to two case studies of regulatory change. The first examines the emergence of a single monopoly in Swedish telecommunications in the early twentieth century; the second case considers recent developments in the regulation of the Swedish rail transport system. The cases reveal the complexity of the processes which are involved in regulating and deregulating network industries. In particular, they reveal that the internal logic of existing regulatory regimes shapes the way in which technological changes or shifts in political ideology impact on new forms of regulation.

Reconsidering explanations of 'deregulation'

What are the assumptions and viewpoints underlying technological determinist and political voluntarist explanations of regulatory change? Let us first consider the technological determinist kind of explanations: *The industry was forced into a reregulatory process due to pressures caused by new emerging technologies.* This kind of technological determinist explanation is often used with reference to the idea of natural monopolies. The idea of natural monopolies assumes that certain industries, and the technologies employed in these industries, have inherent qualities which makes monopoly the only possible form for organizing the industry. The economist Richard Ely, who is said to have coined the concept of natural monopoly, identified three classes of natural monopoly when classified according to the source of monopoly power. The three classes were: 'I. Those arising from some special limitation of the supply of raw material. II. Those arising from secrecy. III. Those arising from peculiar properties inherent in the business' (Ely *et al.* 1923: 184–5; cf. also Ely 1900). He provided a long list of monopolies that according to him belonged to category III:

> By far the most important of all monopolies are natural monopolies of the third class, arising from peculiar *properties inherent in the business.* Among such monopolies are roads and streets, canals, docks, bridges and ferries, waterways, harbors, light-houses, railways, telegraphs, the post office, electric lighting, waterworks, gas works, and street railways of all kinds.
>
> (Ely *et al.* 1923: 187, original emphasis)

Later scholars have often offered the existence of substantial economies of scale as one fundamental property of natural monopoly. Bain, for example, states:

> In certain industries economies of increasing scale are realised for expansion of the firm up to such a point that the whole market would be fully supplied by a single firm before it had reached its lowest-cost or optimum size. Such an industry may be called a 'natural monopoly,' and the firm in question may never grow big enough to encounter the ultimate upturn in its long-run average cost curve.
>
> (Bain 1952: 113–14)

Hence the technological determinist explanation of reregulation of network industries often refers to the ways in which new technologies have changed the 'properties inherent in the business' in such a way as to make the industry acquire or lose the qualities necessary to make it a natural monopoly. There are, however, at least two major problems behind this kind of reasoning. First, it treats technological change as completely exogenous. Technological change is simply viewed as a compelling force coming from nowhere, yet having the power to force large industrial systems into major transformations. Second, and related to the first point, it assumes production technologies – the emerging ones as well as the old prevailing ones – as having inherent properties which are independent of the socioeconomic context in which they are employed.

Voluntaristic explanations tend to assume that an industry can be forced into deregulation and reregulation due to political pressures caused by changes in dominant ideologies. In the recent period, the distrust in government intervention and faith in the power of the market has had clear implications for regulatory processes. Regulatory change tends to become a highly political issue, and it is impossible to deny the political influence on the outcome of a regulatory change. However, this perspective depends on a voluntaristic view that ignores the resistance to change that is inbuilt within large industrial systems.

Although utterly different in important respects, the technological determinist and political voluntarist explanations of regulatory change share one important common feature. They both explain such change by arguing that the decisive force emerges outside of the industry. This ignores what may be termed the 'endogenous' evolution of industries and their regulatory structures.

Regulatory regimes and path dependency

Existing industry structures (or what Commons referred to as 'going concerns' (Commons 1974)) are upheld by rules – today we would perhaps say standards, norms or regulations. These rules constitute a regulatory regime, which in effect promotes certain industrial activities and inhibits others. It creates a 'path dependency'; activities and technological developments follow a certain trajectory, reproducing an industry's 'peculiar properties'. From this perspective, it could be argued that the 'natural technology' implicit in the notion of natural monopolies is as much an effect of a monopoly as its cause. As Capron and Noll noted in 1971, 'many services normally regarded as natural monopolies have remained natural monopolies only because of the interaction between regulation and technological change' (Capron and Noll 1971: 222).

The notion that there is a path-dependent evolution in regulatory regimes can be linked to March's distinction between exploratory and exploitative activities (March 1991). March uses these concepts to discuss certain problems of maintaining a balance between the two in the context of organizations. However, it is also relevant to the discussion of regulation. Under a 'going concern' regime, the exploitation of known economies of scale and scope will be favoured and any exploitation of new commercial and technical opportunities will similarly be adjusted to the regime's prevailing logic. Therefore the drive towards the exploitation of the existing rules will dominate over the exploration of new ones, though this means that certain underexplored entrepreneurial opportunities will arise. But the exploration of new ideas does not suffice for successful innovations. The old has to leave room for the new. The success of the new technology or of the new regulation depends on the possibilities of finding a transition path whereby gradually the new can replace the old. A critical factor in this process is the actors' perception of the switching costs. The following case studies of specific network industries at particular times in their evolution examine the interaction between the path-dependent evolution of the sector and the new possibilities that emerge.

Exploitation, crisis and reregulation in Swedish telephony

From competition to a 'natural monopoly'

Between the late 1890s and 1918, Swedish telephony was dominated by the state-owned Telegraph Administration and privately owned Stockholm Telephone Co. (for further details see Helgesson 1995, 1998). In 1918, the two were merged under the dominance of the state-owned Telegraph Administration, which from this point onwards had a *de facto* monopoly in Swedish telephony. The Telegraph Administration was the larger of the two companies and had telephone switches all around the country interconnected through an extensive interurban network. From 1891, Stockholm Telephone Co. had been confined to operating within an area defined by a 70-kilometre radius from the centre of Stockholm. In early 1910, it had about 54,400 telephone sets within its network, while the Telegraph Administration had about 26,800 telephones within the same area. In total, this area contained more than 81,000 telephone sets, which represented more than a third of all telephone sets in the country. The competition between the two operators had been intense for two decades, especially in efforts to recruit new subscribers, a competition that had resulted in substantially lower tariffs in the Stockholm area than in other parts of Sweden. This competition had become even fiercer after the connection between the two networks was broken on 1 June 1903, following a failure to agree on new tariffs for interconnected traffic, and the Swedish parliament's rejection of a negotiated state acquisition of the private network. In this regime of 'dual service', the two telephone operators competed intensely to enrol new subscribers, since their stock of subscribers defined the extent of the service which they could provide (see

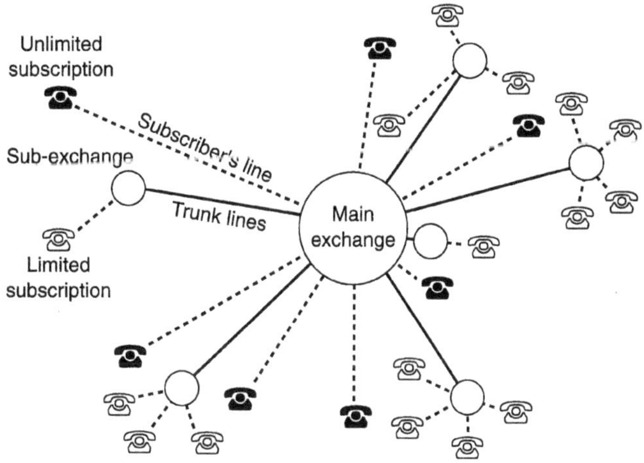

Figure 10.1 Outline of the network principles used in particular by Stockholm Telephone Co.

Mueller 1997 for a discussion of dual service in the USA in the period 1894–1920). However, expansion under these circumstances put strong financial pressure on both companies. Tariffs were kept low in order to attract customers whilst operating costs increased. The reason for this was that a larger network implied larger and more complex manual switches and an increased number of switches as the network grew above the maximum capacity of a single exchange. The greater the number of exchanges, the greater the number of trunk calls, i.e. calls which required at least two operators for their completion (as they required switching between two exchanges). In short, as the networks grew, the number of telephone calls switched per operator and hour tended to decrease, increasing operating costs (cf. Mueller 1989).

Stockholm Telephone, which had the larger network in Stockholm, had devised several practices to manage this situation in which growth was both necessary and problematic. To enrol new kinds of subscribers, the company had offered several kinds of subscriptions since the competition with Telegraph Administration had begun. Along with high-priced subscriptions which allowed for an unlimited number of local calls free of charge, it had gradually introduced several types of subscriptions which only allowed for a limited number of local calls free of charge. In its Stockholm network it had further wired all subscribers who paid for an unlimited number of free calls directly to the main exchange. Other subscribers were, on the other hand, wired to the nearest sub-exchange which in turn was connected to the main exchange with a number of trunk lines (see Figure 10.1). In this way, the company reasoned, it was able to provide a

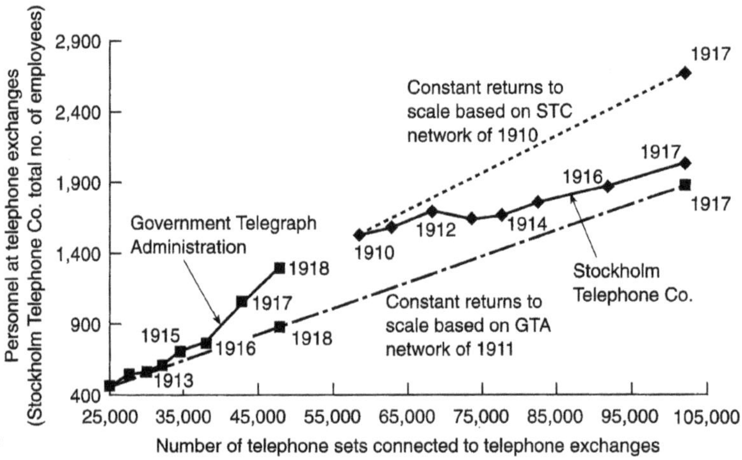

Figure 10.2 Number of employees in the two telephone networks in Stockholm during the last years of competition (Helgesson 1995).

good service to the primarily business subscribers who were heavy callers, and at the same time to some extent reduce the expensive practice of trunk calls. Beginning in 1907, the company had moreover begun to refurbish its network to a new manual switching system, and in 1913 it employed some automatic devices at its main exchange to further increase the number of calls each operator could switch in one hour. The elaboration of the company's commercial and technical practices were intimately intertwined with one another and were moreover heavily contingent on the competitive situation in Stockholm.

These changes enabled the Stockholm Telephone Co. to improve its productivity between 1910 and 1917 (see Figure 10.2, showing that the number of employees per telephone set decreased in this period, compared with what might have been expected had the 1910 productivity level been maintained). Although the Telegraph Administration gradually began to mimic some of the practices of Stockholm Telephone Co., the changes it introduced were less significant and it found its productivity declining rather than rising (Figure 10.2).

What was the government's role in this governance regime of dual service? The so-called 'telephone issue' had been up in parliament three times. In 1901 the parliament had rejected a proposition whereby the Telegraph Administration was to acquire the private network. In 1904 it had rejected a proposition whereby the two competitors would divide Stockholm into two geographically defined monopolies. Finally, in 1906 it had rejected another proposition for the acquisition of the private network. On all three occasions the two competitors had come to an agreement, but parliament had refused to support and fund them. On a few other occasions discussions between the two competing operators were stopped before they reached parliament. Apart from discussing solutions similar to the ones that had reached parliament, they also at one time discussed an agreement for regulating the enrolment of new subscribers between the two networks in combination with a plan for interconnection and coordination of tariffs. The government, however, never proposed legislation for mandatory interconnection. The city council in Stockholm, on the other hand, had for several years attempted to force the operators to reach an agreement on interconnection. To enforce its demands, the city council had used its control over the city streets disallowing the operators from using the streets for running cables as long as there was no interconnection agreement. In 1907 the council had given up on this demand, but it had still required the operators to agree not to increase any fees if they wanted to use the streets.

The regime of monopoly after 1918

The creation of a *de facto* monopoly through an acquisition of Stockholm Telephone Co. was not the only solution of the 'telephone issue' considered since 1903, but it was the solution that finally passed through parliament. In 1918 the Telegraph Administration received parliament's approval to acquire its competitor and Swedish telephony entered into an era of state-owned monopoly. The losses made by the Administration's Stockholm network as well as the possibility of increasing government revenues helped in tipping the balance in favour of an acquisition. Parallel with the physical merger of the two Stockholm networks, the Administration accelerated its efforts to automate the network. The enlarged Stockholm network had become a problem to which automatic switching was put forward as the appropriate solution. In a request for funding sent to the government in 1919, the Administration argued that the introduction of automatic switches was necessary for several reasons. Automation was necessary to merge the two networks, to fulfil public expectations of the merger, as well as to convince the public that it would not have been better served by a non-state business enterprise. In other words, automatic switches were portrayed as necessary to justify the politically supported acquisition of the year before. From 1924 the Stockholm network was automated, drastically decreasing the need for the predominantly female operators used in the manual switching exchanges. The industry gradually acquired properties based on the achievement of economies of scale (see Figure 10.3). With automation, the practice of gathering all heavy callers into one main exchange was abolished, since trunk calls no longer incurred higher switching costs. The tariff structure was moreover gradually redefined during the following decades, and moved towards fewer kinds of subscriptions and more emphasis on metered calls.

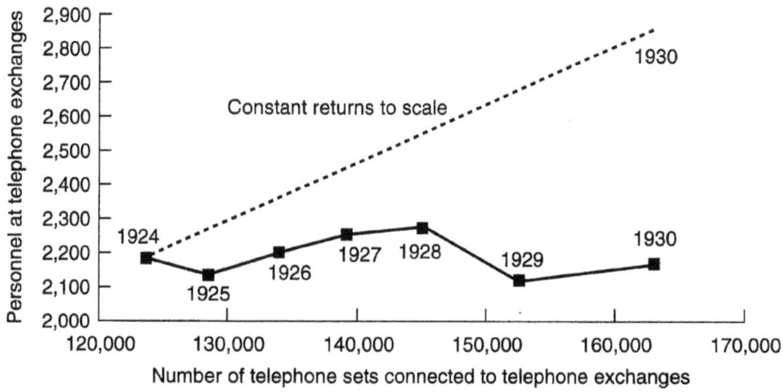

Figure 10.3 Number of employees in the Stockholm telephone network as automatic switches are gradually introduced (Helgesson 1995).

If Swedish telecommunications ever was a case of 'natural' monopoly, it is safe to say that it entered such a state *after* the actual monopoly was in place. Whereas the regime of competition with 'dual service' promoted a rapid diffusion of telephony (as the two operators competed to extend the number of subscribers, almost irrespective of the costs), the regime of a state-controlled monopoly provided the environment in which investments could be made in technology that promoted large economies of scale. Once the investments (and the network) were in place, the state telephone company possessed a 'natural monopoly' but, contrary to expectations, this only came after a *de facto* monopoly had been formed and not before! Moreover, this pattern is not entirely unique to Swedish telecommunications. In the US, AT&T was for a long time reluctant to introduce automatic switches. It was only in 1919, when it was on the verge of regaining a virtual monopoly, that it began to introduce them into its network (see e.g. Lipartito 1989).

The period before the state monopoly was characterized by massive efforts to exploit the possibilities of the manual switching technology, while enlarging the number of subscribers. The layout of the physical network, the large number of subscriptions and the introduction of new kinds of manual switches were all efforts focused on diminishing the diseconomies of scale that were arising. The efforts were effective in important respects; the number of subscribers increased rapidly, and at least Stockholm Telephone Co. managed to maintain an albeit small profit. The monopolization implied a shift of focus. The automatic switching technologies were already being explored before the monopolization, but these efforts were augmented after 1918. With the emerging exploitation of these technologies, changes in tariff structures followed.

Before 1918, growth was the overarching objective pursued by both companies. This proved successful in encouraging a proliferation of telephones. But there were limits to this growth. In fact, it was the impetus of the successful expansion of the telephone networks that finally pushed the regime into a crisis. A proponent of the technological determinist view could say that the crisis simply was the result of the limits of manual switching technology, but such an analysis misses the point that the incessant striving for growth was a consequence of the competitive regime of 'dual service'. Indeed, the operators tried to handle the problems emerging in their growing networks in several ways. Apart from elaborating their switches, the operators also sought to reduce the very need for rapid growth by trying to negotiate cartel agreements, but these were outlawed by the politicians. The emerging problems in the prevailing regime gradually initiated as many efforts to explore new regime alternatives as they propelled efforts to explore new technological possibilities. In the end, the creation of a monopoly became the solution approved by all necessary parties, including the Swedish parliament.

This account goes against the notions embedded in the concept of a 'natural monopoly'. According to the concept of a natural monopoly, a monopoly is forced upon the actors when excessive economies of scale inherent in the employed technology makes competition unsustainable. The prevailing manual switching technology took part in producing the crisis of the regime of dual service, but it was clearly not any inherent economies of scale of the manual switching technology that created the new monopolistic governance regime. The concurrent emergence of new automatic switching technologies could artificially save the argument that the monopoly indeed was created by forces implied by the natural monopoly. But to do this we would have to leave several matters out of account, most importantly that the new automatic switching technologies had nothing to do with the escalating crisis of the prevailing regime. Indeed, there is no evidence that promises of automatic switching technology were used to justify the creation of a monopoly prior to the actual monopolization. The initial Swedish efforts to explore the possibilities of automatic switching technologies were as conditioned by the emerging crisis, as were the efforts to alter the governance arrangements. With the monopoly in place, the further exploration and exploitation of these technologies were to a significant degree shaped by the demands of the new monopolist regime. Over time, the gains from the exploitation of automatic electromechanical switching made the monopolist regime durable as well as less prone to explore new technological and commercial possibilities.

In this case, technology neither plays the role of an autonomous force pressing for change, nor appears as completely subservient to the demands of a prevailing regime. Established technologies are entrenched physical imprints of the prevailing regulatory regime. Technology may indeed be seen as the physical appearance of the ensemble of arrangements (Bijker 1995: 273) that together make up a regulatory regime. The focus on exploitation within the prevailing ensemble of arrangements will sooner or later produce a situation of crisis where new arrangements are explored. This view tries to appreciate the concurrence of changes in technology and regulation, while avoiding interpretations which give technology and technological change the autonomous power to make or break regulatory regimes.

The reregulation of the Swedish railways

The second case we wish to consider involves the role of political intervention in a network industry. The operation of railway networks was believed to be a case of 'natural monopoly' because of significant economies of scale and network externalities. However, during the 1980s, researchers and politicians started to argue that the vertically integrated railway monopoly could be replaced by a disintegrated railway network with competition between firms controlling the rolling stock and firms competing for the railway traffic. The economic and political argument is that the old system, albeit having some advantages, has become obsolete and needs to be replaced by a more efficient structure. From the 1990s, many European countries began to deregulate the railway system in order to introduce a new structure. There were two main steps in the change process. First, the vertically integrated state railway monopoly was to be divided into two parts – one in charge of the railway operation, the other in charge of the infrastructure. Once this had been achieved, it was possible to conceive of other companies competing for routes on the railway timetable against the former state monopoly. However, this process of change need not necessarily be driven by political ideology; the case of the Swedish railway system reveals a more serendipitous process unfolding as the Swedish state sought to find solutions to the problem of the incumbent monopolist Swedish state railways (referred to hereafter as SJ).

During the 1970s, the financial position of the state railways in Sweden was a matter of extreme concern. In an attempt to confront those demanding high subsidies with the financial consequences of their action, the Transport Policy Act of 1979 was passed. It decentralized the control of the local and regional public transport, with the establishment of the County Public Transport Authorities (CPTAs) in Sweden's twenty-four counties. The Act gave the local authorities – the county council and the county's local municipality councils – a formal and all-encompassing responsibility for local public transportation (Nilsson 1995: 175). An advantage of the new structure was that some of the interest groups that opposed branch-line closures got the financial responsibility for these lines. To ease the transition the Act introduced a more complex subsidy system in the railway sector. The state had previously only paid subsidies to cover part of the state railway operator's capital costs and to postpone line closures. With the new system, the CPTAs were to receive a state subsidy that gradually diminished during five years in return for taking charge of some of the local and regional railway services.

The 1979 Transport Policy Act was not sufficient to make SJ profitable and did not address the need for innovation in the railway system. SJ's railway operations were in a vicious circle: the lack of profitability forced the firm to close lines and to postpone new investments which resulted in fewer passengers and high levels of discontent amongst customers which reinforced the profitability problem. A number of political decisions aimed at solving these problems were taken in the 1980s. In 1981 the Swedish parliament financially guaranteed the purchase of a fleet of high-speed trains (Flink and Hultén 1993). Legislation in 1985 meant that the state accepted an increased responsibility for railway infrastructure. The most important change was that only 80 per cent of SJ's investments in the commercial network's infrastructure were added to the firm's debt, the rest was considered as a grant. The Act also directed SJ to separate accounting for infrastructure from other parts of its business, and as a consequence the passenger and freight divisions had to pay fees for their use of the infrastructure. A third novelty in the Act was that SJ had to fund its investments in rolling stock through commercial loans, limited to 600 million SEK the first year. A fourth change in the regulatory framework was an instruction to SJ to reorganize its subsidiaries and to start to divest activities that did not complement its core rail business (Nilsson 1995: 176). (SJ was, however, very reluctant to disinvest these firms and as late as 1993 SJ owned a ferry company, SweFerry, the biggest bus operator in Sweden, Swebus, and two forwarding agents, ASG and Svelast: SJ 1993.) Another important decision was that the Act gave SJ the right to organize itself internally and parliament committed itself not to intervene in the firm's staffing and organizing decisions (Nilsson 1995: 176).

The legislators had hoped that the 1985 Railway Act would function as a way of getting SJ out of its permanent economic problems. However, new projected losses in 1986 and a demand for one billion SEK in additional state aid resulted in a government plan to redraft the 1979 Transport Policy Act. The outcome was the 1988 Transport Policy Act. The Act was motivated by four concerns: 1) the railways were perceived as having environmental and safety advantages that are not appropriately accounted for in an unregulated market; 2) the need to maintain balanced regional economic growth; 3) the road sector was thought to have benefited from the state's responsibility for the road infrastructure; 4) SJ's finances continued to detoriate (Nilsson 1995: 183). The third concern was of major importance for the design of the reform as politicians began to discuss the implementation of a 'Road Sector Model' that would apply to railways.

The basic goal for Swedish transport policy, as it was set out by the 1988 Act, was to provide citizens and industry in the separate parts of the country with satisfactory, safe and environmentally sustainable transport services at the lowest possible cost to society. This socioeconomic viewpoint implies that the transport policy in principle must aid in the effective utilization of society's resources (Swedish National Rail Administration 1994: 8).

The main feature of the 1988 Transport Policy Act was a separation of infrastructure administration (lodged in the National Rail Administration, known as Banverket) from railway operations in SJ. The dividing line between the two entities was drawn between the track and the railway station. SJ was told to improve its results within four years through cost cutting and revenue increases. The government made two major financial commitments. The first was to continue to subsidize unprofitable railway services, both on the national network and on the county lines. The second was to finance the renewal of the railway infrastructure with ten billion SEK. A substantial part of this money was going to be used to upgrade the railway network – signalling, closures of level crossings, etc. – in order to make it possible to run the new high-speed trains. In addition, the state took over the economic responsibility for infrastructure maintenance and a system of levying charges was introduced (Nilsson 1995: 183).

Another important feature of the 1988 Transport Policy Act was the transfer of responsibility for the local and regional passenger services to the regional transport authorities, the CPTAs, in 1990, thereby introducing the possibility for competitive tendering for these services (Nordell 1997). The goal of this policy change was, besides cost savings, to increase the coordination of bus services and railway traffic (Hylén 1995).

From 1989, Banverket was presenting plans for new railway lines in Sweden. The line from Stockholm to Arlanda airport was singled out to be built and operated by private investors. Within a year it became evident that it was difficult to find private investors willing to finance and operate the line. The project start was postponed and the state commissioned investigations into the possibility of attracting private capital (Alexandersson and Hultén 1997).

In February 1991, the Social Democratic government took a first step towards a further opening of the rail-service market, with the decision to map the preconditions for and consequences of increased competition on the state's railway network (Nilsson 1995: 191). Initiated by the Social Democratic government, the objective to open the railways to competition was confirmed by the non-socialist government elected in September 1991 (Nilsson 1995: 192). In January 1992 the new Minister of Transport expressed the goal to put out the non-commercial inter-regional lines to tendering, instead of simply renegotiating the terms with SJ. A committee appointed to investigate the possibilities for competition on the main lines delivered its report in February 1993. It proposed that entry should be open to anyone 'fit, willing and able' and should not be restricted to licensed operators. The assumption was that new operators would prefer to operate in niche markets, since these services were believed to be less risky than the nationwide passenger market. It further argued that even limited entries into niche markets would constitute a threat that would induce the dominant operator to produce what the market wanted at lower cost. The committee recommended that the timetable development function should be taken over by Banverket while SJ should retain the train control and other common functions. Since investment in rolling stock was seen as the major obstacle to entry, the committee suggested that interested parties form an equipment leasing company (Nilsson 1995: 192). While the Ministry worked with its report, that should have formed the basis for a government Bill, other important events occurred. Banverket made a decision to grant the company LKAB the operating rights of ore transport on the important Iron Ore Line, forcing SJ and the Norwegian state railway operator NSB to offer their services at reduced rates (Nilsson 1995: 200). The first result of the tendering for the non-commercial interregional passenger services was made public in September 1993. Despite some competition, SJ won all the bids.

When the Ministry's report appeared in the autumn of 1993, it suggested that SJ was to remain the dominant operator for the foreseeable future and SJ was to keep all the common facilities, including the timetable function (Kommunikationsdepartementet 1993). Therefore it came as a surprise when the government Bill in January 1994 followed closely the recommendations in the original committee report of February 1993. The government's Deregulation Bill proposed that the monopoly positions of SJ and the CPTAs were to be discontinued as of 1 January 1995. Any entrant with sound finances, i.e. not only railways operators, would be permitted to apply for track access on any part of the state's railways. A regulatory agency would be established, having the ultimate responsibility for track capacity allocation. During an interim period SJ would continue to manage the traffic control function and would have the right to plan its railway services before the other actors. Rolling stock was to be made available (buying or leasing) to new operators from SJ's redundant rolling stock on 'commercial grounds'. In May 1994 the government presented the Bill to the Swedish parliament. It was accepted but the Bill met objections from the political opposition, backed by SJ and the railway unions. It was questioned whether the deregulation would promote the development of the railways and less far-reaching changes were suggested as an alternative (Nilsson 1995: 193).

In 1993–94 two important political decisions were taken regarding the future development of the railway sector. The first decision concerned a large-scale investment programme in the Swedish railway infrastructure. Instead of the annual one billion SEK suggested in 1988, 32 billion SEK were to be invested in railway infrastructure from 1994–2003. The parliament had asked Banverket to suggest different plans for infrastructure investment. Banverket developed three plans: 1) regional balance; 2) concentration; 3) accessibility combined with environmental concerns (Swedish National Rail Administration 1994: 3). All three plans included massive investments in upgrading of the core network south of Sundsvall to allow for services with the X2000 – the tilting Swedish high-speed trains. The biggest differences between the projects were that the regional balance plan included a high-speed line in northern Sweden, the concentration plan investments allowing 250 kilometres per hour in the triangle Stockholm–Gothenburg–Malmö, and the accessibility plan a high-speed link Gothenburg–Oslo. The government chose a slightly revised accessibility/environmental plan that included minor parts of the additional investments in the two competing plans. The second decision was to give a private consortium a forty-five-year-long licence to operate the Stockholm–Arlanda airport line. The consortium, that consists of Swedish, French and British firms, pays a substantial part of the construction costs, builds the railway line and supplies the train sets (Alexandersson and Hultén 1997).

When the Social Democratic party regained the power in September 1994, they presented a new government Bill postponing the railway deregulation. The new government launched a renewed investigation of the future organization of the railway sector. This resulted in a Ministry report in June 1995, suggesting similar changes as the reports had during the previous parliament. For example, the functions of allocation of track capacity and train traffic control should be transferred from SJ to Banverket, while other common facilities were to be available on commercial grounds. Instead of permitting open entry for new operators, it was argued that the CPTAs should get the extended rights to run services on the main lines within their respective county, and after special government decisions they should have the right to run services reaching into other counties. The argument was that this would promote the development of the local and regional services. For the freight services the report suggested open access on the whole network (Kommunikationsdepartementet 1995). SJ opposed this and pointed to the risks of destroying the gains from economies of scale. When the government finally presented its Bill in October 1995, it had partly accepted SJ's arguments, allowing SJ 'grandfather's rights' for the freight services it already performed. When the Bill was passed in December 1995 it included a deregulation of the freight services as of 1 July 1996, and extended rights for the CPTAs. SJ's exclusive right to perform inter-regional passenger services was maintained.

While for a couple of years in the 1990s SJ had been profitable, in principle fulfilling the obligations specified in the Transport Policy Act of 1988, in 1996 the firm made a loss of 477 million SEK (SJ 1996). It also had difficulties in financing the new rolling stock needed for the first new railway lines purpose built for high-speed commuter trains. To begin with, the new lines had to be operated with loco-hauled high-speed trains and old, standard Intercity trains.

In the spring of 1997 a special committee on the future of the transport sector, known as KOM-KOM, presented its final report. Its most important suggestions for the rail operations were a new division of the railway network into a business network and an inter-regional basic network, and the abolition of track fees for freight transport. The business network, consisting of SJ's profitable lines, should only be accessed by SJ. This is motivated by a claim that railway operation in a country the size of Sweden should be a natural monopoly due to economics of scale. The railway services on the inter-regional network could, however, be purchased through competitive tenders (Kommunikationsdepartementet 1997). Debates have continued in Sweden on the final structure of services into 1998.

The reregulation of the Swedish railway sector started with measures to ease some of the state-owned monopolist's economic difficulties. Incidentally these actions transformed the regulatory structure. When SJ, despite the additional economic support, was unable to break even and had to seek more state support, the financial aid was accompanied by further changes in the regulatory structure. The regulatory transformations gave SJ more power over its internal affairs but less power over the public transport systems and the freight transport sector. Within a time span of twenty years SJ changed from being a vertically integrated monopoly that controlled competing transport systems and complementary transport activities to a specialized railway operator. In return SJ could extract more state subsidies to itself and to the railway sector.

The new regulatory structure has enabled the politicians to force the railway sector to explore new technologies, new markets and intra-industry competition, and to exploit the potential of high-speed trains and local and regional interconnected public transport systems. These changes have emerged out of dealing with the problems in the old system. They emerged out of these conditions as well as being shaped by political debates and technological changes.

Conclusions

It seems to us that a framework for understanding regulatory stability and change in network industries demands concepts and notions which can appreciate both processes of regulatory transformation as well as the more invisible reproduction of a prevailing regulatory regime. The concepts of exploitation and exploration have in this chapter been proposed to assist us in our understanding of the formation, stabilization, crisis and reformation of regulatory regimes. Our cases suggest that a prevailing regulatory regime will promote exploitation of existing economies, which in turn gradually will produce tensions as the ongoing exploitation in different dimensions will generate advancements with varying degrees of ease. This observation is in accordance with Schumpeter's argument that a system that incessantly exploits given economies in the long run will be inferior to a system that also includes exploration

(Schumpeter 1942: 83). In accordance with this we suggest that incessant exploitation, in itself an important productive force, will over time defeat itself, producing a crisis of the regime.

Although these concepts and notions are only at best one step towards a theoretical framework, this view helps us avoiding at least two frequent shortcomings. First, by separating our understanding of the emergence of a crisis in a prevailing regime from the subsequent reregulation, this view avoids confusing outcomes of a regulatory transformation with causality (cf. Campbell and Lindberg 1991: 320–4). It is, for instance, not uncommon to explain a reregulation by referring to efficiencies gradually unleashed through exploratory and exploitative activities subsequent to the reregulation. This kind of reasoning assumes that the dominant pressures for reregulation are generated by efforts to raise the industry's efficiency, and makes an unjust comparison between two regulatory regimes that are often inherently different as to what exploitative activities they promote. It is seldom possible to assess the workings of a network industry by employing a few objective measurements. The benefits produced by one network industry under one particular regulatory regime are usually qualitatively different from the benefits that would have been produced by the same industry under a different regulatory regime. A regulatory regime will always forcefully influence what economies are explored and exploited and what economies are left aside. The qualities of new technologies developed under the new regime are in the same vein not in this view a valid basis for understanding the emergence of the regulatory regime, since these qualities are themselves the consequence of the reproductive exploitation following upon the reregulation. The technological deterministic explanations of regulatory change are, as we have tried to illustrate, one special kind of explanation that is prone to confuse outcome with cause.

The second shortcoming the proposed view avoids is the use of exogenous forces as explaining the cause behind regulatory change. Both the political voluntarist and the technological determinist understanding of regulatory change lacks a proper division between the opportunity opened up by the crisis in a prevailing regime and the 'heterogeneous entrepreneurial activities' (cf. Law's concept of heterogeneous engineering: Law 1987) thriving to take advantage of these opportunities (even if such entrepreneurial activities may at times appeal to the need for political action or to the 'determined prospects' of technological development). With our emphasis on heterogeneous entrepreneurship, we also avoid seeing the outcome of a reregulatory process as prescribed in the crisis causing it or as prescribed in any exogenous force. *Ex ante*, in a process of regulatory change there is, as our cases show, always more than one new possible regime contesting to become the new prevailing regime. The actors pushing for regulatory change actually try to innovate in the economic system. As with all novelties, nobody can positively anticipate its meaning and implications (Witt 1993: 2). On the other hand, the selection in this entrepreneurial search process is highly constrained and 'unnatural' since the process is contained within a limited number of organizations. Politics might have a weaker power than is usually assumed when it comes to initiating a reregulation, but it is nevertheless often an important part of the process of setting up the new regime and what dimensions it will promote.

The reregulation of network industries is in this view a lasting feature of this type of industry, like any other industry. State intervention in terms of regulating and reregulating will always play an important role in industries characterized by internal scale economies of production and external economies of consumption. Every regulatory regime allowing development, will over time become dysfunctional due to its own success and will accordingly move into transitionary stages, ruptures, which result in a new regulatory regime shaped by a complex interaction of economic, institutional, technological and political factors.

References

Alexandersson, G. and Hultén, S. (1997) 'The Arlanda airport link: railway construction with private sector investors' ('Arlandabanan – järnvägsbygge med privata intressenter'), EFI, mimeo.

Bain, J. S. (1952) *Price Theory*, New York: Henry Holt and Company.

Bijker, W. E. (1995) *Of Bicycles, Bakelites and Bulbs: Toward a Theory of Sociotechnical Change*, Cambridge, MA: The MIT Press.

Campbell, J. L. and Lindberg, L. N. (1991) 'The evolution of governance regimes', in J. L. Campbell, J. R. Hollingsworth and L. N. Lindberg (eds) *Governance of the American Economy*, Cambridge: Cambridge University Press.

Capron, W. M. and Noll, R. G. (1971) 'Summary and conclusion', in W. M. Capron (ed.) *Technological Change in Regulated Industries*, Washington, DC: The Brookings Institution.

Commons, J. R. (1974) [1924] *Legal Foundations of Capitalism*, New York: Sentry Press.

Ely, R. T. (1900) *Monopolies and Trusts*, New York: Macmillan.

Ely, R. T., Adams, T. S., Lorenz, M. O. and Young, A. A. (1923) *Outlines of Economics*, 4th edn, New York: Macmillan.

Flink, T., and Hultén, S. (1993) 'The Swedish high speed train project', in J. Whitelegg, S. Hultén and T. Flink (eds) *High Speed Trains: Fast Tracks to the Future*, Hawes: Leading Edge Press and Publishing.

Helgesson, C.-F. (1995) 'Technological momentum and the national monopoly: monopolisation and the construction of automatic switching in Swedish telecommunications, 1910–1930', paper presented at the conference 'Technological and Industrial Change' ('Teknisk och Industriell Utveckling'), Wik.

—— (1998) 'On the hunt for a natural order: efforts to organize the telephone system in Stockholm' ('På jakt efter en "naturlig ordning": Ansträngningar för att organisera telefonsystemet i Stockholm, 1891–1918'), in P. Blomqvist and A. Kaijser (eds) *The Constructed World: Technological Systems in Historical Perspective* (*Den konstruerade världen: Tekniska system i historiskt perspektiv*), Stockholm.

Hylén, B. (1995) *The County Railways and Deregulation: Effects on Traffic, etc.* (*Länsjärnvägarna och järnvägens avreglering: effekter på trafiken mm*), VTI Dnr 462/95–93.

Kommunikationsdepartementet (1993) *An Open Railway Market in Sweden* (*En öppen järnvägsmarknad I Sverige*), DS 1993:63.

—— (1995) *New Prospects for Railway Traffic* (*Nya möjligheter för järnvägstrafiken*), DS 1995:33.

—— (1997) *A New Traffic Services Policy: The Final Report from the Communications Committee* (*Ny kurs i trafikpolitiken – Slutbetänkande av kommunikationskommittén*), SOU 1997: 35.

Law, J. (1987) 'Technology and heterogenous engineering: the case of Portuguese expansion', in W. E. Bijker, T. P. Hughes and T. J. Pinch (eds) *The Social Construction of Technological Systems*, Cambridge, MA: The MIT Press

Lipartito, K. (1989) 'System building at the margin: the problem of public choice in the telephone industry', *The Journal of Economic History* XLIX(2): 323–36.

March, J. G. (1991) 'Exploration and exploitation in organizational learning', *Organization Science* 2(1): 71–87.

Mueller, M. (1989) 'The switchboard problem: scale, signalling and organization in manual telephone switching, 1877–1897', *Technology and Culture* 3(3): 534–60.

—— (1997) *Universal Service: Competition, Interconnection and Monopoly in the Making of the American Telephone System*, Cambridge, MA: The MIT Press.

Nilsson, J.-E. (1995) 'Swedish railways case study', CTS, working paper 1995: 2.

Nordell, O. (1997) *Organizing the Tasks of Public Authorities and the Common Functions in the Railway Sector* (*Organisation av myndighets – och sektorsuppgifter samt gemensamma funktioner inom järnvägssektorn*), Stockholm: Kommunikationsdepartementet.

Schumpeter, J. (1942) *Capitalism, Socialism and Democracy*, New York: Harper and Row.

SJ (Swedish State Railways (1993) *Annual Report*, Stockholm: SJ.

—— (1996) *Annual Report*, Stockholm: SJ.

Swedish National Rail Administration (1994) *Investment Plan 1994–2003 for Swedish Trunk Railways*, BV/P 1994.

Witt, U. (1993) 'Evolutionary economics: some principles', in U. Witt (ed.) *Evolution in Markets and Institutions*, Heidelberg: Physica Verlag.

Part IV

Regulation, power and inequality

11 The regulation of retail financial services in Britain

An analysis of a crisis

Michael Clarke

Introduction: the 1986 regulatory reform

The claim that the regulation of financial services in Britain is in crisis might seem surprising given the relatively recent legislation (Financial Services Act 1986, hereafter FSA), which led to the implementation of a comprehensive regime in 1988 for the regulation of such services. Although retail financial services are included under that regime, the main impetus for reform came from the wholesale side. In particular, Britain's international role as a financial centre was held to be under threat as a result of the anachronistic, exclusive culture and institutions of 'the City', epitomized by the refusal of the Stock Exchange to allow foreign members and its insistence on managing share dealing through the firmly segregated stock jobbers or market makers and brokers who bought shares for customers, both of them with very limited capitalization by American or Japanese standards (Clarke 1986). It was to the establishment of a level playing field with clear rules of play that the reforms were directed; the regulation of the retail sector at the same time was something of a side show and, in any case, partial. It included only those products and services which could be readily identified as investments, particularly those with long-term implications. In practice, this mainly involved life assurance, unit trusts and personal pensions, followed, when they became available, by personal equity plans (PEPs). Mortgages, which (so far as they were being sold by building societies) had been traditionally regulated by the Building Societies Commission, were excluded. Banking services generally were also excluded, as were term and risk insurance.

While substantial reform of the wholesale side was the primary objective, it was expected that regulation on the retail side would be much less contentious. The main objective was to secure the continued and growing participation of a mass public in savings and investments. It was taken for granted that the industry was sound, dominated, as it was, by large, mainly British firms, many of them with origins in the nineteenth century and earlier and many of them legally constituted as mutual societies formally owned and operated in the interests of their members. Prudential regulation in the sector was long established and, with minor exceptions in small building societies and a few smaller insurers, had operated successfully for many years. The long-term expansion of the large institutions on the back of growing mass affluence produced both a self-confidence in the industry and an acceptance of their benign character by the government. Regulation under the 1986 Act had a large self-regulatory element upon which these great institutions were insistent. Major sectors within the industry were to be overseen by self-regulatory bodies (known as SROs) under the overall supervision of the Securities and Investments Board (hereafter SIB) which was in turn responsible to parliament initially through the Department of Trade and Industry and later through the Treasury. Funding for the regulatory system was through a system of levies on the companies. Membership of the governing bodies was at first primarily from the industry; consumer groups or others capable of putting an alternative view to industry insiders were in a minority, on the argument that it is better to turn 'poachers into gamekeepers' since they know how the system works. The result was, of course, to create an inbuilt propensity towards 'regulatory capture' by the industry and its insiders.

Had the new regime been introduced during a period that was similar to the past – that is with markets expanding calmly – conditions would, as suggested, have been perfect for the capture of the regulators by the industry. As it was, however, the government was determined to use regulation as an opportunity for increasing competition whilst also stimulating greater public participation. There was some suspicion of the cosiness of the great financial services institutions. Reforms were introduced that allowed building societies to diversify and compete with banks and insurers. The building societies' cartel that set interest rates for savers and borrowers was abolished and credit was in a variety of ways derestricted. At the same time sustained practical effort was put into ensuring public participation in financial markets through the privatization of the utilities, the sale of council properties and the promotion of personal pensions. All this created a huge market opportunity for the industry, but also greatly increased competition for market share as the perception grew that the future would belong to very large multifunctional firms operating in almost all sectors of the market. This market turmoil provoked abuses which put the new regulatory regime under great pressure.

Market and regulatory changes in retail financial services

The process of market consolidation also produced in stages a new kind of institution with some regulatory significance, the bancassurer. The 1980s boom initially generated alliances between mortgage lenders and insurers, with the former recommending the latter's products on the basis of a formal tie. This was partly stimulated by a feature of regulation in the retail sector imposed after some acrimonious debate as a principle of investor protection: polarization. Sellers of financial services products, it was decided, can either offer advice over the entire range of the products on the market as independents, or sell only those of one company. Since the costs of training staff in mortgage lenders' branches to advise independently is substantial, lenders successively tied to individual insurers, with NatWest holding out for a while among the banks and eventually only the Bradford and Bingley Building Society surviving of all the major institutions as willing to offer independent advice (Whitaker 1995). It was to become of considerable significance to later regulatory difficulties that polarization was introduced as the primary principle of retail regulation. The argument for it was that it established clarity in the customer's mind as to whether he/she was being sold the products of a particular company, in which case he/she would be advised to shop around for other views before buying, or whether independent advice was being offered. For this reason, multitying to, say, three or six insurers was banned.

The reaction of mortgage lenders over time, however, modified in the realization that, whilst tying generated useful commission from insurers, it was still the case that potentially profitable business was being passed on which could be undertaken in-house. Hence lenders began to set up their own insurance arms, which had strategic advantages as regards selling, since the existing client bank of savers and borrowers could be exploited, not just in the context of a mortgage loan, but over a much longer period – hopefully the customer's lifetime – to sell a range of insurance and investment products. This seemed to offer a considerable advantage over the main established method of selling such products, which was to run a large direct-sales force, pursuing more or less cold contacts with the public.

This, however, is to begin to run ahead of the argument and to enter explicit matters of regulation which cannot be properly debated until two additional contextual elements have been identified: political consensus on the limits of state provision and the role of scandals and abuses. These take us back to the heady enthusiasm of the 1980s. As is so often the case, ideology recognized a development of some importance and, seized of its significance, elevated it into a way of life and so compromised it by excess. The development recognized by the Conservatives in the latter 1970s, and which was resolutely rejected by the Labour government, was the fiscal crisis of the state, that is the incapacity of governments of industrialized nations to continue to increase expenditure on health, education and welfare in line with public expectations, which in turn are based on ever-increasing average incomes and living standards. The Conservative government in the 1980s addressed itself to all manifestations of the fiscal crisis with varying degrees of energy and success – NHS reforms, reduction of unemployment benefits, for example – but it is long-term financial security that provides the focus of our interest. As has already been mentioned, the government took radical steps to expand the market in home ownership and did nothing, until the property boom reached excessive proportions, to deny well-established expectations that home ownership, besides being desirable in itself, was a (indeed the best) long-term secure financial investment, with property prices always rising faster than inflation. Nor, despite the Labour party's commitment to state-rented housing for those in need, and objections to rapidly increasing house prices in a boom, was there fundamental opposition to extensions in home ownership from non-government parties.

In addition, it was increasingly accepted by all parties that the cost of funding retirement pensions related to earning levels was a task that could not be successfully undertaken by the state. By implication, the efforts of the previous Labour government in establishing the state earnings-related pension, whilst of continuing benefit as a safety net, were not adequate for the task of providing a secure old age. Individual self-provision in some form was seen as increasingly essential, especially given the skew of the population structure towards the elderly. In sum there emerged a cross-party consensus on the necessity for individual provision for financial security, especially over the long term, and an acceptance that the state could not be relied upon to provide (Nesbitt 1995; Knights 1997).

The key question was how this self-help was to be achieved. These matters were given considerable point by the gradual realization that the retail financial sector could not be trusted to provide the framework for such self-provision on its own. On the contrary, it became clear that regulation was necessary in order to prevent people from buying inappropriate financial products. Abuses are of course endemic to the financial sector, simply because it deals in money and temptations often prove irresistible, but we are not talking here just about predictable problems, which tend to increase sharply in periods of boom. These can be seen in the crop of rogues and vain-glorious operators, evident particularly among independent financial advisers and tied agents of major product providers. Thriving markets provided ideal conditions for new entrants to markets where entry barriers were very limited, both in financial and competence terms, with the new regulatory regime only formally coming into being in 1988. It proved only too easy for some intermediaries to survive for several years whilst at the same time failing to remit premiums to companies, inflating or inventing business, making false and exaggerated claims about the benefits of products to customers, channelling client funds through personal accounts and, of course, for those licensed to invest and manage clients' funds, making both improper and reckless investments or simply embezzling funds. The autonomy of both independent financial advisers (IFAs) and tied agents meant that it often took some time for product providers and regulators to catch up with them, and it was also possible for the more adept to hoodwink both (Jebens 1997). The most spectacular example of this species was Roger Levitt, whose enterprises were so successful that he had the support of several major insurers who collectively lost £20m by the time he was exposed.

The real problem with the retail financial scandals of the 1980s was not these relatively small fry however, but the willingness of the large, established corporations to become actively and on occasion zealously involved. An example of their willingness to enter into arrangements which were far from sound is provided by home income plans (HIPs), through which elderly home owners remortgaged their properties. The capital sum was then used to buy bonds, the investment income from which was intended to repay the mortgage and leave income to spare. When markets turned and interest rates rose, the bonds did not even yield enough to pay off the mortgages and elderly people faced repossession. These schemes were mainly devised and marketed by IFAs, but the mortgages were supplied by major lenders, who in the aftermath made every effort to distance themselves from responsibility. Court cases and negotiations involving clients dragged on into the middle 1990s as lenders, the Investors Compensation Scheme (ICS) covering for the failed IFAs, and clients battled for their rights. By the time the ICS announced it had paid out a total of £100m at the end of 1995, HIPs accounted for four of its top ten payouts, totalling £24.95m.

Whilst mortgage lenders could seek to avoid liability for HIPs, their responsibility for overlending in the housing boom was painfully evident. The violent crash of the market after August 1988 and its continued weakness in reaction was sustained into the mid-1990s by the huge overhang of negative equity. Borrowers who had been tempted in towards the top of the boom by a track record in which house prices had moved upwards ever since 1945, feverish lending habits which constantly increased the ratio of loans to value and income multiples and relaxed status considerations, found that they now had to pay back a mortgage significantly higher than the value which they could realize for their property. Even worse, hundreds of thousands experienced the horrors of repossession in the early 1990s, often losing all or most of the money they had invested after failing to keep up mortgage payments and being saddled with substantial long-term debts. It was only too evident that, just as the days were past of diligent saving and mortgage queues with an identified building society, so also was cautious advice by the branch manager on the size of the loan in the light of potential changes in circumstances such as job loss or interest rate rises, though of course, as prevailing ideology had it, individuals who borrowed too much had only themselves to blame. Whatever the merits of this argument, it was unlikely to eliminate the political rancour of those subject to negative equity or repossession.

It was, however, less easy to 'blame the victims' in respect of another abuse which emerged during the years of the housing boom and its immediate aftermath. This was the extensive selling of mortgages secured by endowment insurance. The argument to clients was that such arrangements were preferable since they were more tax efficient and in addition offered both insurance protection against the death of a borrower and the prospect that the insurance would generate a surplus over and above the mortgage. From the lender's point of view, endowments generated very welcome commission income, and later business for the in-house life assurance arm. Endowments were at times insisted upon as a condition of lending at the height of the boom, a practice outlawed after public and regulatory protest (Clarke *et al.* 1994). Nonetheless the industry succeeded in reversing the ratio of 80/20 repayment mortgages to endowments at the start of the 1980s to 20/80 endowments by the end of the decade. By this time, however, the appropriateness of endowments for all borrowers on every mortgage had begun to come under attack as it became clear that for certain types of borrowers (such as those who were likely to move frequently) and in certain conditions (e.g. where stock-market growth was low), endowments were not a good idea. More widely, the overselling of endowment assurance came under scrutiny, especially by the Office of Fair Trading (OFT), which began to argue that endowments were poor value for money, an issue made worse by their opaque charging structures which could not be understood by anybody but a few experts (OFT 1993a, 1993b, 1995). The OFT, in conjunction with a number of consumer bodies, therefore began to argue for more and clearer disclosure of charges in the belief that this would reveal the fact that endowments (and many other products) were of poor value. These demands were, of course, resisted by the industry which legitimated its opposition in terms of public 'disinterest in the details', an argument which was supported for some time by the regulators until forced by politicians to rethink their stance and introduce a disclosure system.

These kinds of abuses were central to the biggest scandal of all, personal pensions. Following the 1986 Social Security Act and constant government encouragement, pension providers, most of them insurance companies and including, despite some later denials, all the largest and most respected, engaged in a massive sales drive, involving at times gross misrepresentation of the benefits of personal pensions. Thus, nurses and teachers were encouraged to opt out of their occupational schemes which, apart from being well managed, also meant foregoing the employer's contributions, which usually more than matched that of the employee. Those increasing numbers in all sectors who found themselves redundant with some years' contributions to an occupational scheme were exhorted to cash them in and invest in a personal pension and not told of the value their accrued investment would yield if left in place to retirement age. The industry proved extremely reluctant to admit wrongdoing, even by way of overselling, still less mis-selling. Enquiries by the supervisory regulator, the SIB, in the early 1990s, eventually produced an estimate that 1.4 million people may have been mis-sold personal pensions and had a right to have their cases reviewed and awarded compensation as appropriate. The costs of this were estimated at £2–4 billion. Despite a timetable established by the regulators for reviewing cases, the industry persistently dragged its feet and deadlines for the first tranche of 350,000 priority cases which were supposed to have been dealt with by the end of 1995 were largely missed both by product providers and, on an even more comprehensive basis, by IFAs. It was only with the advent of a new government in 1997 that real pressure began to be applied, with the worst-offending firms named and shamed, and the threat of exclusion from the new government's pension and individual savings schemes based on partnership with the industry used as the ultimate sanction.

Regulatory reform: achieving effective investor protection

By the mid-1990s there emerged, therefore, on the one hand a political consensus that individual citizens should provide much more seriously and extensively for their own financial security than had been the case in the past, and that the state does not have the resources to achieve this, together with an acceptance that the private sector, that is the retail financial services industry, has a substantial part to play in making this possible. On the other hand stood a general recognition of the intimate involvement in and responsibility for a series of abuses of the public by the retail financial services industry and direct personal experience of such abuses by a significant minority of the population. Not surprisingly, public sentiment was decidedly hostile to the industry and business, especially in the insurance sector, was sharply down in 1994 and 1995 and recovered only slowly in the latter 1990s. Between the public and the industry stood the regulators as guardians of propriety and investor protection, and it is scarcely surprising that reform, even of the new regime established only in 1988, was proposed and insisted upon.

Regulatory reform took a more substantial and visible form because of the weakness of the existing structure. By 1993 public and political pressures for improved standards of conduct by product sellers, whether actual providers or intermediaries, particularly as a consequence of recognition of the pensions and endowment insurance mis-selling scandals, had become significant. Media antagonism to the industry on behalf of investors was powerful and levels of business were being threatened. The chair of the supervisory regulator, the SIB, undertook a review of retail regulation and announced the need for a 'step-change' in standards (SIB 1993). Levels of competence and self-restraint in selling products would have to increase sharply and a programme of much more disclosure of information about them and sellers was required: disclosure of commissions, of levels of charging during the life of a product and the impact of both on product performance and of lapse rates (or persistency). A detailed fact-find on customers would be required, to be followed up by a 'reasons why' letter to the customer, justifying the seller's advice and leaving a written record for internal managers and compliance officers as well as external regulators to see.

The import of all this was quite clear. Not only were customers to be told a great deal more about the products they were sold, which would enable them to make informed judgements, but they were to be treated with respect, not oversold or mis-sold inappropriate products. This meant that the sales process would become much lengthier, sales staff training would be very much more extensive and customers were expected to use the additional information to adopt a much more equal and assertive role in the sales process, including actively bargaining to drive down commission levels. This in turn implied, for direct-sales forces, an enormous increase in costs: in training before staff could be put on the road, in time spent to achieve each sale, and in the costs of maintaining sales forces with very high labour turnovers (Whitaker 1995). The traditional strategy of saturating the market with an army of sales staff searching for prospects was also under pressure from the bancassurers (and later, new entrants to the market such as Virgin, Marks and Spencer, Tesco and Sainsbury's) who, it was claimed, could greatly reduce the costs of wasted (cold) calls by selling to their existing client banks, and using friendly customer relations.

Further, the whole strategy of searching out prospects and selling them a limited range of products for which the salesperson was trained was put into question by the new regulatory requirements. These insisted that the customer's entire financial circumstances be identified and appraised, before reaching a reasoned judgement on what was appropriate, which might well be a product type, such as a building society savings account, that was not available from the salesperson. Changes in both the market and regulation hence called the strategy of the big product providers who dominated the industry into question. Not surprisingly, they resisted every regulatory measure tooth and nail, with commission disclosure in cash terms being appealed up to the Chancellor of the Exchequer before becoming a settled matter.

The regulator responsible for the product providers, their direct-sales forces and tied agents, LAUTRO (the Life Assurance and Unit Trust Regulatory Organisation) responded to the new regulatory climate by first making it public that complacency and sloppiness on compliance matters would not be tolerated. It announced that fines would become increasingly heavy, and between 1993 and 1995 began to carry out its threat. The size of fines for regulatory misconduct mounted rapidly from below £100,000 to over £300,000 affecting a wide range of product providers, including leading household names. By 1995 the message had got home and several large corporations pulled their sales forces off the road in panic to engage in retraining and re-evaluation, in some instances for several months at a time (Jebens 1997).

This, however, is to consider only half the picture, that involving the product providers. Regulatory reform was made much more messy in the short term and problematic in the long term by the existence of IFAs. Their position by the early 1990s was chronically problematic. Most were regulated by FIMBRA (the Financial Intermediaries, Managers and Brokers Regulatory Association), but not all. Quite a number opted to remain regulated by the Insurance Brokers Registration Council (IBRC), established under earlier legislation. Others were regulated by IMRO (Investment Management Regulatory Organisation), the wholesale investment regulator, and others still by the professional bodies for accountants and solicitors, recognized under the Financial Services Act. This regulatory confusion was made even worse by the fact that some of the work undertaken by these intermediaries did not fall under the ambit of the FSA at all, notably mortgages and term insurance. Although product providers varied substantially from the newer and smaller to the older and larger, this was as nothing compared with the intermediaries, which ranged from large national networks, employing thousands and comparable in size with product providers, to sole traders with a single office in a small town. Levels of competence also varied enormously. Many intermediaries had traditionally been recruited from the ranks of insurance sales staff, and in the past it had been easy to set up in business with few constraints on the range and nature of advice given. It was thus reasonable enough to sell mainly insurance products and remain largely unsophisticated in respect of other more complex products such as unit trusts and pensions. At the other extreme were specialists in financial planning, investment and pensions who had qualifications from elite bodies. Some of these derived a significant part of their incomes from fees, whereas the majority relied on commission from product sales.

This plethora of circumstances produced chronic financial problems for the main regulator FIMBRA, which started out with a loan from the Bank of England and continued with annual subventions constantly renegotiated from some of the big product providers in recognition of the business they derived from the IFA sector. Subscriptions from its IFA members were never enough to finance FIMBRA's operations and the situation was made worse by the minority of rogues and incompetents who seriously abused the public and went bust. Picking up the pieces was expensive, both in terms of the regulatory enquiries needed and in terms of the consequent need for levies for the Investors Compensation Scheme. It was because of this dissolute and costly minority, and because they argued that IFAs often engaged in the management of customers' assets and the provision of other services that product providers do not, that product providers had insisted on being separately regulated under LAUTRO. As the regime developed after 1988 and FIMBRA's financial position worsened, their views were only confirmed.

In the light of the demand for improved regulatory standards, the situation as regards intermediaries became pressing. On the one hand there was the problem posed by the diversity of regulatory bodies and the danger, if not of active regulatory arbitrage, at least the lack of genuinely uniform standards. The accountants and particularly solicitors came under some suspicion in the latter respect when a review of training was commissioned by the SIB (McDonald 1990). Even more pressing, however, was the fact that FIMBRA was not financially stable, with increases in subscriptions to levels adequate to fund its work likely to drive a good many IFAs out of business. Part of the difficulty here lay in the fact that LAUTRO members could pass on the costs of regulation to customers in their pricing and charging, whereas FIMBRA members could not. Consolidation and a sound financial base seemed to be a precondition for the implementation of higher regulatory standards among independent intermediaries.

IFAs and models of regulatory effectiveness

That, however, was not the whole problem. IFAs are a vital part of the market in regulatory terms and one that was acquiring enhanced significance. The impact of regulation and especially the increased financial burden of it looked likely, as indeed IFA trade associations complained constantly, to drive many out of business. Such a fact could be argued to be the natural and beneficial consequence of improved market regulation acting upon the incompetent and ineffective, but this ignores two things. First, IFAs had traditionally been recruited on a very low cost and capitalization basis using experience to gradually build up a reputation and client bank like other occupations such as accountants, solicitors and estate agents. The danger was that higher regulatory costs – and the proposed introduction of a £10,000 capital adequacy requirement was particularly bitterly complained of – would shut off this supply as regards the honest, hard-working and intelligent as well as the lazy, unscrupulous and stupid. The outcome threatened was a sharp fall in the numbers of IFAs and the increased dominance of the market by the product providers. This is indeed what happened right from 1988 onwards, though the impact was much more powerful in terms of numbers of firms rather than numbers of individuals. Sole traders sought shelter in partnerships, and networks of IFAs showed a dramatic rise, with member firms remaining independent but receiving back-up support on products and the market from the network in return for their subscriptions.

Nonetheless, the impact of regulation on IFAs had been to enhance contraction, in comparison with product providers who, with the exception of limited numbers of mainly foreign mortgage lenders and insurers, were not driven out of the market. The importance of retaining a flourishing and substantial IFA sector lies in its regulatory significance. Product providers sell their own products, where IFAs appraise the market to provide independent advice. They survive in the market by developing knowledge and expertise that a lay investor finds it hard to match simply by shopping around, and can advise the investor which is the best buy, given the investor's circumstances and needs. In this respect they constitute both a market discipline and a regulatory model. As a market discipline IFAs are the only institutions which ensure that real competition between product providers takes place. Although investors may shop around and make comparisons, there is limited evidence that this is at all extensive. Even though much greater levels of disclosure about products and their performance makes comparative appraisal clearer, it remains to be seen either whether investors have the motivation to use it actively, or the capacity to analyse it, given the now substantial and diverse amounts of information becoming available. Such limited research as has been undertaken suggests that only a maximum of a fifth of the public can be termed 'informed market decision makers' (Personal Investment Authority 1996). Product providers who use the IFA channel not only welcome the business it generates, but take a pride in their products selling well on the basis of independent advice, which establishes their merits and underwrites the moral legitimacy of selling them directly.

The investor who buys, as most do, from a product provider or tied agent, receives only part of the advice required; only the IFA, who appraises the products on the market, can provide full advice. As things stand, regulation is somewhat confused on this issue. The seller is required to provide 'best advice' on the basis of the principle 'know your customer', but that has been interpreted by the regulators to mean 'suitable advice' when applied to selling by representatives of single companies. Hence the salesman is required to identify the kind of product that is appropriate to the customer's needs, but of course cannot show that is the best product of that kind unless he is either dishonest, or happens to represent, if not the best company, given the complexity of products and their appraisal, at least one of the top group. The onus is upon the investor to review the advice and information provided – and the entire process, in the light of requirements for a fact-find, may take more than one meeting and several hours – and then compare offers elsewhere. The IFA, by contrast, acts as an independent professional servicing a lay client and undertakes the appraisal both of his circumstances and the market. The 'best advice' that regulation requires of the IFA is the best product available to suit the client's needs.

This leads to the argument that there are in fact two models of the regulatory process in competition within the system. One may be termed the professional–client model. It recognizes the inevitable information deficit that the client suffers due to the complexity of the products and advocates the creation of a body of professional advisers. These advisers would be expected to reach high standards of education and training in order to be able to 'diagnose' and treat the client's needs. They would also be expected to be 'disinterested' and 'objective' about the solution. In other words, they would not be expected to have a monetary interest in recommending one 'solution' (or, in this case, product) rather than another. The logic of this approach is that the client pays the professional a fee for advice. The other model may be termed the market model. Purchasers can be confident that they can get all the 'facts' about products as there is now full disclosure. They can therefore shop around. If they do not do so, it is their decision and they have to live with the consequences – *caveat emptor*! These two models have coexisted since the initial discussions of investor protection. The industry, of course, has tended to reject both, as both imply an end to their traditional sales methods.

The professional–client model of regulatory adequacy is not the one overtly espoused by the regulatory system, however, whose strategy ever since the review by Professor Gower of the provision of investor protection in the period leading up to the Financial Services Act 1986 (Gower 1984), has been to secure protection by disclosure. By forcing the disclosure of amounts of information adequate to permit investors to make informed appraisals of the market for financial services products and decisions based upon them, the object has been to put investors in a position to drive the market to work competitively. Ultimately this model reflects the market's actual dominance by the product providers even if they resisted disclosure for many years. This model, however, can legitimate their selling of their own products through direct-sales forces and tied agents on the basis that the onus is on the investor to make the final judgement. In practice the product providers have also habitually resorted to a subsidiary argument. Since investment and protection products, especially life assurance, suffer from customer inertia, and are not sought out and have hence to be actively sold; and since the population's take-up of long-term investment and protection products has historically been weak, the existence of their large sales forces constantly seeking new prospects is a form of social service. It ensures that a significant proportion of the population have at least some protection and security rather than none; and since their company and its products are sound, only good is done. If investors on the whole do not actively shop around and appraise markets and products they are not seriously disadvantaged.

This argument was persuasive over several generations when backed by the active marketing of product providers as stable, trustworthy and paternalistic. It was on that basis that they entered the new regime under the Financial Services Act, which enshrined the principle of investor protection through information disclosure. The scandals over mis-selling since then have shattered the paternalistic myth however, and product providers are now perceived as powerful and predatory. This development has been influenced by the increased competition in the industry, the credit explosions of the 1980s, as well as by the constant exhortations in television advertising and mailshots for the public to subscribe to both borrowing and investment commitments over the medium and long term. All of this conveys the message 'we want your money', rather than 'we will provide for your security'.

What this and the mis-selling scandals demonstrated was that not only were major product providers unrestrained in stuffing their products down the throats of customers regardless of need or financial capacity at times –

the abuses were not confined to newcomers or fly-by-nights – but that, more importantly, customers were very largely ignorant of what had been done to them, even after the event. Thus, the outcome of the pensions mis-selling scandal has been that the regulators have imposed a timetable upon the industry for recontacting customers according to a series of categories and seeking their cooperation in reappraising the sale, with a view to restoring the customers to the position they should have been in if given proper advice. The industry has been extremely reluctant to comply with this timetable, the first of whose deadlines was reached at the end of 1995, with the regulator recognizing that it had been honoured more in the breach than the observance.

The issue which the mis-selling scandal threw up is, hence, the ease with which the brow-beating and bamboozling of investors took place and hence the hollowness and indeed cynicism with which the principle of informed market choice was espoused by the industry. The customer was never assumed to have a capacity for anything but being manipulated; any customer who did more than that gave the salesperson a hard time. It was easy to argue that most customers had limited investments and protection and hence to pitch for the company's products as a solution. Getting into debate about the competition would not only be time-consuming, but potentially disastrous. For this reason the style of selling was traditionally a combination of sales patter and a caricature of paternalist professionalism usually guaranteed to achieve the subordination of the customer in the face of the salesman's superior knowledge. He could then put himself across as giving helpful advice. The last thing he wanted was an extended debate, and it was for this reason that product providers resisted disclosure, both in principle and in practice. Even after disclosure of status as the tied representative of a single company was required for example, it seemed that there was a widespread habit of failing to do so on the part of those invariably identifying themselves as consultants or advisers rather than salespeople.

The evidence suggests, therefore, that whilst the informed market choice model constitutes the prevailing regulatory strategy and acts decidedly to the advantage of the product providers through the principle of *caveat emptor*, the professional–client model has had an important covert place. Indeed, it is arguable that this model is in practice becoming increasingly important overtly and threatens to supplant the informed market choice model. Covertly, the professional–client model was the practical one by which paternalistic corporations sold their products through direct-sales forces. They lulled the clients into thinking there was a 'professional' relationship when in fact the process was far from professional. The sellers benefited financially not from assessing the needs of the clients and getting a fee for that but by selling their company's products, however well or ill that fitted the client. Overtly, the professional–client model was represented through the IFA sector, though even here few IFAs took a fee.

Instead they were remunerated through a commission received from the company whose product they had sold. Their 'professionalism' then was ultimately flawed because of their financial interest in the outcome of their advice, whatever other requirements they met for knowledge of the industry as a whole.

Most customers then operated as though they were in a professional–client relationship, both with direct-sales forces and IFAs, when the regulators wanted them to act as though they were informed purchasers in a clear and transparent marketplace. They were therefore open to persuasion by the sellers into buying unsuitable products. As the extent of this bad selling became apparent, the contradictions between the two models have heightened. Governments of both complexions want to extend citizens' own responsibilities for their financial futures, but how can this be done in a way which avoids further scandals?

Achieving practical effectiveness in investor protection

The difficulties faced by the SIB (and its successor, the Financial Services Authority, set up after Labour came to power in 1997) as supervisory regulator in reforming and upgrading regulation have been several and substantial. The elimination of the diversity of regulatory bodies responsible for IFAs was obviously essential, as was the establishment of a regulatory body with a sound financial base and prospects. This required the amalgamation of FIMBRA and LAUTRO to create a new front-line regulator, the Personal Investment Authority (PIA). This proved exceedingly hard to achieve given the opposition of product providers to being regulated with IFAs and the permissive nature of the FSA. The SIB was not even able to insist that all those it wanted to join the PIA did so, though it could, in theory, make life difficult for those who refused to cooperate (Clarke 1998).

At the same time the IFA sector posed difficulties, since imposing higher regulatory standards on it looked likely to squeeze its membership. In addition, however, achieving reliable standards of advice by IFAs was essential both for them to continue as a competitive market discipline, and for them to work properly in implementing the professional–client model and eliminate cowboys and incompetents. Yet also the prospect of promoting the expansion of the IFA sector sufficiently to constitute the principal means of providing financial services advice was never entertained, because that would not only present great difficulties of training, but confront the product providers and their sales forces who were adamantly committed to the right to sell just their own products.

How were these difficulties to be negotiated? Both the regulators and the product providers sought ways of squaring the circle. Product providers moved on both their products and the means of delivering them. There was a widespread move to increase flexibility of products so that, rather than a customer buying, say, endowment assurance, and thereby a commitment to a fixed monthly payment for ten to thirty years in return for protection in the event of death and investment, he/she buys a financial plan. The degree of flexibility offered by different companies varies, but in its full form this allows the customer to vary the size of monthly payments according to means and need, switch the balance between investment and protection, to add items such as illness or disability cover, and even to borrow against accumulated funds. Many can incorporate pension provision. The corollary of this is more explicit advice-based, or 'relationship', rather than product selling. The expectation is that customers will have regular contact with the salesperson or adviser to ensure that the amounts and balance of savings and protection is appropriate to changing circumstances and expectations. Not only is this hoped to reduce lapses because of, say, job loss and divorce, but a long-term relationship with a company should ensure that all the customer's disposable resources available for savings and protection are secured by a single product provider. At the same time the best advice principle will be more or less achieved due to the complexity of the plan and difficulties of exact comparisons, coupled with discounting and special offers for the take-up of additional items.

The impact on sales forces has been considerably to increase their costs and this has forced many product providers to rethink their sales strategies. Most have greatly reduced the numbers of sales staff and some have introduced a salary element into their pay, rather than, as in the past, relying on commissions, which were argued by critics to be a powerful inducement to achieving sales at any cost to the customer. Cross-selling to existing customers in the manner of bancassurers has become attractive also to those such as composite insurers, who have other customers. Finally, some companies have sought to enlarge their sales force by buying up those of others, taking advantage of the chance to buy trained people and seeking to achieve economies of scale. In these cases considerable attention has been devoted to training and compliance in an effort to ensure that the letter if not the spirit of the new regulation is respected. Tied agents have on the whole been dispensed with as difficult to control, but IFAs have benefited as a welcome source of business for whose regulatory propriety the product provider is not responsible. IFA numbers stabilized at around 20,000 in the mid-1990s after an initial decline, though the number of firms declined more sharply as regulation and competition brought specialization and larger partnerships and put pressure on sole practice. Their market share began to rise at the expense of direct sellers and bancassurers and reached 50 per cent of sales in 1997. The total size of direct-sales forces fell by 65 per cent over the four years to 1995 and continued to decline thereafter, with the emphasis falling on more productive and better-trained staff.

On the regulatory side, it is pointed out by both companies and regulators that the financial press, which has grown apace in the past decade, now acts as an important source of advice to the public. Critical attention from increasingly sophisticated journalists can exercise a powerful discipline on product providers who engage in doubtful conduct or push unreliable products. Similarly, rogue IFAs are likely to merit warning articles, though not necessarily in time to prevent damage. Direct-product regulation is still precluded, and indeed resisted by the industry as oppressive and uncompetitive. This constitutes a difficulty, given the lack of capacity of some investors to appreciate the risks they may be taking, with home income plans providing a particularly conspicuous example. In their original risky form these are now banned, but settlement of all compensation claims still has not been reached. Once again, not only is the question of the quality of advice in selling raised, but also where the burden of responsibility lies, especially where investment is for long-term security. The most that has so far been done by way of product regulation has been for the PIA (subsumed from 1998 into the new FSA) to establish a product monitoring unit, which will alert the public to new products which seem to pose particular risks. Whether this constitutes product regulation by the back door remains to be seen.

The supervisory regulator, the SIB and now the FSA, has hence been presented with a dilemma. The whole of its investor protection strategy so far has, with the strong support of the industry, been reliant on the informed market choice model, backed by *caveat emptor*. To this end it has enforced a very much greater degree of disclosure, yet in doing so it has exposed the abhorrence of the industry at disclosure and its long-term practical reliance on a biased version of the professional–client model. Real professional advice will be expensive to provide in training costs and, even worse for the industry, endorse the public's desire to shift the responsibility to *caveat vendor*, with absolute rights of redress, along the lines of consumer protection legislation.

It seems that the SIB and now the FSA has recognized these problems and their regulatory origins, for there have been various reviews of the future of regulation. An early contribution to this was the idea of a 'disclosure dividend'. As a result of the information now available to the investor, it was argued that the investor is for the first time in a position to make an informed choice. Consequently, it was suggested that the earlier emphasis in regulation on the sales process and the quality and propriety of advice was becoming less important. Customers now know too much and cannot be bamboozled, and hence constant monitoring of the sales process is less necessary and some of the detailed rules and requirements can be dismantled.

Another suggestion has been that the issue of polarization, which introduced the insidious notion of 'best advice', can be reopened. During the passage of the Financial Services Act it was argued emphatically that a radical distinction between companies selling their own products and IFAs providing advice across the market was essential to avoid confusion, and that allowing a middle path of intermediaries tied to, say, half a dozen companies was unacceptable. There were always practical arguments in favour of multitying, notably that a good many IFAs had neither the capacity nor the inclination to appraise more than a limited number of leading companies and that, providing customers were advised on the comparative merits of the top dozen companies, they were unlikely to receive bad advice, even if they did not, in every case, receive quite the best. From a regulatory point of view multitying takes most of the sting out of the 'best advice' problem, because it fudges the issue. It is not the selling of one company's products alone, but comparative. On the other hand, it does not pretend to appraise the whole market, but is tied, leaving the onus on the customer to range more widely if that is what is wanted, though in the expectation, on the traditional selling model, that most will be hooked and not bother to look any further.

Conclusion

Does this account describe a regulatory system that is effectively the captive of the industry it regulates? A case could undoubtedly be developed to support this, but it would be an oversimplification. Rather the history of retail financial services is one in which the industry has been very lightly regulated until quite recently, and where its paternalistic ascendancy over customers has been historically taken for granted. The recent rapid expansion of the markets, with government support, accompanied by the dismantling of regulatory barriers between its sectors and the creation of new investor-protection regulation has produced a period of turmoil and a number of clear abuses for which the industry as a whole has still properly to accept its responsibility, still less atone. It is fair to say that the industry dominated the regulatory process in the establishment of the Financial Services Act regime, but since then it has been forced more on to the defensive. The belief, both by product providers and intermediaries, that they are providing a vital service to citizens is still widespread and genuinely held, and the commitment to *caveat emptor*, subject to safeguards against abuses, is an ideological one, that is to say, genuinely held as part of a wider market-based philosophy, as well as reflecting material interest. The practical problems posed by the top-heaviness of the industry represented by the product providers are sufficiently great to foster a plausible claim that radical regulatory changes that genuinely put investors, customers and citizens in the ascendant is just not possible at present, and hence that even discussing it as a serious option is pointless.

It is only when such serious discussion begins, probably initiated by government, almost certainly in the light of continued public failings of the existing arrangements, that the outline of coherent regulation will emerge that can ensure that the long-term financial security of investors is achieved with the participation of the private sector. As things stand, it is not clear what the limits on the capacities of the public to make informed choices are; regulation simply asserts those capacities. What products and services need how much regulation, on what terms, for which categories of citizens is hence something yet to be determined and constitutes a major agenda for the industry, the state, the regulators and of course, for academic enquiry.

In the meantime, some features of regulation have changed, but its overall character has not. The abolition of the two-tier structure and the imposition of consolidated state regulation by the new government only confirms what the industry expected and wanted. It had burned its fingers through self-regulation as a result of the scandals and abuses and it was safer to leave responsibility for getting it right to the state, whilst of course continuing to exercise influence. This in a variety of ways it was successful in doing, as the SIB's commendation of the disclosure dividend as the reward for successful regulation showed. This project was taken forward in various ways, by the SIB, IMRO and the PIA, all arguing that overall standards in the industry were now acceptable and regulatory compliance accepted as essential, and that the sensible way forward was to look at risk-rating firms and their activities both for their inherent risks and in the light of the compliance records. Whilst rational enough as an approach, the assumption of general compliance was highly questionable in an industry that continued to drag its feet over pensions mis-selling and, when forced to allocate funds to compensation, showed a general tendency to charge them to the investors' savings funds rather than to profits. Whilst the scandals and toughened regulation might hence be argued to have prevented the simple capture of regulation by the industry therefore, it was far from the case that the regulators had achieved ascendancy (Clarke 1998). Rather the situation was an intermediate one best understood in terms of the industry's continuing truculence. What remedies were likely from the new consolidated regulator for the financial sector, the Financial Services Authority, whose establishment was to be accompanied by new legislation was, at the time of writing unclear.

References

Clarke, M. J. (1986) *Regulating the City*, Milton Keynes: Open University Press.

—— (1998) *Citizens' Financial Futures: Deregulation of Retail Financial Investment in Britain*, Aldershot: Ashgate Publishing.

Clarke M. J., Smith, D. and McConville, M. (1994) *Slippery Customers, Estate Agents, the Public and Regulation*, London: Blackstone Press.

Gower, L. (1984) *Review of Investor Protection*, Cmnd 9125, London; HMSO.

Jebens, K. (1997) *LAUTRO: A Pioneer Regulator 1986–1994*, Salisbury: C. E. Jebens.

Knights, D. (1997) 'Governmentality and financial services: welfare crisis and the financially self-disciplined subject', in G. Morgan and D. Knights (eds) *Regulation and De-regulation in European Financial Services*, Basingstoke: Macmillan.

McDonald, O. (1990) *Report on Training and Competence in the Financial Services Industry*, London: SIB.

Nesbitt, S. (1995) *British Pensions Policy Making in the 1980s*, Aldershot: Ashgate Publishing.

Office of Fair Trading, (1993a) *The Marketing and Sale of Investment Linked Insurance Products*, London: OFT.

—— (1993b) *Fair Trading and Life Assurance Products*, London: OFT.

—— (1995) *Mortgage Repayment Methods*, London: OFT.

Personal Investment Authority (1996) *Consumer Panel Report*, London: PIA.

Securities and Investments Board (1993) *Retail Financial Services Regulation: Making the Two Tier System Work – the Large Report*, London: SIB.

Whitaker, P. (1995) *Effective Distribution*, London: Centre for Insurance and Investment, City University Business School.

12 Price structures in UK utilities

Responses to deregulation

Catherine Waddams Price

Introduction

Since the UK utilities were privatized, government and regulators have combined to bring about changes which are far reaching in their consequences for consumers. The introduction of competition has caused widespread rebalancing of prices, particularly in the residential sector. This chapter discusses such rebalancing from three viewpoints: how it is interpreted in the light of the requirement that these industries should show no undue preference or discrimination between consumers; the implications for economic efficiency; and the differential effects on household groups from the changes.

When the utility industries were privatized they consisted of vertically integrated monopolies. The same company operated the network for its own industry and area (pipes or wires) and supplied services to virtually every consumer in the UK. British Telecom and British Gas were nationwide monopolies, and water and electricity were supplied by regional monopolies. At privatization electricity generation and transmission were separated from distribution and supply, but the latter remained the responsibility of the relevant regional electricity company.

The industries' network activities are a natural monopoly, and will have to remain under single ownership. All suppliers need access to the network. To encourage competition in other aspects of supply the regulators need to ensure that there is access to this 'essential facility' in each case. This has involved accounting separation for industries where the incumbent also owned the network (regional electricity companies, British Telecom and British Gas). Moreover, incumbents need to be prevented from using their market powers in other ways to discourage and disadvantage new entrants.

The structural changes since privatization have been mirrored in a shift of emphasis of regulation from aggregate constraints on the level of prices which incumbents can charge to final consumers, to much more detailed control of prices for competitors to have access to the network, and more specific constraints on the final prices which incumbents can charge. (New entrants are generally not separately regulated, but are effectively constrained by needing to undercut the incumbent's prices to establish themselves in the market.) There is increasing emphasis on the structure of prices which incumbents charge as well as their level, so that market power is not exploited to disadvantage potential competitors. This concern mirrors the considerable rebalancing in tariffs by incumbents as competition has threatened.

Such issues were a major factor in stimulating the Labour government's review of regulation when it took office in 1997, culminating in the Green Paper in the spring of 1998. The issue of price structure is intimately concerned with costs, and the best way to recover the overall costs of supply from different consumer groups, raising the core issue of pricing as a means to promote both efficiency and equity.

The utilities have some cost characteristics in common, though gas, water and electricity have stronger similarities with each other than they do with telecoms. All have fixed networks which are used more and less intensively at different seasons and times of the day or year, leading to peak-load pricing issues. It is generally more expensive (on average) to supply those in rural areas than in more concentrated centres of population, but there may be heavy costs of maintaining networks in city centres where the infrastructure is older. The distance that the commodity has to be carried is a significant factor in the cost of gas, electricity and water, though there is more choice in locating the source for electricity than for the other utilities. In this case the choice depends also on the cost of transporting fuel for generation, including gas. All the industries have some customer-related costs which are incurred by keeping consumers attached to the system (meter reading and billing for example), costs which are independent of the quantities supplied.

The extent to which these costs have been reflected in tariffs has varied. The detailed discussion here concentrates on the residential markets, although we shall draw some broad comparisons between sectors. All levy a fixed charge per consumer, independent of consumption (for unmeasured water services this is the entire charge); for the other industries, at privatization this charge was probably less than the attributable costs of remaining connected, though technological changes in telecoms and increased efficiency in gas and electricity may have lowered this cost. Gas and telecoms prices have been geographically uniform, while water and electricity prices have varied according to the local (monopoly) supplier. Telephones have differentiated peak prices from others, electricity has an optional peak tariff in the residential market, gas and water do not. Such variation is not surprising since the appropriate balance depends both on the difference between peak and off-peak costs and the expense of monitoring peak-load consumption, both of which vary between industries. It is the extent to which such cost differences are reflected in tariffs (particularly to the residential sector) which is the subject of this chapter.

Definition and interpretation of undue discrimination

Undue discrimination is a very nebulous concept and, as one economist acknowledges, 'The more one thinks about price discrimination, the harder it is to define' (Phlips 1983: 5). His criterion is that 'price discrimination should be defined as implying that two varieties of a commodity are sold (by the same buyer) to two buyers at different net prices, the net price being the price ... corrected for the cost associated with the product differentiation' (1983: 6) (e.g. transportation costs). John Vickers suggests that 'a firm's pricing is discriminatory if it sells units of its output at different prices where costs do not differ correspondingly' (Vickers 1997b). By implication both these definitions suggest that it is also discriminatory to charge uniform prices to consumers with different costs of supply. In this case uniform prices are discriminatory, while (cost-reflective) differentiated prices are not.

Moreover, dependence on costs for determining discrimination immediately raises familiar problems of cost allocation, particularly in network industries where there are economies of scale which mean that average and marginal costs differ, and economies of scope which lead to a high proportion of common or joint costs (see, for example, Demski 1994). Ambitious claims are made for activity-based costing, now generally favoured by the regulated utilities, but it cannot solve the problem of allocating to particular activities or groups of consumers those costs which are jointly incurred, particularly capital costs.

The newly privatized industries have generally inherited a highly aggregated accounting system and pricing structure from their nationalized predecessors. In a monopolized market with broadly uniform charges, it was inappropriate to spend significant resources on allocating costs to different consumer groups. It is only in response to the new market situation that many of the cost data are being collected. There have been immense structural upheavals within the industries: two have been subjected to accounting separation; British Gas has been split into two separate companies (British Gas plc, including Transco, the pipeline company, and Centrica which owns British Gas Trading, the gas supply operation); several water and electricity companies have been involved in mergers. In so far as these offer real savings through economies of scope (e.g. between different utilities using a common billing system), it will complicate still further the cost-allocation exercise, and increase its arbitrariness. The numerous studies of cost allocation, including those of the privatized utilities (e.g. Carey *et al.* 1994) merely confirm the arbitrariness of the process of allocating joint costs.

These difficulties may be exacerbated by the regulatory system itself. The industries are subject to a cap on their revenue, and have broadly been free to rebalance within this constraint. Price *levels* are determined by the cap, while the *structure* of prices within it has generally been left to the company to determine, subject to exercising no undue discrimination or preference between consumers. The level of cap is reviewed periodically (five years is typical in monopoly markets) and the company can keep any excess profits which it makes by lowering the cost more than the regulator had anticipated in setting the cap. In effect, the excess of allowed revenue over efficient costs becomes a 'joint cost' to be allocated between product lines and consumers like any other. Moreover, in identifying such 'inefficient' costs, there may be judgements about past decisions which call to mind the problems in US regulatory reviews of determining whether or not costs incurred are allowable in the revenue cap.

In general, issues of price discrimination can be seen as concentrating on the structure of prices – between standing charges and running rates, urban or rural areas, methods by which consumers settle their bills – rather than their overall level, which is controlled by the regulated price cap. The intimate analysis of costs inherent in any investigation of price discrimination is in sharp contrast to the 'hands-off' philosophy of UK regulation which is epitomized by the price cap.

Most of the initial privatization Acts include a provision that suppliers should, in fixing tariffs, 'not show undue preference to any person or class of persons, and shall not exercise any undue discrimination against any person or class of persons' (Gas Act 1986: I-14(3)). The phrase was transferred from most of the nationalization Acts of the late 1940s; it is variously included in the Act itself as a duty of the company (Gas Act 1986; Electricity Act 1989), as a condition to be included in the licence (Telecommunications Act 1984 and in gas after the 1995 Gas Act), and as a duty of the Secretary of State and the industry's regulator (Water Act 1989). The Telecommunications and Water Acts both apply this phrase specifically to those in rural areas. The Competition and Service (Utilities) Act 1992 made further reference to undue discrimination (or preference), amending some of the privatization Acts accordingly.

Each regulator is also asked to take into account the interests of particular groups. In every utility this applies to customers of pensionable age, disabled or chronically sick, and for electricity and water those in rural areas are also included. There are also (unspecified) responsibilities for the environment. None of these is well defined, and they are interpreted somewhat differently by each regulator. Insofar as such considerations include the price charged to consumers for the product, there is no guidance as to the relationship between this responsibility and that to avoid undue preference or discrimination.

General competition Acts are also invoked against undue discrimination, and the 1998 Competition Bill will affect these industries, particularly in the parts which are competitive. The European Court of Justice makes a similar case for allowing such discounts, despite the provisions of Article 86. It is as a deterrent to competition that price discrimination is likely to be most heavily attacked in the courts. The European Commission is also likely to become more involved in utilities as a single European market is established and deregulation completed. Much of the effect of the European Court of Justice depends on progress with initiatives to establish the framework for a single market in electricity and gas. If these are successful it seems likely that Article 86 will be particularly relevant for energy since the incumbent suppliers will remain dominant as competition is introduced, though water may remain largely outside the Council's jurisdiction.

Deregulation of the telecoms market is much further advanced. In this industry the Community has made it clear that cooperation between authorities is allowable 'having first taken steps to ensure that there was no risk that the parties would discriminate against other suppliers of telecommunication services and that there would be no unfair subsidisation of the service by the parties' general telecommunications services' (Whish 1993: 349). If Article 86 is applied to utilities as it has been to other goods, a robust approach to price discrimination can be anticipated, though the cost analyses here are particularly difficult.

The most extensive investigation of price discrimination in the UK utilities has been in the gas industry, where its practices in the 'contract' market were referred to the Monopoly and Mergers Commission (MMC) within a year of privatization. This market was specifically excluded from the price discrimination conditions quoted in the Act above, and the enquiry was conducted under the aegis of the Fair Trading Act 1973, as being against the public interest. The MMC found against the company, imposing price schedules and other conditions which promoted the development of competition in this market (MMC 1988). Although it recommended that both the individual nature of the company's contracts and their secrecy be ended, they did suggest that quantity discounts be allowed. The large quantities which all the firms concerned bought is likely to have exhausted any economies of scale in supply, so quantity discounts must be a reaction to demand characteristics rather than costs. This is a classic case of second-degree price discrimination, where price depends on quantity purchased, though costs are unlikely to do so.

The 1988 MMC report dealt with discrimination in the contestable part of the market, where the price discrimination was seen as one of a number of mechanisms whereby British Gas discouraged new entrants. However, it is unlikely that this particular practice was *designed* to prevent new entry into piped gas supply, since it had been common during the industry's nationalized period and predated the removal of British Gas's legal monopoly (the market was liberalized *de jure* in the 1982 Oil and Gas (Enterprise) Act, but no new entrants appeared until 1990). Pricing structures were aimed more at countering competition from other fuels in the bulk heat market. This case was outside the jurisdiction of the regulator (who at that time was responsible only for encouraging competition in piped gas supplies).

However, the gas regulator, Ofgas, has dealt with two further referrals on price discrimination in final markets, looking at the differentials between tariffs in the residential market. In early 1998 it allowed price changes by the incumbent supplier (British Gas Trading) after detailed consideration of the relative reductions to be allowed. Both reports (Ofgas 1995, 1996: 330) noted that the 'important objective in attributing "joint" costs is to ensure that no customer or class of customer is required to bear an undue burden of ... "joint" costs as compared with others' and that 'fairness in the recovery of "joint" costs is one of the main issues to be addressed'. In electricity, similar issues of the balance between charges made to those paying by different means are arising as the market faces new entrants, with similar concerns about prepayment meter users, who are more expensive to supply and include a high proportion of vulnerable households.

This has distributional consequences as we shall see below, which may cause some concern. Regulators sometimes intervene in this process to prevent rebalancing and so perpetuate price discrimination on distributional grounds, as in the standing charge/rental cap example discussed above. By not requiring rebalancing to reflect costs, regulators implicitly condone other cross-subsidies, which will be eroded by competition rather than regulation. British Gas offered to lower the tariffs of those who paid by direct debit only after it was confirmed that the residential market would be opened up to competition, even though it could have increased its profits (and reflected costs more closely) by such a change in the monopolistic market. The regulators are far more concerned with potential new cross-subsidies than with those which have been inherited. In telecommunications the burden of proof is shifted from the regulator having to demonstrate that a pattern of prices is 'plainly wrong' to the industry having to justify its own price differentials to the regulator *ex ante*. In water the main issue has been in the balance of revenue collected from consumers paying for measured and unmeasured water supplies.

In the pricing of access to the monopoly networks, both electricity and gas regulators have influenced the structure of the prices charged. In the early 1990s, the electricity regulator constrained the extent to which the National Grid could rebalance prices to reflect the higher costs of transmitting power to the south of England, on grounds of containing sharp increases for particular regions. The gas regulator has limited the charge per consumer to be made to shippers for each residential consumer supplied, probably on the basis that this would make entry easier for new competitors in the market. All these constraints effectively perpetuate existing price discrimination on distributional or competitive grounds, though these are rarely made explicit.

The tension between monopoly regulation and competitive markets was also seen as the residential gas market was opened to competition in staged geographical areas. If British Gas were to defend its market in the initial competitive phase in the south west, it would need to lower its prices to meet those of competitors; but the non-discrimination clause would at first sight prevent it from doing so for these half-million consumers, unless it simultaneously did so for the remaining eighteen million. Lower prices in the south west certainly cannot be justified on the basis of *lower* costs; if anything, distance from the gas fields indicates higher than average costs. If the regulator allowed the prices to be lowered within the price cap, then British Gas could raise the prices elsewhere to balance the lower prices in the south west. If the regulator prevented any difference in price, competing in the south west would become too expensive for the incumbent, who would have virtually to abandon that market. The solution was effectively to apply separate caps in the competitive and non-competitive areas, so that British Gas could lower prices in the south west differentially, but not use these to trade against higher prices elsewhere within the overall cap. As the competitive market opens for both gas and electricity, the cap on average prices is being replaced by individual caps on each tariff to remove these undesirable incentives. The disadvantage of such caps lies in introducing rigidity into the price structure, and perhaps discouraging competition in some sectors of the market by constraining prices below costs.

The increasing move to multiutilities, where one company supplies several commodities to the same customer, raises other questions. The fixed costs of joint provision may be less than where separate companies supply the services, though the marginal costs of providing additional utilities is unlikely to be zero. Offers to provide extra services at zero 'standing charge' as has been suggested by some electricity companies offering gas to their consumers, or other discounts for customers who buy more than one service from the company, might be challenged in the courts as constituting a loyalty bonus, in contravention of both UK and European law. The size of the discount which such multiutility suppliers can offer may well depend on detailed analysis of their cost structures.

Price structure, price caps, competition and discrimination

Individual constraints on the structure of tariffs such as those outlined above are in stark contrast to the philosophy underlying the price cap, which is to allow the firm maximum freedom within a simple constraint which is easy to impose and monitor (Littlechild 1983). It may also prevent the firm from choosing the most efficient pricing structure.

In many circumstances discriminatory prices can maximize economic efficiency (Armstrong *et al.* 1994). This is particularly true where there are fixed or common costs incurred across several product or consumer groups, and where charging attributable or marginal costs to each group will not recover the total costs of supply. Such cost structures are frequently observed in the network industries where there are significant economies of scale and scope, even in those areas which do not constitute a natural monopoly. In cases such as these, the best way to maximize total efficiency is to raise most above marginal costs the prices of products and services whose demands are least responsive to such price increases. In this way demand is disturbed as little as possible from the first best level in which prices are equal to marginal costs. But such pricing is clearly discriminatory since prices are determined by demand factors and not just by costs. Some economists have suggested that demand aspects can be included so that prices which maximize social surplus are not discriminatory even if they do not reflect costs in the sense outlined above (Heald 1994). This would entail prices which reflected both costs and demand characteristics, raising prices most above marginal costs for consumers who will adjust their demand least in response. When demand considerations are explicitly included, this not only affects the argument in principle, but considerably broadens the range of prices which do not constitute discrimination. Legal considerations generally take a much narrower view: most arguments are couched solely in terms of the costs of supply, without reference to consumers' willingness to pay.

Efficient prices may have adverse distributional effects if the products with non-price responsive demands are basic necessities. For regulated industries this is a particular concern with respect to the standing/rental charges for staying connected to the system. Again it may be possible to incorporate distributional considerations in identifying the optimal prices, as Feldstein (1972) has suggested. However this is a complex process, requiring consensus on the relative weights to be attributed to the income of different members of society, and it is difficult to implement. In addition, problems may arise where the size of the market served by a firm is changing rapidly, and the marginal costs of serving an extra consumer are very different from the average costs of serving the market as a whole. For example an incumbent with high fixed costs of serving a particular market may lose market share rapidly as new entrants compete; the average costs of supplying the remaining consumers will rise because their fixed costs are spread over fewer consumers. In effect, the competitive system may be more expensive in the short run as the suppliers adjust their capacity to new circumstances.

Moreover, the economically efficient pattern of prices (defined above) is very difficult to identify, since it needs considerable information about demand patterns, as well as the problems of cost attribution already discussed. Such 'Ramsey pricing' is usually abandoned as impractical for regulators to impose (and if the nationalized industries achieved a pattern similar to Ramsey pricing it was likely accidental). But a pattern similar to Ramsey pricing might emerge from price-cap regulation, if it were in the regulated company's own interests to choose such prices. The company presumably has considerably more information about its consumers' reactions than the regulator, and some forms of price-cap regulation can induce such price patterns (Bradley and Price 1988). Such prices are discriminatory in the sense that demand as well as costs determine their pattern, and it is likely that they would result in higher standing/rental charges per consumer than at present permitted. The regulators' interventions could then be seen to be to prevent such rebalancing on the grounds of avoiding discrimination, though in practice it is more likely to result from (coincidental) social and distributional concerns.

The desirable incentives for allocative as well as productive efficiency from some price caps are less clear when competition starts to emerge unevenly across its markets. When a monopolist faces no competition, then it can be induced to balance prices efficiently in the economic sense. If there is competition (real or actual) in all markets, it becomes a price taker and regulation should no longer be necessary. But partial competition presents a more complicated issue. A price cap here may actually exacerbate predatory behaviour if both competitive and monopolized markets are included in it. For if prices in the monopolistic market are effectively constrained, lowering them in threatened markets gives the supplier a reward not only in that market (by deterring would-be entrants) but enables them to raise prices in the monopolized markets by giving some 'head room' within the aggregate price cap (Vickers 1997a). Perhaps the most important lesson for regulators is to recognize the incentives of the regulated firms to raise prices above costs in particular ways and markets, and to be vigilant against such behaviour if it is thought to be undesirable – remembering that discretion in how costs are allocated means that the firm may well be able to justify such moves on other grounds.

Here there are real dangers that the regulator will get sucked into a detailed examination of costs, where allocations are inevitably somewhat arbitrary. Regulated companies will soon learn their regulators' attitudes to appropriate recovery of cost, and costs will shift accordingly to justify what the regulated company wanted in the first place. The two referrals of British Gas supply (Ofgas 1995, 1996) to the regulator already reveal this tendency. The undue discrimination clause becomes ineffective, since the firm can always find some cost argument which will justify the pattern of tariffs it seeks, and both company and regulator expend large resources over the arguments. There is no perfect or impartial accounting rule, and regulators may have to abandon ambitions for very detailed cost allocation in the interests of a broad view. Moreover, this also avoids the danger of regulatory capture which may be present if there are detailed discussions on cost minutiae with a company which holds all the cost information and has considerably more resources at its disposal, and a much higher stake in the exercise, than does the regulator.

Very odd effects can occur in some price caps when competition is introduced, as the gas market has experienced. In this industry the current weighting of the cap meant that in the markets subject to competition, the company would simultaneously lower prices and lose market share, and so the quantity weight for that lower price; the effective cap on the rest of the market became harsher (since the lower prices now had lower weight), a phenomenon recognized by the MMC in recommending that British Gas's nominal price cap be lowered (MMC 1993). Similar distortions may arise if sliding-scale regulation is introduced, depending on exactly how the price cap relates to the sharing of profits.

Competition should remain a means rather than an end in itself, and may not always be desirable throughout these industries (parts of which are acknowledged to be natural monopolies). Moreover, there is a danger that in encouraging transparency regulators may unwittingly enable anti-competitive behaviour. For example, the requirement that incumbent firms publish price schedules provides a legitimate means of collusion for new entrants, particularly in a market where they are not fiercely competitive with *each other* for market share. The promises of new suppliers to the gas market to give discounts of a certain percentage on British Gas's prices is a good illustration of such 'price pegging'.

As competition is introduced, the emphasis on regulation shifts from controlling the prices of an incumbent monopolist to encouraging competition by making available the naturally monopolistic elements of the industry to new entrants. As a result, the issue of discrimination is likely to become more significant in access prices than in final market prices. Regulators themselves have expressed concern about allowing all suppliers access to the common network on the same terms. The structure of prices becomes crucial here, particularly the relationship of the incumbent's final prices to access prices charged to competitors (the fact that they are charged also to itself, as now required for telecommunications, is not a real constraint, since the allocation is merely an internal transfer so long as the two parts of the firms remain in common ownership). It is the gap between the incumbent's final prices and the access prices charged to entrants which determines the potential profitability of entry. The structure of that gap (i.e. for which consumers and types of supply it is greatest) determines where entrants are likely to concentrate their efforts.

Moreover, there is an important dynamic element, as incumbents anticipate entry (which has to be timetabled well in advance for legislative and operational reasons). They may anticipate that there will be constraints on how frequently they can alter their tariffs once competition is established. Ofgas has indicated that it would not expect British Gas to introduce new tariffs more than twice a year. The incumbent will then 'position' itself to face new entry, and may be able to affect the type of entrant by the structure of both its final and access prices (e.g. making it attractive for only large competitors by raising the fixed costs).

There may also be cross-subsidy over time. Where the incumbent must invest in new systems to meet changing market conditions, it may prefer to recoup the investment before competitors enter, charging present consumers the full cost of a system which will be operational over a number of years. This is a familiar problem of appropriate depreciation, given a new twist for an incumbent who is a regulated monopoly in the short-term, but faces competition in the more distant future.

Rebalancing observed: empirical evidence and distributional consequences

We have seen that there is no reliable and unique cost basis for tariffs, and that non-discriminatory tariffs may have adverse effects on both equity and efficiency; however, we can observe the rebalancing in prices which privatized firms have undertaken since their flotation.

We deal first with broad trends in the industrial and residential markets, and focus on the gas and electricity markets. Figure 12.1 shows that the gas and electricity suppliers have raised prices more, or lowered them less, for residential than for industrial users. This might either have increased or decreased the extent of discrimination. Nationalized industries were apt to undercharge in their residential markets, suggesting that recent rebalancing will have brought price patterns closer to costs. Moreover, there are obvious benefits for a firm to allocate as many costs as possible to its regulated sector (see Bradley and Price 1991), so increasing its apparent, if not real, costs of these activities. Industries have faced competition in their industrial markets, but only its threat in residential markets, so this may be an anti-competitive ploy which increases price discrimination. The timing for the divergences is also interesting. In the gas industry, two periods appear critical: 1985, around the time of privatization, and ten years later when competition in the industrial market was becoming truly effective (the incumbent had lost more than half its market by this time). Since 1996, as competition has extended in the residential market, the gap is narrowing again. In the electricity industry the gap has widened fairly steadily since 1990, when the industry was privatized with the prospect of competition being introduced into its large industrial markets first.

Moreover, in the gas industry we can identify a more detailed response to the regulatory environment and its changes. In the access market, the industry reversed its move towards more cost-reflective peak prices when it became clear that the price cap would be mainly determined by rate of return. In response it sought to lower charges for use of the system at peak

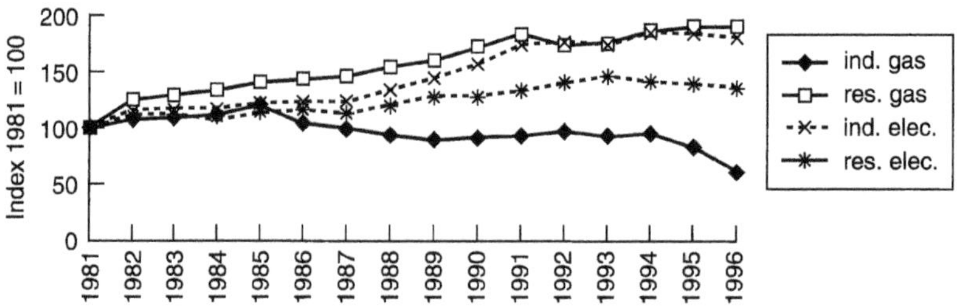

Figure 12.1 Changes in average gas and electricity prices charged to the industrial and residential sectors.

periods. This moved price structures away from costs, and was accepted by the regulator somewhat reluctantly (see Table 12.1). Since 1997 British Gas Transco has sought tariff structures which are more cost reflective. One possible explanation is the demerger of gas supply from the pipeline business, so the latter no longer had an incentive to protect the interests of the former, which might have been served by subsidizing peak demand.

On a more micro scale there has also been rebalancing within the residential sector. In the period since privatization British Gas has altered the balance between its tariffs considerably, raising the standing charge

Table 12.1 Gas industry: tariff structures since privatization

Date	*Regulation*	*Industrial market*	*Residential market*	*Access price*
1986	Privatization, no gas-to-gas competition	Perfect discrimination	Uniform tariff: standing and commodity charge	None
1987				Indicative
1988	MMC report	To be developed		
1989				Schedules introduced; repeatedly lowered
1991	OFT report	Insufficient competition		Changing structure
1992	Referral to MMC; regulation of access price, rate of return discussed			Shift of costs from capital to commodity and national to regional charges
1993	MMC report		Competition announced	
1994	Residential competition confirmed		Price differentials introduced	Lower long-distance charges to SW
1995	Structure of access standing charge determined	Price schedules suspended	More price differentials	
1996	MMC referral for pipeline charges		Competition introduced	
1997	Price caps agreed		Continued rebalancing	Rebalancing in favour of large consumers

Table 12.2 Reductions in annual gas bills since privatization

Payment method	*Number in sample*	*£ saved p.a. 1986–96*
Slot meter	622	122
Standard credit	9,473	94
Direct debit	6,060	141
All	16,155	113

Source: Based on analysis of Family Expenditure Survey Data for 1991–93 by Ruth Hancock.

more than the running rate (but still within the formula's constraint) and rebalancing between the prepayment and the credit tariffs. Consumers have therefore gained different amounts, and we can see on average how particular tariff groups have fared in the years since privatization (1986–96; see Table 12.2). This is a very crude estimate, and assumes that consumers have not switched between payment methods over the period.

We see that those paying by direct debit (receiving the discounts outlined in Table 12.2) have saved more from the tariff rebalancing than those on the standard tariff. It is interesting to note that the slot meter users have also benefited more than the average, despite a general perception that they have suffered under privatization, and the fact that their average consumption is generally lower than in the other categories, though the table does not show the effect of British Gas's transfer of many consumers on to the more expensive prepayment tariff in response to debt problems. The rebalancing among residential gas consumers has continued, as Figure 12.2 demonstrates. This shows both reductions in favour of direct debit payers, and a mixed picture for prepayment consumers. These changes will benefit more high-income than low-income consumers.

The erosion of cross-subsidies in residential markets is not distributionally neutral, though the pattern varies between utilities. In energy,

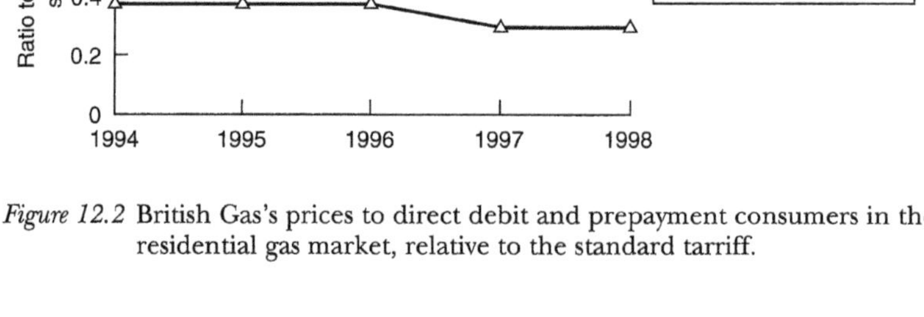

Figure 12.2 British Gas's prices to direct debit and prepayment consumers in the residential gas market, relative to the standard tarriff.

Table 12.3 Characteristics of gas-consuming households (% in each category)

	Characteristics of gas-consuming households	
	With no bank account	*With bank accounts*
Poorest quintile	59	16
Richest quintile	1	23
Pensioner household	42	23
Single parent	13	3
On income support	53	9
Disabled	16	9
Sample size	360	4,941

Source: 1991 FES data from Hancock and Waddams Price 1995.

demand increases with income but at a declining rate; water is still largely unmeasured, and charges levied are related to the value of the house occupied, though within unmeasured charges there has been considerable rebalancing between the fixed element, independent of this value, and the value-related charge. Telephone expenditure is much more responsive to changes in income, though this is reflected as much in which services are used as in the quantity of calls.

Moreover, those whose historical cross-subsidies are threatened by competition contain a disproportionate number of vulnerable families. This is most obvious, both intuitively and statistically, for those who do not have a bank account and cannot take advantage of lower charges for direct debit payers. Table 12.3 shows the characteristics of gas consumers who have no access to a bank account (and so are denied the savings from cheaper direct debit tariffs), compared with gas consumers who do have bank accounts, most of whom can take advantage of the discounts.

This pattern is common across the utilities, so that changes to reflect the lower costs of payment through bank accounts are broadly regressive. However, there is a discrepancy in how such costs are charged to households by different utilities, reflecting both different degrees of competition in the residential sector, and different attitudes to social issues. As an example, the discounts available to a residential consumer living in the English Midlands in February 1998 are shown in Table 12.4.

It should be noted that Severn Trent provides subsidies for customers paying weekly or fortnightly at post offices. Other utilities do not, but gas and electricity provide prepayment meters (almost always at higher charges) for consumers with debt problems. British Telecom offers some discount for quarterly variable direct debit payment, and a variety of other discounts.

The range of discounts offered by the different utilities seems very difficult to justify on cost grounds alone, and may more accurately reflect the extent of competition in each industry. Severn Trent justified their flat-rate

Table 12.4 Annual discounts available against 'standard tariff' for paying by monthly direct debit

Gas	£24.50 + 0.12p/kWh (average £47.12 p.a.)
Electricity (EMEB)	£5.00
Telecom	none
Water (Severn Trent)	none

fee and their subsidy to frequent-paying customers on the grounds that this helped most those who might have difficulty paying a lump sum annually or biannually (the standard charging procedure). The discounts given by the other utilities for payment through banks clearly disadvantages those without access to a bank account. 'Social pricing' may be a luxury that only the water industry, with little immediate threat of competition, can afford. The impact on different household groups of changes up to 1996, across the utilities, are as shown in Table 12.5.

Again we see that higher-income households have benefited more, and pensioners less than others. Other inherited subsidies which will be eroded by competition also probably help vulnerable families, so their removal will also be regressive. Table 12.6 shows the characteristics of households who consume very small and very large quantities, showing that more pensioners and poor households will suffer if the present subsidy on connection continues to be eroded, raising the price for small usage and lowering it for large usage, though multiutilities may be able to achieve economies of scope between commodities and lower some of these charges. Even more important than these average figures are the consequences for individual households of what may seem comparatively small changes in tariffs.

Responsibility for the effects of such rebalancing is unclear and politically sensitive. It seems unreasonable to expect the industries concerned to continue their 'social role' once privatized. Anyway, they cannot do so in the face of competition even if they wanted to, since any attempt to do so will make vulnerable to their competitors the markets providing the subsidy, and so the subsidies themselves will be sacrificed. The rebalancing is a direct result of the government's drive for competition, which seems to have delivered benefits to consumers on average by passing on some of the lower costs (Newbery and Pollitt 1997). The problems caused by these price changes result primarily from low income, and are exacerbated by simultaneous changes across the utilities, which form a large proportion of the expenditure of low-income families. It is unclear how far the Labour government elected in 1997 expects regulators or industries to play a social role. Social security payments and pensions are uprated by the Retail Price Index (RPI), which measures the change in price in an average expenditure basket. But this may well go down, even while the charges to vulnerable groups are increasing, so compensation is far from automatic. This

Table 12.5 Mean gains from price rebalancing, separately for each industry since privatization, £ p.a. (consumers only)

	Telecom	*Gas*	*Electricity*	*Indicative total*
All	0.0	0.0	0.0	0.0
Pensioner household	–10.5	–1.7	–1.2	–13.4
On disability benefit	–1.3	0.0	–1.6	–2.9
On income support	1.9	–0.1	0.0	1.8
Lowest income quintile	1.6	–0.7	1.1	2.0
2nd income quintile	–5.0	–0.4	–0.9	–6.3
3rd income quintile	–2.5	0.4	–0.3	–2.4
4th income quintile	–1.2	0.7	0.6	0.1
5th income quintile	6.8	–0.2	–0.7	5.9
Nos. in sample	17,621.0	15,906.0	6,717.0	

Source: Waddams Price and Hancock 1998.

Table 12.6 Characteristics of households consuming small and large amounts of gas (% in each group)

	Annual gas consumption		
	100 therms or less	*Over 1,500 therms*	*All*
Poorest quintile	26	17	18
Richest quintile	21	32	21
Pensioner household	31	13	24
Single parent	6	6	4
On income support	16	13	12
Disabled	7	7	9
Nos. in sample	264	218	5,301

Source: Hancock and Waddams Price 1995.

adds to the double jeopardy already posed by price-cap regulation, under which discounts offered to one section of consumers leaves more room for raising prices to others who cannot take advantage of the lower tariff. In such cases, optional tariffs may not always improve consumer welfare, if the 'standard' is thereby raised more than it otherwise would be and some are denied access to all the options. Regulators have addressed this by imposing individual price caps as an interim measure. While this provides short-term price protection, it may also discourage competition in high-cost (relative to revenue) markets with consequent long-term disadvantages for the very groups which such caps seek to protect.

The most obvious people to *monitor* the effects are the regulators, though it is unclear that they have either a duty or a right to rectify any adverse distribution, even for those groups for whom they have a statutory responsibility. Regulators have no special brief to help poor consumers, but they are mandated to take account of the needs of elderly consumers (in an unspecified way).

Conclusion

We see that regulators have a complex set of obligations, only one of which is to prevent undue preference or discrimination, and that all the utilities seem to be practising considerable cross-subsidy in response to historical inheritance and/or market pressures. Regulators' enthusiasm to prevent this varies considerably with the circumstances, and they are more vigilant to prevent new discrepancies than to erode inherited discrimination. As competition develops, prevention of undue discrimination is likely to become the mainstay of remaining regulation, probably increasingly administered under competition law both in the UK and under European regulation. It remains unclear exactly what is meant legally by undue discrimination, particularly with respect to the allocation of joint costs. Until this is resolved, companies are likely to continue to enjoy considerable latitude in setting their relative prices. Competition forces regulators to pay more attention to the structure of prices than to their aggregate level, which has been the traditional focus in regulating monopoly utilities. How far this should extend to identifying and eliminating cross-subsidies is crucial for the industries and their consumers in the future. It will affect the attractiveness of different markets to new entrants, the efficiency with which competition develops, and has significant distributional implications, particularly for vulnerable households.

Acknowledgements

I am grateful to participants at the EMOT Workshop, Manchester Business School and at a seminar at London Business School for comments on versions of this paper. Thanks are also due to British Gas Trading for supplying information on tariff changes. A revised version of this paper was published in *Utilities Law Review*, September/October 1997 under the title 'Undue discrimination and cross-subsidies: price structures in UK utilities'.

References

Armstrong, M., Cowan, S. and Vickers, J. (1994) *Regulatory Reform*, Cambridge, MA: The MIT Press.

Bradley, I. and Price, C. (1988) 'The economic regulation of private industries by price constraints', *Journal of Industrial Economics* XXXVII(1): 99–106.

—— (1991) 'Partial and mixed regulation of newly privatised UK monopolies', in W. Weigel (ed.) *Economics Analysis of Law*, Vienna: Schriftenreihe der Bundeswirtschaft-skammer.

Carey, A., Cave, M., Duncan, R., Houston, G. and Langford, K. (1994) *Accounting for Regulation in UK Utilities*, London: Institute of Chartered Accountants in England and Wales.

Competition and Service (Utilities) Act (1992) London: HMSO.

Demski, J. (1994) *Managerial Uses of Accounting Information*, Lancaster: Kluwer Academic Press.

Electricity Act (1989) London: HMSO.

Fair Trading Act (1973) London: HMSO.

Feldstein, M. (1972) 'Distributional equity and the optimal structure of public prices', *American Economic Review* 62: 32–6.

Gas Act (1986) London: HMSO.

—— (1995) London: HMSO.

Hancock, R. and Waddams Price, C. (1995) 'Competition in the British domestic gas market: efficiency and equity', *Fiscal Studies* 16(3): 81–105.

Heald, D. (1994) 'Cost allocation and cross-subsidies', report for the European Commission.

Littlechild, S. (1983) *Regulation of British Telecommunications Profitability*, London: HMSO.

MMC (1988) *Gas*, Cm 500, London: HMSO.

—— (1993) *Gas and British Gas, plc*, Cm 2314–2317, London: HMSO.

Newbery, D. and Pollitt, M. (1997) 'Restructuring the CEGB: was it worth it?', *Journal of Industrial Economics* XLV(3): 269–304.

Ofgas (1995) *Referral by the Gas Consumers Council Relating to Discounts for Customers Paying by Direct Debit: the Director General's Decision*, London: Ofgas.

—— (1996) *Decision on Referral on Option Pay*, London: Ofgas.

Oil and Gas (Enterprise) Act (1982) London: HMSO.

Phlips, L. (1983) *The Economics of Price Discrimination*, Cambridge: Cambridge University Press.

Telecommunications Act (1984) London: HMSO.

Vickers, J. (1997a) 'Regulation, competition and the structure of prices', *Oxford Review of Economic Policy* 13(1): 15–26.

—— (1997b) 'When is discrimination undue?', IEA/LBS lecture, 18 November.

Waddams Price, C. and Hancock, R. (1998) 'Distributional effects of liberalising UK residential utility markets', *Fiscal Studies* 19(3): 295–319.

Water Act (1989) London: HMSO.

Whish, R. (1993) *Competition Law*, Oxford: Butterworths.

13 Regulating money laundering

A case study of the UK experience

Prem Sikka and Hugh Willmott

In this chapter, we focus upon the UK state's response to allegations of money laundering against accountants to interrogate the regulatory dynamics of the fight against this activity. By detailing a money laundering court case, our study illustrates how this activity is undertaken and the role which accountancy firms play in this. Our study then explores the operations of the regulatory apparatus in the UK in addressing cases of money laundering. Despite the court judgement, we note the reluctance of regulatory authorities to investigate evidence and allegations brought out in this case. This indicates, in our view, an alarming degree of inertia and buck-passing within the UK regulatory process. The evidence of this case suggests the existence of a deeply ingrained indifference to the apparent involvement of major accounting firms in money laundering activity, or, at least, it suggests an institutionalized disinclination to undertake vigorous and open investigation of such cases.

Money laundering in context

During the 1980s and the 1990s, market capitalism became an unrivalled global economic system. To attract financial flows, nation states have increasingly been obliged to restructure their economies by promoting an 'enterprise culture' and by lowering international barriers to the free flow of goods, services and money. Though globalization is an uneven process (Hirst and Thompson 1996), its intensification is clearly evident in the world of finance where the development and application of communication and information technologies has fostered an increased mobility of capital, enabling money to roam the world and be traded as a commodity (Harvey 1989; Giddens 1990; Herring and Litan 1995).

In liberal democracies, it is widely expected that the state enacts legislation to protect its citizens and to facilitate the necessary stability for smooth accumulation of economic surpluses by business enterprises. At the same time, regulation by the state is often resisted by those who perceive their 'private interests' or 'freedom' to be detrimentally affected by such regulations (Angell 1996). They strive to apply pressures, individually and collectively, upon the state to limit and dilute restrictions upon their activity. There are also questions about the implementation and enforcement of laws, especially as the state does not have any direct means of examining business life and intruding into its daily affairs. In order to secure even minimal compliance and enforcement with some laws – for example against corporate crime, fraud, institutionalized lawbreaking – vigilance is required inside private organizations. The separation of 'public' and 'private' spheres in modern societies means that, to a greater or lesser extent, the state depends upon the business sector to monitor and report compliance.

Globalization and money flows

The geographical mobility of capital has been vastly increased by the development of global stock markets, money, futures, derivatives, currency, interest rates and other markets, a condition which encourages intensification and interdependence between competing states and societies. The freer flow of money has been facilitated by the development of new financial centres which ask few questions, guarantee secrecy to their clients and obstruct inquiries by international regulators (Kerry and Brown 1992; Hampton 1996)). Even in the major international financial centres (e.g. London, New York), the technological and organizational structures used for legitimate business transactions (e.g. limited liability companies) can easily be used to enable the proceeds of drug trafficking, smuggling, terrorism, tax evasion, bootlegging, art theft, vehicle theft, fraud and other illegal activities.

The deregulatory environment has also encouraged a 'cynical disregard of laws and regulations' (Department of Trade and Industry 1997: 309). The combination of entrepreneurialism, deregulation and financial globalization has given rise to what Castells (1997) calls 'the mother of all crimes – money laundering' (p. 260), a process which enables knowledgeable elites to transmit 'illicit funds through the banking system in such a way as to disguise the origin or ownership of the funds' (Bingham 1992: 25). The amounts being laundered are estimated to be anything between US$750 billion (Castells 1997: 260) and a trillion dollars (Wiener 1997), figures which dwarf the Gross Domestic Product of many nation states.

Money laundering is not the preserve of a few deviant individuals occupying some Dickensian dim and sleazy 'den of crimes'. Rather, it is planned, executed, minuted and concealed in clean, respectable, warm and well-lit city centre offices. As the forced closure of the Bank of Credit and Commerce International (BCCI) showed, money laundering is facilitated through 'the use of shell corporations, bank confidentiality, secrecy havens, layering of corporate structures, the use of front-men and nominees, guarantees and buy-back arrangements; back-to-back financial documentation, kick-backs and bribes, the intimidation of witnesses, and the retention of well-placed insiders to discourage government action' (Kerry and Brown 1992: 1). Those who facilitate money laundering command very high fees – as much as 20 per cent of the money laundered (Hook 1998).

The laundered amounts are large enough to stimulate and/or destabilize financial markets, national/world economies and social order (Home Affairs Committee 1994; Rider 1996). Bribery and corruption at senior policy-making levels can play havoc with democratic politics. The loss of taxation revenues and the large amounts of illicit proceeds make it difficult for some governments to manage national economies. The resulting instability poses a threat to the relatively stable economic and political environment necessary for smooth accumulation of profits and revenues by capitalist enterprises.

The regulation of economic activity by nation states is a product of recurrent conflicts which involve a process of negotiation and bargaining between representatives of the public and private sectors. Exemplifying this process of negotiation, social policy on combating money laundering is constantly in the making: a relaxation of legislation that inadvertently undermines business confidence and/or mass support is followed by pressures for increased regulation. Members of the business world may contest and resent the direct encroachment of the state into what they often prefer to represent as their private affairs. Yet, in addition to demands for 'stability' and 'predictability', there are ideologies of justice, fairness and accountability as well as pressure-group activity which demands that the state place restrictions upon private businesses and, to some extent, holds them accountable to the wider public.

The role of nation states: the UK case

Nation states have responded to the threat of money laundering by re-regulating at both the international and national levels. Through legislation they have sought to redefine the limits of lawful conduct. At the international level, the 1988 United Nations (Vienna) Convention has encouraged nation states to cooperate by sharing information and tracing laundered proceeds across their territorial boundaries. The Vienna Convention also shaped the European Union's Directive on Prevention of the Use of Financial Systems for the Purposes of Money Laundering. The UK government implemented the Directive by creating the Criminal Justice Act (CJA) 1993. Under the CJA and the money laundering regulations made thereunder (for a discussion, see Bosworth-Davies and Saltmarsh 1994; Auditing Practices Board 1997; Wiener 1997), it is an offence to knowingly launder, or assist another person to launder, the proceeds of crime. The CJA's main focus is banks and financial institutions but it also places special responsibilities on all citizens to report money laundering, or suspicious transactions, to a specially designated agency, the National

Criminal Intelligence Service (NCIS). It is an offence to fail to disclose knowledge or suspicion of money laundering to the authorities, or to tip off any person about an actual or impending investigation by the authorities into any alleged money laundering activity.

One of the conclusions of the NCIS is that 'Criminals continue to use … professional money launderers (including solicitors and accountants)' (1996/97 report of the NCIS: 9). However, the World Bank is encouraging nation states to place greater reliance upon accountants/auditors to monitor company transactions and inform the regulators of any suspicious transactions (Wolfensohn 1998). The reason for this is simply that accountants claim to have the necessary expertise to identify, investigate and report suspicious transactions (Bond 1994; ICAEW 1994a; Auditing Practices Board 1997) and assist the state to manage the risks generated by the liberalization of markets.

In the UK, the state already places considerable reliance upon accountants/auditors to monitor the activities of financial businesses and report suspicious transactions to designated regulators, even without the knowledge of their clients (Power 1993; Auditing Practices Board 1995; Sikka and Willmott 1995; Sikka *et al.* 1998). The calls for greater reliance upon accountants are based upon an image of accountants as altruistic and public spirited 'professionals'. It ignores the fact that, as managers and owners of significant businesses, accountants are not immune to the structural pressures of a capitalist economy and need to make profits to survive. Hanlon notes that the socialization processes within accountancy firms are mainly concerned with 'being commercial and on performing a service for the customer rather than on being public spirited on behalf of either the public or the state' (Hanlon 1994: 150). Accountancy firms have shown a considerable capacity for 'turning a blind eye on the wholesale abuse by client company directors of [legal] provisions' (Woolf 1983: 112) and 'disclosing considerably less than what they actually know' (Woolf 1986: 511; also see Sikka and Willmott 1995). The recent statistics published by the NCIS (see Table 13.1) suggest that accountants do not easily notice

Table 13.1 Total number of disclosures made to NCIS since 1992

	Total disclosures	*Disclosures by*	
		Accountants	*Solicitors*
1992	11,289	1	4
1993	12,750	2	4
1994	15,007	6	86
1995	13,710	38	190
1996	16,125	75	300
1997	14,148	44	236

Source: Annual Reports of the National Criminal Intelligence Service (NCIS).

instances of money laundering; or perhaps they are unwilling to communicate suspicious transactions to the regulators (80 per cent of notifications are from banks and building societies).

The remainder of this chapter is organized into four further sections. The first section presents our case study in which an accountancy firm (Jackson & Co.) was judged to have used a series of shell companies to launder money. It is based upon evidence given in open court and from a review and summary of the judgement read out by Mr Justice Millett in the case of *AGIP (Africa) Limited* v *Jackson and Others* [1990] 1 Ch 265 (also see Mansell 1991a; Robinson 1994: 293). By drawing upon the court judgement, we detail how large sums of money passed through the offices of this firm, though the only benefit derived by those involved took the form of standard fee income. We also note that the High Court judgement stated that a number of contacts and schemes were provided to Jackson & Co. by a Grant Thornton partner. The second section examines this link. We submit that the clarity of the High Court judgement and the many unanswered questions surrounding the comparatively high-profile AGIP case might reasonably have attracted the attention of UK regulators. More specifically, allegations made during the course of the court case were, we submit, of sufficient seriousness to merit an investigation of the involvement of the larger accountancy firm in the AGIP affair. The apparent lack of action prompted us to engage in a dialogue with the regulators in an effort to stimulate their interest in the case. Through a series of questions raised in parliament and numerous letters to regulators and ministers, including the Prime Minister, we sought to discover how the regulatory apparatus was responding to the revelations of the AGIP case. This correspondence is reported in the third section. On the basis of the findings derived from our investigation of the response of the regulators and ministers, the fourth section concludes that one possible explanation of the blindness and/or indifference of the regulators to accountants' involvement in the AGIP case is a disarmingly and disturbingly close relationship between the UK accountancy profession and the state.

The AGIP court case

In the late 1970s and early 1980s, AGIP (Africa) Limited, a company incorporated in Jersey, was engaged in drilling for oil in Tunisia, on its own behalf and in joint ventures with other companies under permits and concessions granted by the Tunisian government. Jersey is part of the Channel Islands which are British, but not part of the United Kingdom. They enjoy the status of self-governing dependencies of the British Crown, but the UK is responsible for their defence and foreign affairs. Nor are the Channel Islands part of the European Union. The islands are tiny, but a large number of multinational companies are based there to avoid taxation in their host countries. Corporate laws in these islands are relatively lax. Secrecy is preferred to public accountability (Grey 1994; Hampton 1996). The Tunis branch of AGIP held a US$ account at Banque du Sud from which overseas suppliers were paid. Over a period of many years (since 1976), both before and after 1983 when accountants Jackson & Co. became involved in the matter, AGIP was systematically defrauded of millions of dollars by its chief accountant, a Mr Zdiri (see the Appendix for the full 'cast of characters' in this drama). Though not a director of the company or a signatory of any bank account, he was responsible for collecting invoices and matching them to the completed payment orders prior to obtaining approved signatures for the same. He was also responsible for banking. The court judgement recorded that Mr Zdiri had used his position to misappropriate the funds by altering the name of the payee on the payment orders after obtaining authorized signatures.

Mr Justice Millett's judgement stated that between March 1983 and January 1985, Mr Zdiri defrauded AGIP of US$10.5 million by altering some twenty-seven orders which found their way to England. The payees were all companies registered in England and managed by Jackson & Co., based in the Isle of Man. Seven different companies, each holding a US$ account at a major branch of Lloyds Bank (a major British bank) were used in succession to receive the monies. However, AGIP did not bring a criminal case for fraud or even a case for the recovery of US$10.5 million or anything (said to be in excess of US$17 million) dating back from 1976. Instead, it took civil action under 'law of trust' to recover only the sum of US$518,822.92 (being the last of the diverted monies), paid on 7 January 1985 to Baker Oil Services, on the ground that this was all that Jackson & Co. could reasonably afford to repay.

The case was defended by Mr Barry Jackson and a Mr Edward Bowers (the court found no case against the latter), who practised as chartered accountants in Douglas, Isle of Man, under the name of Jackson & Co. The third defendant, a Mr Ian Griffin, was an employee of Jackson & Co. The defendants, the judge noted, were acting on the instructions of a French lawyer, Monsieur Yves Coulon, who in turn was acting for principals whose identity is not known. The court judgement recorded that Jackson & Co. were introduced to Coulon by Roger Humphrey of Thornton Baker (now Grant Thornton). Each of the companies into which the funds had been paid had a nominal share capital which was usually registered in the names of service companies provided by Jackson & Co. In each case, Mr Jackson and Mr Griffin were the directors and the authorized signatories on the company's bank account. Roger Humphrey was also a director and a signatory in the case of the first few companies. None of the companies had any assets or carried on any genuine business activity. In the case of each company, except that of Baker Oil, after two or three payments had been received and paid out, the account was closed and a new account opened for the successor company. Its predecessor was then put into liquidation and either Mr Jackson or Mr Bowers was appointed liquidator. All bank statements of the payee companies showed the receipts to be derived from payments made by AGIP.

When a payment was received by the payee company, it was immediately transferred, usually on the same day, to another company, Euro–Arabian Jewellery Limited, which also maintained a US$ account at the same branch of Lloyds bank. Euro–Arabian was registered in England with Mr Jackson as one of its three directors. Jackson, Humphrey and Griffin were the authorized signatories of its bank account, with the agreement that either could act as a signatory in his own right. The court judgement recorded that there was 'no evidence to show that Euro–Arabian carried on any genuine business activity' (quotations from Mr Justice Millett's judgement in *AGIP (Africa) Limited* v *Jackson and Others* [1990] 1 Ch 276). As soon as it received any payment from a payee company, it paid it out to parties located abroad. Most of the money went to Kinz Joaillier SARL, incorporated in France, which appears to be a subsidiary of Euro–Arabian Jewellery. Mr Jackson was a director of the company with Yves Coulon acting as its legal adviser. Coulon had no authority to operate the bank accounts of any of the payee companies or Euro–Arabian, but the bank's assistant manager (who was not involved in the fraud in any way whatsoever) was authorized to disclose information about the accounts to him. Indeed, Coulon visited the bank during his travels to London and lunched with him, and he believed Coulon to be the man behind all the arrangements. The bank's assistant manager was told to expect payments of about US$500,000 per month from Tunis. When a payment was expected, the assistant manager would be notified by Jackson & Co. Upon receipt of money, he would telephone Jackson & Co. and inform them that the sums had been received. After a short interval, but usually on the same day (presumably after instructions from someone, e.g. Coulon), upon Mr Jackson's instructions, the monies would be paid out.

The case brought by AGIP centred on a payment to Baker Oil, which was incorporated on 12 December 1984. Baker Oil's immediate predecessor compay was Parkfoot Limited, which had been put into liquidation on 6 December 1984, shortly after receiving and paying out to Euro–Arabian on the same day US$502,458.33. Baker Oil had authorized share capital of £2,000 with two shareholders and bank signatories who were also its directors. Mr Jackson and Mr Griffin held the entire issued share capital of £1 each. Baker Oil opened a US$ account at the same London bank branch on 17 December 1984. Just a day later, a Mr del Sorbo, an AGIP official, had signed a payment order of US$518,802.92 in favour of Maersk Supply (Tunisia) Limited, payable at Morgan Guaranty Trust Company of New York. After the signature, the payment had been altered and made payable to 'Beker–Service Cie' with the address of the London branch of Lloyds Bank and the correct number of Baker Oil's dollar account. The altered payment order was executed by Banque du Sud on 7 January 1985. Jackson & Co. had already told Lloyds Bank to expect a payment and asked to be informed of its arrival. On 7 January Mr del Sorbo also became aware of the fraud as he visited Banque du Sud. He asked the bank to stop the payments, but due to time differences between London, Tunis and New York, payments had already been made and could not be reversed. The sum of US$518,822.92 was received to the account of Baker Oil and then transferred to the account of Jackson & Co. (opened in March 1984), held at the same branch of Lloyds, and Baker Oil's account was immediately closed. These transactions were confirmed in a letter to Baker Oil. On 9 January 1985, the same amount was transferred to Jackson & Co.'s 'Client's' account at the Isle of Man Bank Limited. On 15 January, US$400,000 was paid out from this bank account to Kinz Joaillier SARL. US$70,000 was paid out to Mr Chouck ben Abdeaziz (who has not been traced) and US$ equivalent of FF34,330.70 to M. Coulon. Subsequently, Baker Oil, Euro–Arabian and Kinz were all put into liquidation. AGIP brought proceedings in Tunisia against Banque du Sud and also sought to recover US$518,822.92 from Baker Oil (which no longer existed) and Jackson & Co.

During the court case, Jackson & Co. 'elected to call no evidence' (*AGIP (Africa) Limited* v *Jackson and Others* [1990] 1 Ch 276). Therefore, the court attached considerable importance to some documents presented to it. One of these related to the minutes (dated 22 March 1984) of the first meeting of Keelward Limited, another of the payee companies. The minutes noted that 'the receipt of monies from Tunisia ... formed part of a long standing arrangement ... the arrangements resulted in the extraction of monies from Tunisia in circumvention of the Tunisian Exchange Control Regulations'. In another document, a letter (dated 14 August 1984) addressed to Mr Jackson by a firm of solicitors noted that 'AGIP may be able to establish a cause of action by claiming that the payments were obtained by fraud. AGIP could also rely on English law as the fraud would presumably have taken place within England, at the time when monies were transferred out of AGIP's account into the account of the UK company ... although AGIP may be able to establish a cause of action, it would still be necessary for AGIP to establish fraud (as defined under English law) for any action for the recovery of the monies to be successful ... Because of the general principle of banking confidentiality, it would be extremely difficult for the Tunisian Government or AGIP to obtain an order requiring Lloyds Bank to disclose banking transactions, unless disclosure is ordered by the English Courts ...' (*AGIP (Africa) Limited* v *Jackson and Others* [1990] 1 Ch 277–8).

In his judgement, Mr Justice Millett stated (also see *The Times*, 20 May 1989: 3; 5 June 1989: 41) that:

> Mr Jackson and Mr Griffin knew ... of no connection or dealings between the Plaintiffs and Kinz or of any commercial reason for the Plaintiffs to make substantial payments to Kinz. They must have

> realised that the only function which the payee companies or Euro–Arabian performed was to act as 'cut-outs' in order to conceal the true destination of the money from the Plaintiffs ... to make it impossible for investigators to make any connection between the Plaintiffs and Kinz without having recourse to Lloyds Bank's records; and their object in frequently replacing the payee company by another must have been to reduce the risk of discovery by the Plaintiffs. Mr Jackson and Mr Griffin are professional men. They obviously knew they were laundering money ... It must have been obvious to them that their clients could not afford their activities to see the light of the day. Secrecy is the badge of fraud. They must have realised at least that their clients might be involved in a fraud on the Plaintiffs.
>
> (*AGIP (Africa) Limited* v *Jackson and Others* [1990] 1 Ch 294)

To recap, monies were being transferred from AGIP to Kinz Joaillier SARL via a number of other 'cut-out' companies and their bank accounts. In this process, accountants Jackson & Co. were judged by the courts to have dishonestly assisted in the misapplication of funds. As Mr Justice Millett's judgement also noted, Jackson & Co. were introduced to various schemes and payee companies by a Grant Thornton partner. We now consider this link.

The Grant Thornton connection

The High Court judgement stated that:

> Jackson & Co. were introduced to the High Holborn branch of Lloyds Bank Plc in March 1983 by a Mr Humphrey, a partner in the well known firm of Thornton Baker [now part of Grant Thornton]. They probably took over an established arrangement. Thenceforth they provided the payee companies ... In each case Mr Jackson and Mr Griffin were the directors and the authorized signatories on the company's account at Lloyds Bank. In the case of the first few companies Mr Humphrey was also a director and authorised signatory.
>
> (*AGIP (Africa) Limited* v *Jackson and Others* [1990] 1 Ch 275)

So how did Roger Humphrey and Grant Thornton become involved? Before joining Grant Thornton, Roger Humphrey was employed during 1979/80 by Minet Financial Management Limited in London (this section is based on press reports of the High Court judgement and a 'proof of evidence' drawn up by Roger Humphrey in the presence of Grant Thornton solicitors: for the press reports see Mansell 1989a, 1989b, 1991a). Minet Financial Management had a subsidiary in Guernsey, Minet Trust Co. (International) Limited. In common with other off-shore havens, Guernsey legally enables individuals and companies to hold nominee accounts and facilitates secrecy/privacy concerning their financial dealings. Over the years, major finance houses have located in places like Guernsey and offer services to a variety of clients. In common with many other financial intermediaries, part of Minet Trust's business involved the handling of funds through trusts and other arrangements for wealthy clients who wished to keep their monies in secret 'off-shore' tax havens, such as Guernsey. In late 1979/80, Humphrey made a business trip to Guernsey. By chance he met the managing director of Minet Trust who was accompanied by Yves Coulon, a French lawyer. Coulon eventually invited Humphrey to act as an intermediary, an offer which Humphrey accepted as it required him to pass on, rather than execute, the instructions. These instructions were dictated to Humphrey and Coulon did not put them in writing.

During the course of his dealings with Coulon, Humphrey became aware that payments were being received from Tunisia and that the amounts were placed to the account of various shell companies created by Minet Trust. The first such company, Humphrey recalls, was Anderfield Limited (incorporated in February 1980). Humphrey was not an officer of this company but became aware that funds received were transmitted onwards to various bank accounts in France in accordance with Coulon's instructions. He also became aware that the arrangements were being operated for the benefit of a prominent Tunisian, Sophie Ben Hassine (for further details of her involvement see Mansell 1991a, 1991b). Humphrey understood that Ben Hassine had substantial funds which she wished to transfer to France via England and knew that although she lived in France, she did not wish to have her funds in France in her name. There was nothing unusual in these arrangements, as Minet Trust was routinely and quite legally engaged in the handling of funds off-shore for prominent and wealthy European clients.

Humphrey left Minet in November 1981 to join banking house Tyndall Trust in London. In common with other respected businesses, Tyndall Trust was also engaged in the provision of off-shore services to clients. Coulon suggested that the existing scheme or arrangements should also move with him. Humphrey suggested the idea to John Botting, a director of Tyndall Trust International (IOM) Limited. Humphrey recalls that Botting and Coulon probably met without his presence; he is not sure what enquiries were made of the links with Coulon or Ben Hassine. Humphrey was not concerned since he was acting as a messenger/intermediary. During his employment at Tyndall, Humphrey also eventually met Ben Hassine.

On 14 December 1981, shortly after Humphrey had moved to Tyndall Trust, Euro–Arabian Jewellery Limited was incorporated (originally under the name Boldford Limited) and Humphrey became an authorized bank signatory to its account held with Midland Bank in London. One of the initial directors of the company was John Botting of Tyndall Trust

International who was replaced in 1984 by Barry Jackson. Jackson resigned in 1985 to be replaced by Ian Griffin. Humphrey was also a signatory for Lenthorpe Limited and Palmerstone Limited and three further shell companies (or 'cut-outs') created by Tyndall Trust. In his capacity as a signatory on the account of Lenthorpe Limited, Humphrey became aware, for the first time, that the funds in question were being remitted from AGIP (Africa) Limited.

In November 1982, Humphrey left Tyndall and joined Thornton Baker (now Grant Thornton). Once again, Coulon suggested that the schemes move with him. Humphrey was not certain whether this would be possible but soon became aware that Grant Thornton had a 'correspondent firm', Jackson & Co., in the Isle of Man which engaged in similar operations. In January 1983, Humphrey introduced Coulon to Barry Jackson, but for many months Coulon continued to pass his instructions to Jackson & Co. through Humphrey. Thereafter, Humphrey claims that Coulon dealt directly with Jackson & Co. and that May 1983 was the last time he was actively involved in relation to instructing the bank to effect transfers through another payee company, Windlist Limited. The relationship between Grant Thornton and Jackson & Co., however, continued until 1989 when, in the wake of the 1989 High Court judgement, Grant Thornton announced (on 30 October 1989) that in light of the judge's comments, the agreement between the firm and Jackson & Co. had been suspended.

(In)action of the UK regulators

AGIP won the court case and Jackson & Co. were required to repay around $700,000 (the Baker Oil money plus interest) even though the monies had passed through various bank accounts and eventually reached Sophie Ben Hassine. Jackson & Co. went out of business as Barry Jackson was unable to obtain sufficient professional indemnity cover. The AGIP court case raised a number of questions about the involvement of accountants and accountancy firms in money laundering. A Grant Thornton senior partner acknowledged, 'I don't think there is any doubt that Humphrey met this man [Yves Coulon], passed on instructions, did things for him' (cited in Mansell 1989b; also see Mansell 1991c). In addition, there were questions about the efficiency of external audits (*Accountancy Age*, 20 April 1989: 3; 18 May 1989: 2; 13 July 1989: 3; 20 July 1989: 1; 30 May 1991: 2; also Mansell 1991d), especially as auditors and accountants are assumed to be in the front line of the war against fraud. In the case of AGIP, a number of questions are relevant. For example, as the payments by AGIP were fraudulently diverted, how did the original creditors get paid? Following standard auditing procedures (Coopers & Lybrand 1984; Woolf 1986), auditors may have examined supplier statements or obtained direct confirmation of outstanding balances from suppliers. What did this evidence reveal, or were the frauds too well concealed? Either way, the high profile of the AGIP case might have prompted the regulators to examine the implications of the case, including the involvement of accountants and accountancy firms in money laundering.

In an effort to raise such issues, a Member of Parliament (Austin Mitchell MP) invited the Secretary of State for Trade and Industry to investigate the role of accountancy firms in money laundering. In response, the Minister of Corporate Affairs replied that he would be pleased to consider any case which is referred to him (*Hansard*, 30 January 1991, col. 523). The Minister was then sent a letter (12 February 1991) accompanied by a 'Law Report' from *Financial Times* (18 January 1991: 36) and an article on the subject matter (Mansell 1991b). The Minister's considered reply (28 February 1991) took the form of a letter that denied responsibility for such matters, arguing that it was either a criminal issue (it should be recalled that the AGIP case was a civil case) which should be referred to the police; or, alternatively, it was a matter of 'professional misconduct' to be taken up with the relevant accountancy body: The Minister added:

> I have no power under the Companies Act to investigate the role of accountancy firms in this affair. Any question of their criminal involvement would be a matter for the police. The investigation of professional misconduct is a matter for the relevant professional body.
>
> I understand that the Institute of Chartered Accountants in England & Wales had noted the criticisms of one of its members made by the judge ... and is making enquiries. However, the progress of the investigation is at present delayed by the continuing litigation. The Institute is also aware of the unsupported allegations in the press about the auditors, and a report will be made to its investigation committee at its next meeting.

Since the Minister is directly responsible for corporate affairs, which includes the regulation of accounting and accountants, he was then urged (8 March 1991) to set up an independent investigation, especially as the court judgement had ruled (see above) that 'Mr. Jackson and Mr. Griffin ... obviously knew they were laundering money'. This was followed by a further letter on 22 March. The Minister rejected calls for an independent investigation and reiterated his contention that it was either a matter for the police or for the Institute of Chartered Accountants in England and Wales (ICAEW):

> The police may have been alerted by the recent press articles, which is the only information that I could have given them. If you wish to pursue this matter I suggest that you speak to the police to find out any action taken by them.
>
> (Letter dated 27 March 1991)

Dissatisfaction with the Minister's approach was again communicated on 29 April 1991. The demand for an independent inquiry was repeated. Then the AGIP affair took an unexpected turn. In June 1991, Yves Coulon, the French lawyer and middleman in the money laundering schemes was due to give evidence in France to the Tribunal de Grand Instants in Paris, in relation to the criminal charges (no immunity of any kind had been given to him) associated with the AGIP theft. He never gave this testimony because he was the recipient of a single bullet through the head. This murder occurred only a day before his supposed co-conspirator Sophie Ben Hassine was found guilty in France of defrauding AGIP of US$11.8 million and sentenced to three years in prison (Mansell 1991b). Coulon had feared that he would be murdered. He was therefore keen to put some information on the public record. In particular, he made the claim that:

> a former Conservative [UK] cabinet minister still very prominent in politics ... was available to provide protection ... a major organization involved in the affair had the powers of 'a government'. They've got an important politician in England who is looking after their interests in this and he will make sure things won't get out.
>
> (Mansell 1991b)

In the light of the allegations about the involvement of a former Conservative cabinet minister made by Coulon before his murder, correspondence with the Prime Minister, John Major, was opened on 26 June 1991. The Prime Minister followed the line provided by the Minister for Corporate Affairs, urging that 'If you have evidence of wrongdoing the correct course is for you to pass it to the police' (letter dated 22 July 1991). Regarding the alleged involvement of a former cabinet minister, the Prime Minister remained silent. He neither confirmed it nor denied it and would not say what investigations, if any, he had made. When reminded (9 August 1991) of his silence, the Prime Minister avoided any direct reply, but added:

> The allegations are vague. If the suggestion is that a particular person, no matter who, is deliberately covering up criminal activity, then that is itself a criminal matter; as with the allegations of money laundering by accountancy firms, it is something for the police to investigate ... if you have evidence of wrong doing, the correct course is for you to pass it to the police.
>
> (Letter dated 11 September 1991)

On 8 August 1991, a letter was sent to the Serious Fraud Office (SFO) (see Widlake 1995 for a discussion of the role, powers and purpose of the SFO). We urged the SFO to investigate the allegations against the former Minister and also the role of accountancy firms in money laundering, especially in view of the High Court judgement. The SFO Director declined to investigate these issues and added:

> ... our jurisdiction is limited to suspected offences which took place in England and Wales and Northern Ireland.
>
> I understand that the Metropolitan and City Police Company Fraud Department conducted an investigation into allegations of fraud involving AGIP (Africa) Limited in 1985. A report outlining the results of the police investigations was sent to the Director of Public Prosecutions who advised that in his opinion there was insufficient evidence to justify the institution of any criminal proceedings for offences within the jurisdiction of the English Courts.
>
> (Letter dated 4 September 1991)

Referring to the court judgement, the SFO Director added:

> I do not regard the words of the Court of Appeal in this respect, where they were considering the question of whether a constructive trust existed, as a sufficient basis to justify re-opening the investigation which was concluded in 1985 ... I am empowered ... to investigate any suspected offence of serious or complex fraud, this Office is able to investigate only limited number of cases. Of necessity we have to be selective in the cases which we accept ... I have been informed that the Institute of Chartered Accountants is actively reviewing the role of members and members' firms in this affair and expect to conclude their deliberations shortly.

In a letter dated 9 October 1991, the SFO's claims to lack jurisdiction over the matter were challenged: the shell companies were formed and registered in England; the money was laundered through banks in England; one of the accountancy firms was based in England and it was the English High Court which judged that Jackson & Co. 'knowingly' laundered money. Since the High Court had 'sufficient' evidence to reach a judgement against Jackson & Co., how did the SFO come to conclude that the evidence was 'insufficient'? Despite bringing these inconsistencies to the attention of the SFO (letter dated 18 October 1991), the position set out in its letter of 4 September was repeated.

In a letter to the Prime Minister (16 September 1991), we noted that the SFO claimed to have no jurisdiction for investigating the money laundering. Once again he was invited to say something about the alleged involvement of a former cabinet minister in money laundering. Although he would not be drawn on this allegation, the Prime Minister added:

> I understand that the authorities in the Isle of Man are currently considering complaints by a former employee of one of the auditing

> firms alleged to be implicated in the affair to see whether there are grounds for further action.
>
> (Letter dated 7 October 1991)

When pursued, a spokesperson for the Isle of Man police stated that, 'At the moment we are not doing anything ... We are writing to [the Director of] the Serious Fraud Office as we want to know who's dealing with it' (*Accountancy Age*, 24 October 1991: 2).

On 18 November 1991, the Prime Minister again reiterated the view, first articulated by the Minister for Corporate Affairs, that it was up to the profession to investigate the role of accountancy firms.

Correspondence with the ICAEW over this issue had been initiated during the previous month. The ICAEW replied by noting that it was considering the matter (letters dated 16 October 1991; 29 January 1992). Following an extended period of silence, a request for information about progress on this matter drew the response that 'It is not the Institute's practice to make announcements on the conduct of an investigation in progress' (letters dated 28 May 1992; 26 June 1992; 21 July 1992). The silence from the regulators, including the ICAEW, continued during 1993 and into 1994. Correspondence was reopened with the DTI and the SFO on 4 March 1994. The SFO Director replied on 17 March 1994 and said:

> I can confirm, from recent contact with the Institute, that they have recently concluded their consideration of this matter and have made a decision not to pursue the matter any further. No report will be sent by them to this office ... [the SFO] would expect to receive a report only if the Institute found evidence of serious or complex fraud. It would seem, therefore, that none has been found as enquiries of the Institute have confirmed.

Seemingly, the SFO were happy for the ICAEW to decide whether evidence of 'serious or complex fraud' existed, regardless of the court judgement. However, the view that the ICAEW had concluded their consideration of the case and had elected not to pursue the matter seems to be contradicted by a letter written by the Minister for Corporate Affairs (15 April 1994). He stated that 'My officials are discussing the AGIP case with the Institute of Chartered Accountants in England and Wales, and I shall write to you again when these enquiries are complete.' He then added, 'I understand that the ICAEW are writing to let you know about the outcome of their investigation' (letter dated 9 May 1994). Coincidentally, the ICAEW wrote on the same day:

> It has been concluded that there is insufficient evidence available to the Institute to justify the bringing of a disciplinary case against any of its members.

> The Committee was fully aware of the comments made in the course of the civil proceedings. However, the test to be applied is not that used in civil proceedings but rather the standards used in criminal cases. A formal complaint cannot properly be preferred unless there is adequate evidence supporting the contention that the members concerned knew or ought to have known that the activity with which they were associated was illegal or that they were recklessly indifferent as to whether or not the activity was wrong. No compelling evidence to satisfy the test required has been obtained.

It seems, in our view, that the ICAEW considered itself better placed to evaluate the evidence than the High Court judge who concluded that Jackson and Griffin were 'professional men' who 'obviously knew that they were laundering money ... They must have realised at least that their clients might be involved in a fraud on the Plaintiffs.' Subsequently, all questions relating to the possible involvement of accountancy firms and a former cabinet minister in money laundering continued to be parried by the Department of Trade and Industry (DTI) (*Hansard*, 29 June 1994) and the Prime Minister by saying that the ICAEW has already investigated the matter, and that there was no basis for pursuing the issue further.

With a change of ministers at the DTI, another attempt was made to persuade the Minister for Corporate Affairs not only to address the matter, but to make a public statement about it, especially as neither the ICAEW nor any other regulatory body had published any report of its investigation of the case. In response (14 January 1995), the Minister of Corporate Affairs confirmed that he and his officials had seen a report by the ICAEW which, as we have already noted, claimed that there was insufficient evidence. However, few other people have had sight of this report or, relatedly, the opportunity to scrutinize its contents and the basis for its conclusions. The ICAEW has claimed (letter dated 31 March 1995) that 'Mr Jackson's representations were taken into account when preparing the report ...'. These representations included the argument that his company had merely continued with ongoing arrangements and schemes passed on to him by Roger Humphrey of Grant Thornton. However, the failure to make this report available to Mr Jackson makes it impossible to assess this claim. Despite requests (19 June 1995; 4 August 1995), the Prime Minister and the Minister of Corporate Affairs were unable (letters dated 28 July 1995; 7 September 1995) to refer us to any statutory basis which empowers the ICAEW to interview witnesses, demand evidence and investigate cases of money laundering.

Summary and discussion

New opportunities for mobility of capital have accompanied the globalization of financial markets. These developments have also produced new risks, predatory and antisocial activities. One of the major risks is money laundering, associated with social, economic and political uncertainty and instability. In response, nation states have been obliged to reregulate through the introduction of various anti-money laundering laws.

The regulation, detection and curtailment of money laundering remains problematic. This is not least because any business engaged in legitimate transactions and international financial transactions can also be used as a vehicle for illicit activities (McCormack 1996). Processes of implementation and enforcement may also have complex and contradictory effects. For example, a severe regime of investigation and enforcement may persuade the public to believe that the government is serious about fighting financial crime and protecting its citizens. But, equally, the same policies may also send a 'negative' signal suggesting that British business is corrupt or that money laundering tendencies are institutionalized, something which has a capacity to erode confidence in capitalism and can have serious consequences for the long-term viability of a government.

It may be tempting for the regulators to justify their existence and demonstrate their vigilance by taking high-profile actions against 'bent' individuals, especially if they are non-Establishment figures like Roger Levitt or Peter Clowes. However, such policies are unlikely to help in effectively combating money laundering. For money laundering is best understood as an activity undertaken by organized groups, corporations and members of elite occupations. In our introduction to the AGIP case, we suggested that much of the reported increase in money laundering in the 1990s is connected with historical changes in the nature of capitalism in the Western world where profits are increasingly made from speculative ventures such as currency trading, takeovers, futures trading, land speculation, insider trading, beating exchange controls; or what might be called 'placing good bets'.

Accompanying and amplifying these shifts has been an erosion of moral restraint and 'gentlemanly conduct' (so far as this ever existed). 'Bending the rules' for personal gain is often regarded as a sign of business acumen (Coleman 1994; DTI 1997) or as stealing a march on a competitor rather than acting in a criminal way. *Ceteris paribus,* it is to be expected that 'rule bending' shading into money laundering will increase where competitive pressures increasingly link promotions, prestige, status and rewards profits, securing markets, niches and meeting business targets. In this environment, any 'deal' becomes acceptable as long as it is profitable and unlikely to be detected. Increasingly, the crime resides more in being caught than engaging in dishonourable or illegal activity. Indeed, 'smart' business activity resides in constructing mechanisms through which benefits are derived from illegal or suspect activities whilst escaping any (legal) responsibility for their operations (McBarnet 1991).

Faced with the numerous contradictions that accompany efforts to regulate business activity, the UK state has forged a well-developed alliance with accountants – the trusted foot-soldiers who in return for favours (e.g. a statutory monopoly of external audits) are asked to report suspicious transactions and financial irregularities to the regulators. This approach to regulation is reliant upon the capacity of accountants to place a duty to 'the public interest' above their own self-interested pursuit of business opportunities. The advisability of depending upon accountants to report suspicions of money laundering is further placed under question when it is appreciated that money laundering on any scale is difficult to accomplish and conceal without the active or tacit involvement of professionals (e.g. accountants) who are able to form nominee companies and create a bureaucratic labyrinth which impedes the tracing of the illicit transactions. In the case of AGIP, the fraudulent payments passed through Tunisia, England and France, with shell companies often obscuring the origins and destination of illicit funds.

Our interrogation of the regulatory apparatus has revealed that the UK regulators were aware of the possible involvement of accountants in the illicit transfers of monies from AGIP as long ago as 1985. When reminded of this, each of the regulators deemed it to be a matter for some other body. After several years, the ICAEW produced a report that allegedly found no hard evidence of misconduct. The other regulators were then able to point to this conclusion to legitimize their earlier and continuing inaction. Since the ICAEW report remains unpublished, it is impossible to access the thoroughness of the investigation or the reasoning for its recommendation that there was no basis for taking further action. Whether or not such evidence was found, the unavailability of this report for public scrutiny is symptomatic of the unaccountability of the regulatory system. How, then, might the evidence of the operation of this system as presented in our paper be interpreted?

One possible interpretation of this case is that every assessment made by each regulator at every stage – from the judgement in the court to the alleged ICAEW report – was entirely in accordance with the law. Whereas there was a case to be answered by Jackson & Co., the activities of other accounting firms associated with AGIP amounted to no more than very marginal involvement or minor incompetence which did not merit further investigation. In short, the matter was effectively dealt with by the courts and there was no reason for the regulators to pursue the case further. If this interpretation is accepted, then we submit that fundamental questions need to be asked about how the regulators operationalize and interpret the law. By the judge's own account, Jackson & Co. 'probably took over an established arrangement', yet as far as we have been able to determine, equivalent regulatory investigations were not applied to other parties.

Another interpretation is that those associated with the AGIP case were effectively protected from criticism by the reluctance of regulators to act. During the period in question, the UK government was very actively using major accountancy firms to restructure the state through the privatization of public utilities (e.g. accountants valuing assets and reporting on the privatization prospectuses of gas, electricity, water and other industries), the management of the public sector (e.g. accounting- and auditing-based regulations to control schools, hospitals, universities and local authorities) and the redesign of the tax collection system (e.g. the introduction of income tax self-assessment). Perhaps there was a reluctance to do anything which might openly undermine the carefully constructed aura that accountants are somehow independent, objective, trustworthy and honest. On this interpretation, the government did not wish to endanger the implementation of its New Right political project by opening up the potentially embarrassing issue of the possible involvement of major accounting firms in money laundering.

To conclude, this chapter has explored how the UK regulatory system reacts to allegations of money laundering against accountants. It has exposed a process of indifference and buck-passing that can be interpreted as further evidence of a close and cosy (but complex) relationship between the UK state and major accountancy firms in mediating the crisis of legitimation (Mitchell *et al.* 1994; Sikka and Willmott 1995). We anticipate that anxieties about money laundering and the reputation of the City will not abate. New pieces of legislation will be passed. But the costs to the Exchequer, the political risks associated with a more independent regulatory system and the state's continuing reliance upon forms of self-regulation and accountancy firms make it unlikely that any strenuous effort will be made to investigate the involvement of major firms in money laundering. These problems are further compounded by the secrecy afforded to UK accountancy firms who, despite enjoying statutory monopolies of auditing and insolvency, are not required to publish any information about their affairs (Kerry and Brown 1992).

Postscript

Since the drafting of this chapter, we managed to secure (Mitchell *et al.* 1998; *Accountancy Age*, 17 September 1998: 12–13; *Accountancy*, November 1998: 18) a copy of the unpublished ICAEW report (ICAEW 1994b) which supposedly found 'insufficient evidence' to warrant an investigation of the alleged involvement of accountants in money laundering.[1]

Much of the report prepared is by an internal ICAEW investigation team. It primarily consists of summaries of newspaper reports and the publicly available transcripts of the court judgements and speculation thereupon. There is nothing in the ICAEW report to show that any steps were taken to secure information, evidence and files from other jurisdictions (e.g. the Isle of Man, Jersey, Tunisia or France). No attempt has been made to request to secure any files from any accountant, accountancy firm or its associates. No attempt has even been made to look at the bank statements of the shell companies allegedly used to launder money.

We had always argued that the ICAEW did not have the capacity to investigate matters relating to allegations of money laundering. It had no independence from the auditing industry. The ICAEW certainly could not subpoena accountants or non-accountants (e.g. Ian Griffin, Roger Humphrey) or interview them and/or any witnesses. It had no capacity to examine their files and other relevant documents. The Secretary of the ICAEW investigation committee stated that, 'the public face of this case, that is the way in which *Accountancy Age* has criticised the Institute, is that "money laundering" has not been clamped down upon. The Institute's disciplinary procedures do not however lend themselves to this task' (ICAEW 1994b: 2). These admissions raise further questions about the public statements made by the ICAEW, the DTI, the SFO, the Prime Minister and others in which they continued to argue that allegations of 'money laundering' were investigated or even could be investigated by the ICAEW.

Further comments show that the ICAEW did not treat the matter as urgent. It would be recalled that matters relating to AGIP had been reported in the newspapers since 1985. The High Court case was concluded in 1990/91. We had been pressing various regulators to act since early 1991. Given the High Court revelations, one might have expected the ICAEW to move with some urgency, but its report shows little concern. The Secretary of the investigations committee wrote, 'I should like nothing better than to close the file on AGIP, not least because ... I have contributed to delays by putting this matter aside in favour of more pressing and less intractable problems' (ICAEW 1994b: 2). One can only speculate on the nature of the 'more pressing' problems. Seemingly, the views expressed by a High Court judge and the involvement of accountants in money laundering are not considered to be urgent enough. There is nothing in the report to explain the delays. The correspondence with external parties is minimal and there is no indication that any face-to-face meetings took place with any of the parties. No evidence had been invited from Griffin (found dead with a noose around his neck on 8 July 1998) and Humphrey. No correspondence had been sent to any of the journalists who investigated the AGIP affair. There appears to be no operational reason for the delay.

The ICAEW report is not based upon any sworn affidavits from any of the parties concerned. There is no list of any questions that any individual accountant or accountancy firm had been asked to answer. The report speculates on three possible interpretations of events. These are framed from the transcript of the publicly available High Court judgement and press reports rather than from any original investigation by the ICAEW. The investigation committee's favoured belief is 'the possibility that the funds were intended as bribes to Tunisian officials or ministers' (ICAEW 1994b: 2). However, the report does not contain any evidence to show why the committee believes this version of events rather than any other interpretation. There is certainly no indication of any weights that might have been attached to any of the evidence to enable the committee to reach its favoured conclusion. The ICAEW does not appear to have asked for the sight of any of the allegedly forged bank drafts. The report does not contain names of the directors, or the bank signatories of the companies through which the money was laundered.

The report may be deemed to be inadequate, yet it enabled the DTI, the Prime Minister and others to parry all searching questions.

Appendix: the cast

Name	*Details*
Sophie Ben Hassine	Prominent Tunisian; assumed grand-daughter of the Bey of Tunis
Edward Bowers	Partner, Jackson & Co.
Yves Coulon	French lawyer and middleman, shot dead
Carlo del Sorbo	AGIP official
Ian Griffin	Employee, Jackson & Co.
Roger Humphrey	Tax manager, Grant Thornton (previously known as Thornton Baker)
ICAEW	Institute of Chartered Accountants in England and Wales, the UK's largest professional accountancy body
Barry Jackson	Partner, Jackson & Co.
Jackson & Co.	Firm of chartered accountants, operating from the Isle of Man
Kinz Joaillier SARL	Company incorporated in France, and a subsidiary of Euro–Arabian Jewellery Ltd
Lloyds Bank	Major British commercial bank
John Major	British Prime Minister, 1990–97
Philip Monjack	Chartered accountant and insolvency expert, partner in Leonard Curtis, appointed as liquidators for Euro–Arabian Jewellery Ltd
Mr Mongi Zdiri	Chief Accountant, AGIP (Africa) Ltd

Note

1 The report can be found on the Internet site http://visar.csustan.edu/aaba/aaba.htm

References

Angell, I. O. (1996) 'Economic crime: beyond good and evil', *Journal of Financial Regulation and Compliance* 4(1): 9–14.

Auditing Practices Board (1995) *Statement of Auditing Standards 120: Consideration of Law and Regulations*, London: APB.

—— (1997) *Practice Note 12: Money Laundering*, London: APB.

Bingham, The Honourable Lord Justice (1992) *Inquiry into the Supervision of the Bank of Credit and Commerce International*, London: HMSO.

Bond, M. (1994) *Accountants Digest No. 324: Money Laundering*, London: Accountancy Books.

Bosworth-Davies, R. and Saltmarsh, G. (1994) *Money-Laundering: A Practical Guide to the New Legislation*, London: Chapman and Hall.

Castells, M. (1997) *The Power of Identity*, Oxford: Blackwell.

Coleman, J. W. (1994) *The Criminal Elite: The Sociology of White-Collar Crime*, New York: St. Martin's Press.

Coopers & Lybrand (1984) *Manual of Auditing*, 4th edn, London: Gee.

Department of Trade and Industry (1997) *Guinness PLC*, London: The Stationery Office.

Giddens, A. (1990) *The Consequences of Modernity*, Cambridge: Polity Press.

Grey, S. (1994) 'The blue chip islands', *Accountancy*, September: 34–8.

Hampton, M. P. (1996) *The Offshore Interface: Tax Havens and Offshore Finance Centres in the Global Economy*, London: Macmillan.

Hanlon, G. (1994) *The Commercialisation of Accountancy*, London: St. Martin's Press.

Harvey, D. (1989) *The Condition of Postmodernity*, Oxford, Basil Blackwell.

Herring, R. J. and Litan, R. E. (1995) *Financial Regulation in the Global Economy*, Washington, DC: The Brookings Institution.

Hirst, P. and Thompson, G. (1996) *Globalization in Question*, Cambridge: Polity Press.

Home Affairs Committee (1994) *Organised Crime: Minutes of Evidence and Memorandum*, London: HMSO.

Hook, P. (1998) 'No laughing matter', *Accountancy Age*, 12 February: 16–17.

Institute of Chartered Accountants in England and Wales (1994a) *The Recognition and Action to be taken in respect of Money Laundering* (Technical Release FRAG 11/94), March, London: ICAEW

—— (1994b) *The AGIP Report*, London: ICAEW.

Kerry, J. and Brown, H. (1992) *The BCCI Affair*, Washington, DC: US Government Printing Office.

McBarnet, D. (1991) 'Whiter than white collar crime: tax, fraud insurance and the management of stigma', *British Journal of Sociology*, September: 323–44.

McCormack, G. (1996) 'Money laundering and banking secrecy in the United Kingdom', in P. Bernasconi (ed.) *Money Laundering and Banking Secrecy*, Amsterdam: Kluwer.

Mansell, S. (1989a) 'Firms face institute's wrath over AGIP', *Accountancy Age*, 20 July: 1.

—— (1989b) 'Grant Thornton man linked to AGIP affair', *Accountancy Age*, 5 October: 1.

—— (1991a) 'Ripples of uncertainty offshore', *Accountancy Age Magazine*, February: 9–14.

—— (1991b) 'Death of an AGIP middleman', *Accountancy Age*, 20 June: 13.

—— (1991c) 'Invoices show Grant Thornton AGIP role', *Accountancy Age*, 28 February: 3.

—— (1991d) 'Coopers' alleged AGIP role: English ICA knew', *Accountancy Age*, 28 March: 1.

Mitchell, A., Sikka, P., Puxty, T. and Willmott, H. (1994) 'Ethical statements as smokescreens for sectional interests: the case of the UK accountancy profession', *Journal of Business Ethics* 13(1): 39–51.

Mitchell, A., Sikka, P. and Willmott, H. (1998) *The Accountants' Laundromat*, Basildon: Association for Accountancy and Business Affairs.

National Criminal Intelligence Service (1992–97) Annual Reports. London: NCIS.

Power, M. (1993) 'Auditing and the politics of regulatory control in the UK financial sector', in J. McCahery, S. Picciotto and C. Scott (eds) *Corporate Control and Accountability*, Oxford: The Clarendon Press.

Rider, B. (1996) *Money Laundering Control*, Dublin: Round Hall, Sweet and Maxwell.

Robinson, J. (1994) *The Laundrymen*, London: Simon and Schuster.

Sikka, P., Puxty, T., Willmott, H. and Cooper, C. (1998) 'The impossibility of eliminating the expectations gap: some theory and evidence', *Critical Perspectives on Accounting* 9(3): 299–330.

Sikka, P. and Willmott, H. (1995) 'Illuminating the state–profession relationship: accountants acting as Department of Trade and Industry investigators', *Critical Perspectives on Accounting* 6(4): 341–69.

Widlake, B. (1995) *Serious Fraud Office*, London: Little, Brown and Company.

Wiener, J. (1997) 'Money laundering: transnational criminals, globalisation and the forces of "redomestication"', *Journal of Money Laundering Control* 1(1): 51–63.

Wolfensohn, J. D. (1998) 'Accountants and societies – serving the public interest', *Accounting and Business*, January: 12–14.

Woolf, E. (1983) 'Banks: the substance over the form', *Accountancy*: 111–12.

—— (1986) *Auditing Today*, 3rd edn, Hemel Hempstead: Prentice-Hall.

Yule, I. (1994) 'Keeping the right company overseas', *Financial Director*, April: 78–80.

Index

www.ingramcontent.com/pod-product-compliance
Ingram Content Group UK Ltd.
Pitfield, Milton Keynes, MK11 3LW, UK
UKHW010955180926
475701UK00004B/380

* 9 7 8 1 1 3 8 5 6 9 0 7 2 *